D0630612

REVISITING *THE WASTE LAND*

LAWRENCE RAINEY

Revisiting
The Waste Land

YALE UNIVERSITY PRESS   NEW HAVEN & LONDON

Set in Scala by Duke & Company, Devon, Pennsylvania.
Printed in the United States of America.

Library of Congress Cataloging-in-Publication Data
   Revisiting The waste land / Lawrence Rainey.
      p.   cm.
   Includes bibliographical references and index.
   ISBN 0-300-10707-2 (alk. paper)
 1. Eliot, T. S. (Thomas Stearns), 1888–1965. Waste land. I. Title.
   PS3509.L13W3639 2005
   821'.912—dc22
2004017255

A catalogue record for this book is available from the British Library.

The paper in this book meets the guidelines for permanence and durability of the Commit-
tee on Production Guidelines for Book Longevity of the Council on Library Resources.

10 9 8 7 6 5 4 3 2 1

For Evan Rainey
who has a wicked backhand

CONTENTS

PREFACE

"What are you thinking of? What thinking? What?
"I never know what you are thinking. Think."

—*T. S. Eliot,* The Waste Land

Think, pig! (Pozzo jerks the rope. Lucky looks at Pozzo.) Think, pig!

—*Samuel Beckett,* Waiting for Godot

MORE THAN EIGHT DECADES after it was first published in 1922, *The Waste Land* has lost little of its lacerating power or its uncanny capacity to startle and disturb. Though it may never acquire a readership as broad as, say, that which currently follows the work of Stephen King, its status remains secure as the greatest long poem written in English in the twentieth century. And though too many readers first encounter the poem in a classroom setting that sometimes encourages a style of reading inimical to the poem's grotesque and grim extremism, many others first encounter it through the prompting of simple curiosity, returning to it with pleasure again and again. In writing this book, I have attempted to address not just scholars of Eliot's work but also that large body of nonspecialists who continue to take an intelligent interest in understanding a poem that has been so central to the culture of the twentieth century.

Readers under a certain age will not recall the enormous excitement produced in 1971 when Valerie Eliot, the poet's second wife, published a facsimile edition of the poem's prepublication drafts, typescripts, and other working materials (*The Waste Land: A Facsimile and Transcript of the Original Drafts* [New York: Harcourt Brace, 1971]). No book review section of the time was complete without an extended essay whose author tried to assess how the new materials altered our understanding of the poem. Reviewers generally agreed that the poem's composition had been more troubled

than one might have supposed, or that its evolution had been more tentative and confused than critical accounts of the poem might have led one
to surmise. They got no farther than this elementary observation, however,
because only a tiny proportion of the prepublication materials had been
assigned tentative dates by Mrs. Eliot. The rest was a chaotic jumble.

In Chapter 1 I take up this long-standing problem, one that has troubled
critics and interested readers for more than thirty years. I do so by applying a method that is regrettably lacking in grand theoretical premises,
one buttressed only by the everyday dictates of common sense. If we compare the papers that were used in the *Waste Land* manuscripts with those
that were used in T. S. Eliot's contemporaneous letters, we will have reasonable grounds for inferring the dates of the working materials that make
up the *Waste Land* manuscripts. Dates by themselves, of course, are inert
information, raw data; they must be integrated into the connecting tissue
of analysis and argument that will enable us to organize them into a meaningful story: an account of how *The Waste Land* was composed, of the
choices and impasses that Eliot faced as he wrote, and of the solutions
that he adopted to address them. Discovering that story, in turn, enables
us to appreciate more fully the distinctive aesthetics of the histrionic that
Eliot was elaborating, both in the poem and in his contemporary essays
(only recently republished after more than eighty years; see Lawrence
Rainey, ed., *The Annotated "Waste Land" with Eliot's Contemporary Prose* [New
Haven: Yale University Press, 2005]), and so to read his poem in a key
that differs sharply from most accounts of the last eight decades.

In Chapter 2 I take up the poem's publication history, an unusually
protracted and complicated one. Our received myth is that the poem was
either neglected or reviled in the 1920s after it first appeared. Quite the
contrary: publishers who had read not so much as a word of the poem's text
competed fiercely with one another to bring it out, and the story of that
competition—or rather, the story of what they thought they were competing for—can tell us much about how institutions shape the horizons of
expectations that readers bring to a text. (This chapter, it should be noted,
has been published in a previous collection of essays; but I have significantly
revised and updated it here to take into account new information.)

Confronted with the poem's intransigent opacity, and deprived of the
numerous guides which have subsequently turned its enigmas into something as tidy as a schoolboy's lunch box, readers and critics struggled in

1922 to find a vocabulary that would enable them to describe or make sense of the poem's mordant ferocity. In Chapter 3 I identify the fault lines that ran through these early discussions and go on to consider reasons why it may be that *The Waste Land* will always prove resistant to the kind of account that most critics, simply by virtue of being human, want to give of it.

This book, in short, is not a systematic overview of *The Waste Land*, nor does it offer a line-by-line commentary or analysis. In it I take up three topics: the poem's production, transmission, and reception, or how it came to be written, published, and read. And although I do introduce and summarize research that will be new even to scholars of Eliot's work, I hope that I do so in ways that make it accessible also to anyone who takes an interest in Eliot's masterpiece. Ideally, even a reader who has encountered the poem for the first time only recently should be able to turn to these pages with profit.

One last prefatory comment is in order. To discuss the large and disorderly body of manuscript materials which have come to be known as the prepublication manuscripts of *The Waste Land,* we need a few technical terms that can help us economically designate the various states that a text undergoes in the course of its production. One term is familiar to all of us: a *draft* is a tentative or provisional form of a text. Another term has somewhat less currency in everyday speech: a *fair copy* is a version of a text that has been prepared for a readership, even if that readership comprises only the author himself. Whereas a draft will typically have cancellations or alternative readings which show an author actively at work, a fair copy will typically be neatly written out in longhand or, if the author lived after the invention of the typewriter, in typescript. If the fair copy is written out by the author in longhand, it is called an *autograph fair copy.* That term is not meant to indicate that the author has signed it or otherwise appended his signature or "autograph" to it; instead it harks back to the Greek etymology of the word "autograph": "self-written." If, instead, the fair copy has been prepared with a typewriter, it is a *typescript fair copy.*

There are a few more terms we need for our account. One is *watermark,* which is a distinguishing mark or device that has been impressed in the substance of a sheet of paper during manufacture, usually barely noticeable except when the sheet is held against the light. Watermarks were once fairly common in finer papers for writing letters, though in recent decades they have become more rare and are chiefly used for documents that seek

a certain degree of formal dignity. Another term is *chainlines,* which desig-
nates a series of faint little lines, typically about 25 mm apart, that can be
arranged either horizontally or vertically on a leaf of paper. Chainlines,
like watermarks, are usually barely noticeable except when the sheet is
held against the light. Like many terms, *chainlines* has a history attached
to it. When paper was still made by hand, the pulp (a paste that had been
manufactured from undyed linen rags) was poured or "laid" into a mould,
a rectangular wooden frame which had a series of tiny wires running par-
allel to the long sides of the rectangle. The wires acted as a sieve for the
liquid pulp as it dried. These tiny wires, in turn, were crossed perpendicu-
larly at regular intervals by heavier little chains that supported them. When
the paper dried, the chains left marks at regular intervals across the page,
called chainlines. Once paper began to be machine- rather than handmade,
chainlines should logically have disappeared. But enough people have
continued to prefer the appearance of traditionally made papers, with their
watermarks and chainlines, that manufacturers have continued to produce
paper that *appears* to have chainlines and watermarks, even though these
no longer reflect the manufacturing process and are simply patterns impressed into the paper.

We need know only two more terms and one abbreviation. Many people
like to buy paper that not only has a pattern of horizontal lines printed on
it to facilitate writing but also has a pattern of vertical lines and so resembles
graph paper. These are called *quadruled* papers—not a very lovely term,
it must be conceded, but one that will have to do. Finally, textual critics
prefer to refer to a *leaf* rather than a sheet of paper, and so to designate
four (let us say) leaves with the abbreviation "4 ll." But with that little tech-
nicality out of the way, we are now prepared to venture ahead. Fortified
with our modest array of seven technical terms—*drafts, autograph* and
typescript fair copies, watermarks and *chainlines, quadruled* papers, and *leaves,*
or *ll.*—we can now address what has been a compelling scholarly mystery
for more than three decades: the corpus of manuscripts and typescripts
that make up the prepublication materials of *The Waste Land.*

"Corpus," of course, is the Latin word for "body" and reappears in the
cognate term, "corpse." We might think of ourselves, then, as beginning
at that familiar starting point of a classical mystery or detective fiction,
the discovery of the corpse. Like many of those classical detectives, we
shall first have to take note of a great many details, and no doubt we shall

have to do a bit of tedious measuring, recording the precise size and weight of objects that must have played some role in the events that resulted in our corpse, or corpus of documents. But if we persevere past that preliminary stage, we may suddenly find that in the reconstructed light of our imagination, the corpse once more takes on the semblance of life and once more speaks its strange and haunting tongue:

> "That corpse you planted last year in your garden,
> "Has it begun to sprout? Will it bloom this year?
> "Or has the sudden frost disturbed its bed?
> "Oh keep the Dog far hence, that's friend to men,
> "Or with nails he'll dig it up again!
> "You! hypocrite lecteur!—mon semblable,—mon frère!"

ACKNOWLEDGMENTS

I AM GRATEFUL TO many people and institutions for their assistance in the course of researching and writing this book. My first debt is registered in the dedication to Chapter 1. Donald Gallup kindly allowed me to consult his collection of letters by Eliot, which were indispensable to the project. I am also grateful to Craig Simmons, a former student of mine, who examined Eliot's letters at Northwestern University, the University of Chicago, the Lilly Library at Indiana University, the University of Virginia, Princeton University, the Rosenbach Museum and Library in Philadelphia, the McKeldin Library at the University of Maryland, the University of Bonn Library, the Schiller Nationalmuseum in Marbach am Neckar, Germany, and the Schweizerische Literaturarchiv in Bern. His help was invaluable. His travels were funded by an NEH Junior Scholars Grant, for which I am also thankful. I also wish to thank the Bibliographical Society of America for a grant which enabled me to travel to a number of libraries; and the Harry Ransom Humanities Research Center at the University of Texas, Austin, which permitted me to survey its holdings of letters by Eliot. I am deeply grateful to private owners who made their collections available for consultation: Prof. David G. Williams, Prof. John Waterlow, and Herbert T. Greene. Several scholars were also kind enough to read and comment on early drafts of the book. I wish to thank Ronald Bush, David Chinitz, John Roe, Ronald Schuchard, and John Whitter-Ferguson for their helpful suggestions.

REVISITING *THE WASTE LAND*

CHAPTER ONE

With Automatic Hand

WRITING *THE WASTE LAND*

In memory of Donald Gallup (1913–2000),
Bibliographer of T. S. Eliot and Ezra Pound

TO STUDENTS OF TWENTIETH-CENTURY modernism, 1971 was the
year when Valerie Eliot published a facsimile edition of *The Waste Land*'s
prepublication manuscripts. The event invited new accounts of the poem's
development and fresh assessments of how that might bear on our understanding of the poem.[1] One year later Hugh Kenner and Grover Smith
published essays which, while differing sharply in premises and procedures,
reached a consensus that part III, "The Fire Sermon," was the earliest portion of the poem to have been written, probably around midsummer 1921,
followed first by parts I and II and then by IV and V (these latter completed in December 1921).[2] Their efforts were followed in 1977 by Lyndall
Gordon's attempt at "Dating *The Waste Land* Fragments," a wide-ranging
survey which addressed both the principal parts of *The Waste Land* and
the various drafts and ancillary poems.[3] In the end, however, Gordon remained divided over the claims of two sharply incompatible hypotheses
for dating the principal parts of *The Waste Land* and concluded that the
question was, at least for the present, "unresolved" ("DTWLF," 146). In
1979 there was still another consideration of the dating by Peter Barry.[4]
Barry urged a complicated chronology which assigned priority to the first
leaf in the typescript for part I, a passage recounting a rowdy night on the
town in Boston (assigned to April–May 1921), followed by all of part III (September–October), then the rest of part I and all of part II (early November),

and finally parts IV and V (November–December). Finally, in 1984, Ronald Bush offered a reading of the poem which echoed Smith's and Kenner's thesis assigning priority to part III, and relied on Gordon's conjecture that a specific fragment, the one beginning "London, the swarming life," might date from as far back as 1918.[5]

By 1985, however, debate had come to a standstill, and since then a lack of new evidence or argumentation has effectively put a halt to discussion. What had once seemed a new dawn has turned into a lunar landscape, with critics condemned to retracing the dusty tracks left by Kenner, Smith, Gordon, and Barry. At the same time, as Christine Froula has lately noted, more recent criticism has increasingly drawn upon the prepublication manuscripts to offer "readings that cross easily between the 1921 and 1922 texts," despite legitimate uncertainty about the date or status of virtually all the prepublication manuscripts.[6] Indeed, as Froula's repeated references to "the 1921 manuscript" and "the 1921 text" indicate, the specificity of the prepublication materials—their heft, their material and historical density—has been leveled by a process of abstraction into "text," or even "the 1921 text," that definite article urging a monolithic entity that is at odds with the experience of pondering the undated, disordered scraps that jostle one another in the facsimile edition. That experience inevitably raises a host of questions. Did one passage or fragment antedate the others and preserve the trace of an original program which had later dissolved? Were specific passages composed all at once or in discrete and discontinuous moments? Were the ancillary poems conceived as independent works or meant to form part of the poem's texture? Was the poem's composition a straightforward progress or did it entail more entangled loopings? If we are to address these questions, if we are to restore the specificity of the prepublication materials and assess their bearing on critical understanding of *The Waste Land*, we must first return to the manuscripts themselves, revisiting the debates which ground to a halt in the mid-1980s. More concretely, we must resolve the vexing question concerning the priority of parts I and II versus part III, a question that hinged on the identity of a typewriter that mysteriously disappeared. Then we must establish a chronology for the entire corpus of prepublication materials to furnish a coherent account of the poem's production, assaying its significance for long-standing debates about the plan or program which shaped the poem's composition. And last, we need to integrate those considerations into a history specific to the early twentieth century, a culture of the book that gravitated around that epitome of modern communication flows, the typewriter, and that recognizably modern protagonist, the typist. "Such an exercise needs no apology," wrote Hugh Kenner at the outset of his own attempt to address the prepublication manuscripts some thirty years ago. "*The Waste Land* is still a determinant of modernist consciousness, postmodernist also if it has come to that, and the profit . . . may be that we shall learn a little more about the history of our own minds" ("UA," 24). Or, as Ezra Pound put it in his preface to the facsimile, "The more we know of Eliot, the better" (*TWL:AF*, vii).

CONFESSIONS OF A TYPEWRITER

The first two scholars who attempted to date the *Waste Land* manuscripts, Hugh Kenner and Grover Smith, agreed that the principal question was the problem of the typewriters—three of them, to be exact. One was especially distinctive: its characters were discernibly larger than those of the others, and, as Valerie Eliot noted that it had been used with the kind of "violet ribbon used by Pound" (*TWL:AF*, 63), both critics inferred that this machine was Pound's. Eliot must have worked on it while visiting him in Paris in January 1922, they reasoned, and it had been used to type fair copies of parts IV and V of the poem because these were apparently the last to be drafted and had still not been typed when Eliot came to Paris ("UA," 24; "MOTWL," 131). That left a more difficult question: what was the relationship between parts I and II, typed on a second kind of typewriter, and part III, typed on a third? The facts were both suggestive and confusing: suggestive because in theory the different typewriters offered a key to identifying discrete levels or times of composition; confusing because in practice there seemed to be no way of establishing the chronology of their usage.

These typewriters produced characters generally rather similar in appearance. Yet on closer scrutiny they can be distinguished from each other by several features. One is the minuscule forms of the letters t and f. In the typewriter used for parts I and II (Fig. 1), the descender of the lowercase t ends with a finishing stroke that seems oddly constricted, curving back sharply as it rises toward the cross-stroke above. Similarly, the ascender of the lowercase f concludes with an arc that curls back toward the character's body, giving it a crabbed appearance, and it ends at a point high above the level of the cross-stroke. The characters from the other typewriter, the one used for part III, are recognizably different (Fig. 2). The finishing stroke of the lowercase *t* culminates in a wide, stately curve, arcing beyond the length of the cross-stroke above, while the ascender of the lowercase *f* also finishes with a wide, graceful arc, circling downward until it nearly touches the cross-stroke below. Moreover, this machine produced apostrophes and quotation marks that are notably elongated; numerals such as *2* and *3* without serifs; alignment that is straight and even, as opposed to the often wobbly alignment of the other machine; and characters that are crisp and well-defined, as opposed to the worn appearance of the other machine ("UA," 24; "MOTWL," 131–132). There is one other distinction that Kenner and Smith did not notice: the machine with apparently wider characters, the one used for part III, actually allocated less space per letter than the other, 2.10 mm, while the machine with the crabbed finishing strokes (parts I and II) allocated more, 2.12 mm.

Both Kenner and Smith concluded that part III, typed on the 2.10 typewriter, was the earlier material, though they did so on very different grounds. Kenner noted that much of the material in part III was written in elegiac quatrains (a stanza pattern so named because of its use by Thomas Gray in his famous "Elegy in a Country Churchyard"). The same stanza, he observed, had also been used by John Dryden in his "Annus Mirabilis," a poem that celebrates the reconstruction of London after the fire of 1666 and elaborates a sustained analogy between modern London and ancient Rome. Eliot published a review of a new book on Dryden on 9 June 1921, allowing us to infer that he was reading in Dryden in May. Further, on 9 May he had notified John Quinn that he had "a long poem in mind," and that it was "partly on paper" already.[7] Thus, Kenner concluded, the material "partly on paper" was probably the typescript draft for part III. And even if this typescript draft was not completed by 9 May, it was certainly completed shortly thereafter, and certainly preceded the composition of parts I and II. The 2.10 machine, with its rounded, stately finishing strokes was Eliot's "London typewriter" ("UA," 25), which had first been used to type part III; while the 2.12 was "the one he used at Lausanne" ("UA," 38).

Grover Smith reached the same conclusion by a complex body of assumptions and inferences. First and foremost, Smith assumed that the passage depicting Madame Sosostris in part I derived from Aldous Huxley's

```
The Chair she sat in, like a burnished throne
Glowed on the marble, where the swinging glass
Held up by standards wrought with golden vines
From which (one)tender Cupidon peeped out
(Another hid his eyes behind his wing)
Doubled the flames of seven-branched candelabra
Reflecting light upon the table where as
The glitter of her jewels rose to meet its it,
From satin cases poured in rich profusion;
```

1 Text typed with the typewriter that allocates 2.12 mm per character, used for parts I and II of *The Waste Land*. From Valerie Eliot, ed., *The Waste Land: A Facsimile and Transcript of the Original Drafts* (New York: Harcourt Brace, 1971), 10.

portrait of a fortune-teller in *Crome Yellow,* a novel published in November 1921. If so, he reasoned, parts I and II, both typed with the 2.12 machine, could not have been written earlier. Second, Ezra Pound had once remarked that the passage beginning "Summer surprised us . . ." contained "snatches of conversation heard by Eliot from his fellow patients" in Lausanne ("MOTWL," 132).[8] If so, Smith inferred, it reinforced the hypothesis that parts I and II were written after Eliot's journey there in November 1921. Third, Vivien Eliot's written comments on one copy of part II indicated that she was surprised when she saw it for the first time; and though Smith did not explicitly state this, apparently he assumed that "the first time" could only have been in Paris in January 1922. If so, it corroborated the view that parts I and II were primarily composed and typed in Lausanne. That inference, in turn, became the premise for another. If parts I and II were composed and typed in Lausanne, then Eliot must have taken this typewriter with him: "It is assumed that Typewriter [2.12] was a portable machine and that Eliot took it to Lausanne" ("MOTWL," 133). And from this premise, yet another inference followed: part III was neither composed nor typed in December in Lausanne, for Eliot would have used the same typewriter to do so; "it follows, then, that the fair [typescript] copy of Part III was made before Eliot left England on November 18" ("MOTWL," 133). Indeed, it was very likely that "Part III, or some prototype of it, existed by the time Eliot and Vivienne went to Margate about the middle of October" ("MOTWL," 133).[9]

```
Twit twit twit twit twit twit twit
Tereu tereu
So rudely forc'd.
Ter
```

2 Text typed with the typewriter that allocates 2.10 mm per character, used for part III of *The Waste Land*. From Valerie Eliot, ed., *The Waste Land: A Facsimile and Transcript of the Original Drafts* (New York: Harcourt Brace, 1971), 30.

Kenner and Smith, then, agreed that part III, typed on the 2.10 machine with the rounded *t*'s and *f*'s, had been written and typed before parts I and II, typed on the 2.12 machine. Part III was for Kenner "the earliest continuous stretch of the poem" ("UA," 25), for Smith "the first germ of *The Waste Land*" ("MOTWL," 133). They also agreed on its date of composition: Kenner assigned it to May 1921, or not long thereafter; while Smith thought it had "probably" been composed by early May, and in any case sometime before Eliot left for Margate in mid-October 1921 ("MOTWL," 133). Finally, they concurred that the 2.12 typewriter, the one with the crabbed finishing strokes used for parts I and II, was firmly linked with Eliot's experience in Lausanne: for Kenner it was "the one he used at Lausanne" ("UA," 25), for Smith "a portable machine . . . that he took . . . to Lausanne" ("MOTWL," 133). But that claim entailed an obvious puzzle: if Eliot used this typewriter in Lausanne to type parts I and II, why did he not use it to prepare a typescript of parts IV and V as well? Why, in fact, bother to prepare a fair copy of parts IV and V by hand if one had a typewriter at one's disposition? Smith never considered the question, but Kenner clearly anticipated it: when Eliot prepared part IV, he reasoned, "a typewriter" was "for some reason inaccessible" ("UA," 41). It was at least an answer, however vague. ("For some reason"? What reason?) To Smith's hypothesis that Eliot had taken a "portable machine" with him to Lausanne there was a still stronger objection. For when Eliot went on to Paris in January 1922, why did he use Ezra Pound's typewriter to prepare type-scripts of parts IV and V? Had he jettisoned his own typewriter while in Lausanne, or lost it while en route to Paris?

Lyndall Gordon, writing seven years later, struggled to address these questions. She was the first to consult the manuscripts themselves and to focus on evidence offered by study of their papers. By collating the kinds of paper used in the *Waste Land* manuscripts with those used in poems whose dates of composition were already established, she hoped to date not just the major parts of *The Waste Land* but all the fragments and inde-pendent poems. For our purpose, her comments on the chronology of parts I and II, versus part III, are the most important. Having examined the typescripts of other poems by Eliot, Gordon was aware that the 2.12 typewriter, the one with the crabbed finishing strokes, was used not only for parts I and II of *The Waste Land* but for numerous poems that Eliot had composed much earlier. Gordon, in fact, dubbed it "his Harvard type-writer" ("DTWLF," 144), implying that he had used it at least since 1914, perhaps even earlier. But if so, its usage typified not Eliot's stay in Lausanne but his everyday life in London, and therefore it would seem that parts I and II had been written not late in 1921 in Lausanne but earlier. And this suspicion was buttressed for Gordon by other evidence. First, parts I and II were written on the same kind of paper as a poem titled "Song for the Opherion," and since "Song" had been published already in April 1921, in the *Tyro,* parts I and II presumably had been composed long, long before the Lausanne period (late November–December) urged by Kenner and Smith. Second, the original opening of part I had described a raucous evening in Boston, a scene redolent of the Night-town episode in *Ulysses,* which Eliot was reading in manuscript in early May 1921, so corroborating an earlier dating of parts I and II. And third, Eliot's letter of 9 May to Quinn, stating that his "long poem" was already "partly on paper," could be deemed further confirmation: "on paper" might refer not to part III or some part of it, as Kenner and Smith had urged, but to parts I and II.

But against this scenario were two arguments that Gordon found compelling. Eliot, she assumed, would always show any new poems almost immediately to Pound. Eliot and Pound are known to have met briefly in mid-October 1921, when Pound returned to London for a week, and since Pound's letter describing their encounter to John Quinn made no reference to Eliot's new poem, it could only be because no major poem was yet in existence. Also, Gordon accepted Smith's assumption that the name of Madame Sosostris came from "Sesostris the Sorceress" in Huxley's *Crome Yellow,* published in November 1921 and completed only in August 1921 —much too late to permit the inference that parts I or II had been composed in the spring of 1921. On these grounds Gordon rejected her first hypothesis and advanced another. Since nothing about a major poem had been mentioned to Pound in mid-October, nothing had yet been composed. Immediately thereafter, Eliot went to Margate, taking only a few fragments assembled from poems written much earlier, and there wrote part III, "The Fire Sermon." The different typewriter used for this manuscript, the 2.10, was "an office typewriter" ("DTWLF," 145) that he presumably borrowed from Lloyds Bank. (The idea that a bank would lend out office equipment may strike some readers as a bit far-fetched.) After leaving Margate, Eliot had returned to London, then traveled to Paris for a few days. It was there that Pound made his first comments on part III. Eliot next proceeded to Lausanne, where he composed parts I and II, then IV and V. Gordon confessed, however, to being puzzled by an obvious objection to this view: why had Eliot typed only parts I and II in Lausanne, and not IV and V? She concluded: "The story of *The Waste Land*'s composition in 1921 remains, as yet, unresolved. There are two possible hypotheses and one can do no more at present than weigh one body of circumstantial evidence against the other" ("DTWLF," 146).

Gordon's account revealed the impasse which had been reached in efforts to date the *Waste Land* manuscripts which were based primarily on the facsimile edition. Even her attempt to draw on the papers used in Eliot's earlier poems rested on a documentary base too slender to resolve the outstanding questions. It was only in 1988, when Valerie Eliot published the first volume of Eliot's letters through 1922, that scholars could gain a panoramic view of his correspondence, a precondition for an account of his writing practices that would have sufficient breadth to address not only the vexed debate about the typewriters but also the papers used in the fragments and independent poems affiliated with *The Waste Land*. If we could collate data about the papers that were used in the *Waste Land* manuscripts with corresponding data from Eliot's letters from 1914 to 1922, we would have reasonable grounds to infer the manuscripts' dates, for most of Eliot's letters are dated, and those that are not can be conjecturally dated with sufficient accuracy.

Mrs. Eliot's edition of *The Letters of T. S. Eliot,* vol. 1 *1898–1922,* printed transcriptions of 509 letters by Eliot. (It also contained 37 by his first wife, Vivien, and 40 by various third parties.) Not all the 509, however, were derived from extant originals. For 16 letters included in Valerie Eliot's edition, the text was taken from published transcriptions, the originals being no longer extant (chiefly letters to the editors of periodicals); for another 13 letters, the originals turned out to be held in private collections that could not be consulted. In addition, there are 6 letters for which the originals have been lost since they were first located by Mrs. Eliot; and for 2 other letters, both from Eliot to his brother Henry and both dating from December 1922, I did not obtain permission to examine the originals (though these last two would not affect the dating of the *Waste Land* manuscripts).[10] In short, there were 37 published letters whose originals I could not examine, leaving 472 of the published letters whose originals I consulted. In addition, I have examined another 166 unpublished letters which were omitted from the 1988 edition: all together then, 638 letters, written on more than 900 leaves. These letters, together with synoptic descriptions of the paper on which they were written, are registered in Table 1, pages 158–175. In addition, I have examined more than 200 leaves of Eliot's student papers, which range in date from 1910 to 1915 and are held at the Houghton Library of Harvard University. These are described in synoptic form in Table 2, pages 194–195. Finally, I have also examined more than a hundred leaves containing poems and essays by Eliot in a variety of libraries, and these are described in Table 3, pages 198–199. Taken together, more than 1,200 leaves of Eliot's writing have been examined, ranging over a decade, from 1913 to the end of 1922.

The evidence from these documents tells an unequivocal story about the 2.10 and 2.12 typewriters. In all of Eliot's student papers from 1913 to 1915, in all his typed letters from 1914 up through 6 July 1921, and in all the typescripts of his poems and essays during the same period, Eliot uses only one typewriter, the 2.12 machine with the crabbed finishing strokes, the one also used in typing parts I and II of *The Waste Land.* Type from the 2.10 machine with wider finishing strokes (the one used in typing part III) appears for the first time in a letter to Richard Aldington, dated 8 September 1921 (*LOTSE*, 468–469), and it appears in every typescript letter and essay that Eliot wrote thereafter until the end of 1922. Moreover, evidence of the 2.12 machine vanishes forever, at least in Eliot's usage.

What brought about this change of typewriters is sketched in a letter by Vivien Eliot to Eliot's brother Henry, written only three days after Henry, together with his mother and sister, had left England on 20 August 1921. Eliot's mother and sister had been staying in the Eliots' flat at 9, Clarence Gate Gardens for some ten weeks since their arrival on 10 June, while Eliot and Vivien had moved to a temporary flat at 12, Wigmore Street. Returning to their old flat in August after the Eliot family had vacated it, Vivien wrote to Henry: "And the typewriter? What does that mean please? You can hardly have mistaken them *in* (as Tom insists) the circumstances. But whatever it means, you are shown up as an angel. A bloody angel, as they say over here. . . . Tom will write about the typewriter" (*LOTSE*, 465–466). As he did finally, though not until six weeks later, on 3 October: "I was most painfully touched at finding that you had secretly left your typewriter behind instead of my old wretched one, which I hope will not fall to pieces" (*LOTSE*, 472). Henry, it is now clear, had done something remarkable when he left the Eliots' flat and England on 20 August: he had taken away Eliot's old typewriter, the 2.12 with the crabbed finishing strokes, the one Eliot had used a few months earlier to type parts I and II of *The Waste Land*, and in its place left behind his own, newer machine, the 2.10 typewriter with the wider strokes, the one that Eliot would soon use to type part III of *The Waste Land*.

In retrospect, we can see all too plainly how the speculative arguments about the dating of *The Waste Land*'s parts went astray. One mistake was the repeated attempt to postulate an opposition between a "London typewriter" ("UA," 25) and "the one [Eliot] used at Lausanne" ("UA," 38) or even "a portable machine . . . that he took . . . to Lausanne" ("MOTWL," 133), or "an office typewriter" ("DTWLF," 145) which Eliot borrowed and then mysteriously lost while in Lausanne. The other was the assumption that the name of Madame Sosostris in part I could only be derived from the character of Sesostris the Sorceress in *Crome Yellow*, and hence that part I could have been written only after Huxley's novel was published, in November 1921.[11] As if Eliot were incapable, on his own account, of using that most common expression "so so" to invent a name meant to suggest equivocation.

PAPER TIGERS

Evoking the holidays in France which he had spent together with Eliot in the summer of 1919, Wyndham Lewis recalled that his companion possessed a curious habit: "I hope I shall not be destroying some sentimental illusion if I record that to my surprise my companion entered most scrupulously in a small notebook the day's expenses. This he would do in the evening at a café table when we had our night-cap. There was not much more he could spend before he got into bed."[12] Eliot was a frugal man, at least in the years 1914–1922. Despite earning a relatively substantial salary at Lloyds Bank from 1917 onward, he was beset by worries over money, prompted chiefly by Vivien's many medical expenses and the need to keep a cottage in the country where she spent much of her time. His frugality extended to his consumption of paper as well: he seems to have purchased relatively small batches of paper that would last at most a few months, often only a few weeks, before he would purchase another (see Table 1). As a consequence, his letters can serve as a control base for establishing the dates of the prepublication materials of *The Waste Land*. No, we cannot identify the precise day on which a given passage or poem was composed; but often we can establish the week or weeks, and more broadly we can establish a working account of the poem's documentary evolution and an understanding of its composition—up to a point. And yes, the boundaries of that point will need to be carefully delineated later.

The twenty-six documents which make up the *Waste Land* manuscripts can be divided into four principal groups. One consists of the manuscripts and typescripts which contain the text (or a large block of it) for each of the five parts of the published poem:

1. Burial of the Dead, typescript, 3 ll.
2. A Game of Chess, typescript, 3 ll.
3. A Game of Chess, carbon copy typescript, 3 ll.
4. The Fire Sermon, typescript, 5 ll.
5. The Fire Sermon, carbon copy typescript, 5 ll.
6. Death by Water, autograph fair copy, 4 ll.

7. Death by Water, typescript, 4 ll.
8. What the Thunder Said, autograph fair copy, 6 ll.
9. What the Thunder Said, typescript, 2 ll.

A second group consists of autograph fragments and independent poems which were written contemporaneously with the main text of *The Waste Land;* the fragments were wholly or partly incorporated into parts I and III, while the independent poems were ultimately set aside:

FRAGMENTS

10. "Those are pearls," autograph, 1 l., incorporated into part I
11. "O City, City," "London, the swarming life," autograph, 1 l., incorporated into part III
12. "The river sweats," autograph, 1 l., incorporated into part III
13. "Highbury bore me," autograph, 1 l., incorporated into part III
14. "On Margate Sands," autograph, 1 l., incorporated into part III
15. "From which, a Venus Anadyomene," autograph, 1 l., incorporated into part III, then rejected

INDEPENDENT POEMS

16. "Elegy"/"Dirge," autograph, 1 l.
17. "Dirge," autograph fair copy, 1 l.
18. "Exequy," typescript, 1 l.

A third group consists of four poems, conserved in five documents, which are known to have been written some years before *The Waste Land,* though there is no agreement concerning their precise dates:

19. "The Death of St. Narcissus," autograph draft, 1 l.
20. "The Death of St. Narcissus," autograph fair copy, 1 l., of which five lines, with alterations, are incorporated into part I
21. "The Death of the Duchess," typescript, 2 ll., of which six lines, with alterations, are incorporated into part II
22. "So through the evening," autograph, 1 l., of which eight lines are incorporated into part V
23. "After the turning," autograph, 1 l., of which one line was incorporated into part V

A fourth group consists of two brief poems, of which no part was ever incorporated into *The Waste Land:*

24. "I am the Resurrection," autograph, 1 l.

25. "Song [for the Opherion]," typescript, 1 l.

Finally, there is the title page, which was added to the manuscripts in January 1922, after Eliot had returned from Paris to London.

The earliest stratum of materials consists of three poems, of which two ("After the Turning" and "So Through the Evening," *TWL:AF*, 108–109, 112–113) provided lines incorporated into part V, while the third ("I am the Resurrection," *TWL:AF*, 110–111) left no traces in *The Waste Land*. "From the handwriting," Valerie Eliot urged that all three "were written about 1914 or even earlier" (*TWL:AF*, 130). Certainly all three are on the same kind of paper, which measures 267 × 205 mm and has a thickness of 0.12 mm. Each has a watermark reading "Linen Ledger," which measures 36 × 124 mm, and a distinctive pattern of quadruled lines. Though Eliot used several varieties of paper bearing the watermark "Linen Ledger" during the academic year 1913–1914 (see Table 2), these can be distinguished from one another by their thickness and different patterns of printed lines. Only two exemplars match the paper used in the three poems. One is Eliot's "Notes on Eastern Philosophy," dated 3–10 October 1913, the other his notes on "Perry: Philosophy 25," dated 2 October 1913. These leave little doubt that the three poems should be dated to the same period, between 2 and 10 October 1913.

The second stratum of materials consists of two poems, one of which ("The Death of St. Narcissus," *TWL:AF*, 90–93) is conserved in both draft and fair-copy form. Five lines from this poem became, after revision, lines 26–29 of part I of *The Waste Land*. Six lines from the other poem, "The Death of the Duchess" (*TWL:AF*, 104–107), became, after alteration, lines 108–110 and 136–138 of part II of *The Waste Land*.

The draft version of "The Death of St. Narcissus" is written on paper which measures 262 × 203 mm and has a thickness of 0.09 mm. The paper is laid and has eight chainlines which appear as vertical lines on the leaf at intervals of 28 mm. It also has a watermark reading "EXCELSIOR / FINE / BRITISH MAKE," measuring 71 × 125 mm. The same sort of paper turns up only once in Eliot's correspondence, in a letter to Ezra Pound which is dated 15 April [1915] from Merton College, Oxford (Fig. 3). Tellingly, however, the same type of paper also was used for three of Eliot's student essays, titled "[On Matter]," "[Matter and Form]," and "[Aristotle: Definition

3 Excelsior Fine watermark, with chainlines; letter from T. S. Eliot to Ezra Pound, 15 April [1915]; courtesy of the Beinecke Rare Book and Manuscript Library, Yale University.

of . . .]" (see Table 2, items 35–37.1). None is dated, but all clearly stem from the same period when, as he explained in a contemporary letter, he "was writing papers for Joachim on Aristotle" (*LOTSE,* 98; Harold Henry Joachim was the Fellow and Tutor in Philosophy at Merton College). The penciled first draft of "Mr. Apollinax" appears on the same paper (see Table

3, item 16), and we may assume that this poem should also be assigned to the same period, mid-April 1915.[13]

The fair-copy version of "The Death of St. Narcissus" is written on paper which measures 250 × 198 mm and has a thickness of 0.10 mm. The paper has no watermark, but it does have eight horizontal chainlines at intervals of 27 mm. The paper is also quadruled, forming an identifiable pattern: the horizontal lines begin 29 mm from the top edge of the leaf, occupy a block of space that measures 207 mm and contains 24 lines, and come to an end 14 mm from the bottom edge of the leaf (or: 29.207(24).14). No such paper appears in Eliot's correspondence, nor among his student papers. The same sort of paper is used, however, for the autograph fair copy of "Mr. Apollinax," written in black ink (Table 3, item 17). Since Eliot typically made fair copies shortly after writing a draft, the fair copies of both poems should be assigned to May 1915.

"The Death of the Duchess" is written on paper which measures 258 × 202 mm and has a thickness of 0.07 mm. It has no watermark but is laid, with nine horizontal chainlines at intervals of 27 mm. The same paper appears in a small group of five letters by Eliot, all written between 5 and 7 September 1916 (to Eleanor Hinkley, his mother, Henry Eliot, Harriet Monroe, and J. H. Woods; see Table 1). The poem should also be assigned to the same period, early September 1916.[14]

The third stratum of material for *The Waste Land* consists of a single poem, "Song [for the Opherion]" (*TWL:AF*, 98–99). A brief work of fifteen lines, it was published under the pseudonym Gus Krutzsch in the first issue of Wyndham Lewis's new journal the *Tyro*, which appeared on 9 April 1921.[15] The typescript, with corrections in black ink and pencil, is on paper which measures 263 × 200 mm and has a thickness of 0.07 mm. The paper is laid, with eight vertical chainlines at intervals of 26 mm. It also has a watermark, "BRITISH BOND / [device: S entwined with B]," which lies horizontally on the leaf and measures 65 × 125 mm. There are three different papers among Eliot's correspondence which have the British Bond watermark, but this one (which I shall designate British Bond [B]) is distinguished from British Bond [A] and British Bond [C] by having chainlines (Figs. 4, 5).[16] In Eliot's correspondence it was used for sixteen letters which date from 13 September 1920 to 30 January 1921, a period comprising nearly twenty weeks.[17] I suspect, however, that "Song" was written at the very end of this period, around 23–30 January 1921. For on 30 January,

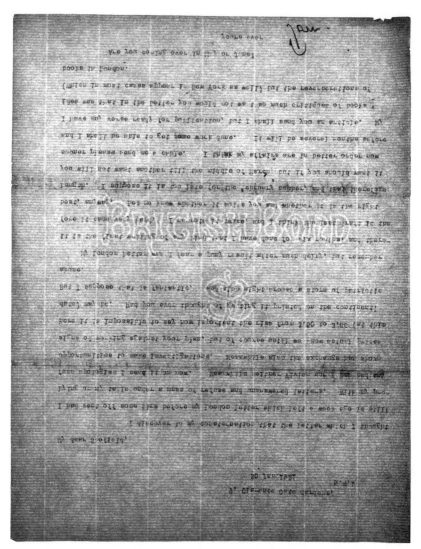

4 British Bond [B] watermark, with chainlines; letter from T. S. Eliot to Scofield Thayer, 30 January 1921; courtesy of the Beinecke Rare Book and Manuscript Library, Yale University.

when Eliot wrote to Scofield Thayer, the editor of the *Dial,* to apologize for the poor quality of a "London Letter" he had sent him only "a week ago," he added a comment about his recent writing: "But remember it is the first writing of any kind that I have done for six months; and therefore it came very hard" (*LOTSE,* 435). There is every reason to credit Eliot's testimony, and on the basis of it we should assume that "Song" was written not long after his "London Letter," in late January 1921.[18]

The fourth stratum of materials for *The Waste Land* marks the beginning of the poem as it was eventually published. It comprises four documents: first, a verse fragment beginning "Those are pearls" (*TWL:AF*,

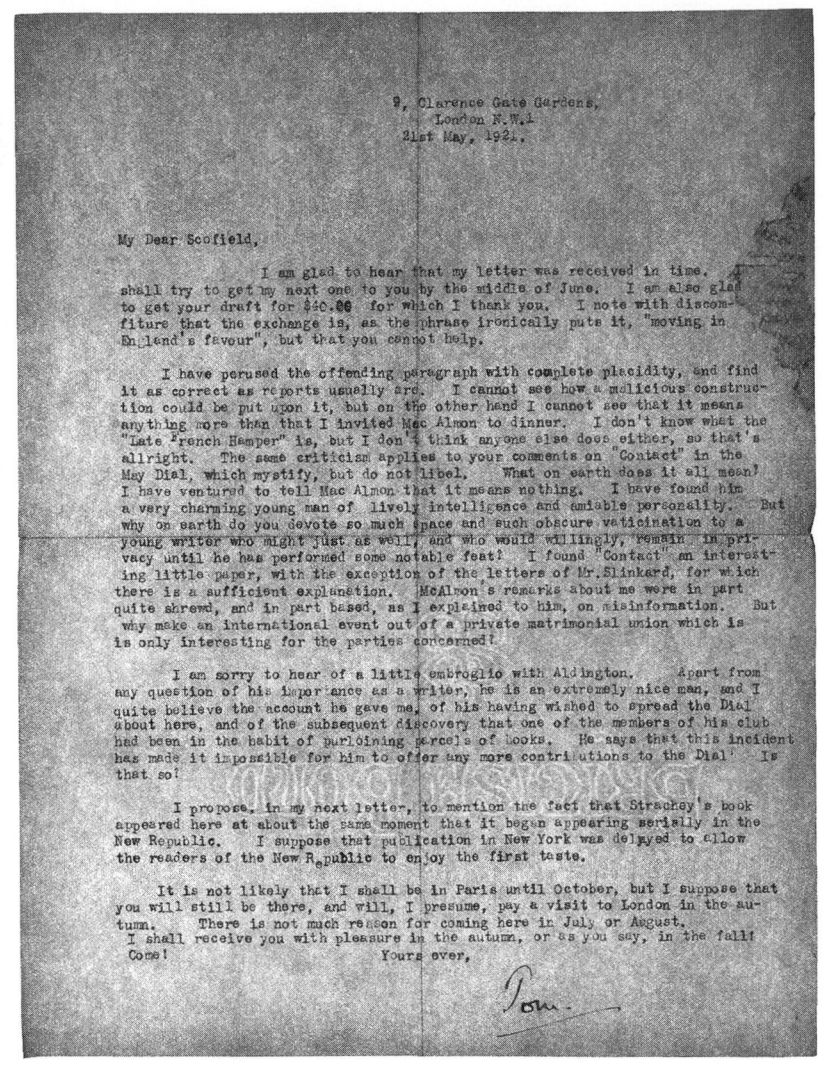

122–123), one line from which is incorporated into the next document; second, the typescript of part I (*TWL:AF*, 4–9); third and fourth, the typescript and carbon of part II (*TWL:AF*, 10–15, 16–21). All these are found on paper which measures 264 × 203 mm with a thickness of .08 mm. The paper has a watermark reading "BRITISH BOND / [device: S entwined with B]," which lies horizontally on the leaf and measures 66 × 123 mm. What distinguishes this paper from the British Bond paper used in "Song" is that is has no chainlines.

The British Bond [C] paper also was used for seven letters by Eliot from the first half of 1921:

DATE	RECIPIENT	*LOTSE* PP.	NO.
13 February	Mother	436	T.329
9 May	John Quinn	450	T.343
21 May	Scofield Thayer	453	T.345
22 May	Robert McAlmon	449	T.342
22 May	Dorothy Pound	456	T.347
[15 June]	Mary Hutchinson		U.82
15 June	Leonard Woolf	457	T.349

(The letter to Robert McAlmon is incorrectly assigned to 2 May in Mrs. Eliot's edition.) In addition, the same paper appears in the typescript of Eliot's "London Letter, May 1921" for the *Dial,* which appeared published in the June issue.

In his correspondence from this period, Eliot made three references to his work on the poem. Writing to Sydney Schiff on 3 April, he commented (*LOTSE,* 444): "My poem has still so much revision to undergo that I do not want to let any one see it yet, and also I want to get more of it done—it should be much the longest I have ever written. I hope that by June it will be in something like final form. I have not had the freedom of mind."

Nearly three weeks later, on 22 April, apparently replying to a query from John Middleton Murry, Eliot observed: "It is true that I have started a poem" (*LOTSE,* 444). More than two weeks later again, on 9 May 1921, Eliot wrote to John Quinn: "I am not anxious to produce another [book of criticism] for a year or two; and meanwhile have a long poem in mind and partly on paper which I am wishful to finish." But there were also problems: "The chief drawback to my present mode of life is the lack of *continuous* time, not getting more than a few hours together for myself, which breaks the concentration required for turning out a poem of any length" (*LOTSE*, 451).

Given the preponderance of letters on British Bond [C] which date from the period 9–22 May, as well as the "London Letter, May 1921," which must have been posted by 1 May or thereabouts, it seems safe to say that the typescripts of parts I and II were produced during this period, and that they represented a summation of work that had been in progress since March or February, perhaps even the last week of January.[19] Eliot had good reason for attempting to sum up his work on the poem at just this time: his mother, together with his sister Marian and brother Henry, was due to arrive in England on 10 June, and since Eliot and Vivien were to vacate their flat for them, now was an appropriate time to summarize his progress to date. No doubt there were other autograph drafts and fragments, aside from "Those are pearls," which were jettisoned when Eliot prepared the typescripts in mid-May. How many, we shall see later.

Two qualifications need to be added to this account. The first concerns the first leaf of the typescript for part I, "The Burial of the Dead," which portrays several incidents in the course of a drinking binge that takes place one night in Boston. The protagonists go to a vaudeville show, stop in a brothel, and later are saved from being arrested by the police through the intervention of a Mr. Donavan, a respectable citizen who boasts about his influence down at City Hall. The episode loosely recalls the closing portions of the "Circe" episode in *Ulysses,* with Mr. Donavan playing much the same role as Corny Kelleher. Joyce evidently sent a copy of both the "Oxen of the Sun" and "Circe" episodes to Ezra Pound in April 1921. On 20 April Pound wrote to a friend: "Joyce's new chapter is enormous—megalo-scrumptious—mastodonic."[20] Four days later he reiterated this view to his mother: "Joyce next chapter great stuff."[21] It is not clear whether Pound forwarded the manuscript to Eliot or Joyce sent it to him independently, though it is far more likely that Pound did so just after 9 May.[22] Eliot must have read the material quickly, since he returned the manuscript to Joyce on 21 May and commented specifically on what he termed "the Descent into Hell," or "Circe": "I have nothing but admiration; in fact, I wish for my own sake that I had not read it" (*LOTSE*, 455). The very next day he also wrote to Robert McAlmon, praising "Oxen of the Sun" for its "marvellous parody of nearly every style in English prose from 1600 to the *Daily Mail"* (*LOTSE,* 450), and in a letter written the same day to Dorothy Pound he exclaimed: "The unprinted manuscript [of *Ulysses*] is even finer stuff than the printed" (*LOTSE,* 456). While the precise chronology of this complex of events is unclear at several points, it seems likely that the Boston incident, typed on a separate leaf, was a late addition to the typescript which had originally begun on leaf two, with "April is the cruellest month." If so, it may explain why what was then the provisional title of the poem as a whole, "He Do the Police in Different Voices," is so conspicuously out of alignment with the block of the text on the first leaf of the typescript. In this scenario, both the title for the whole poem and the page numbers of leaves two and three were added when the Boston incident was incorporated into the already existing typescript in late May 1921.

That scenario invites a second qualification to our tentative dating of parts I and II. For if it is true that the first leaf of part I, the leaf that follows a lead from Joyce in recounting a drinking binge in Boston, was added to the typescript only sometime after 9 May, it follows that the earlier or original version of part I consisted only of the four verse-paragraphs that we also have in the published poem, the result of Pound's having deleted the drinking episode when he later edited the poem in Paris. That scenario is confirmed by a letter from Wyndham Lewis to Sydney Schiff, the generous patron who was funding the first issue of Lewis's new journal, the *Tyro.* Reporting on his progress in gathering materials for the issue, on 7 February 1921, Lewis wrote: "Everything is practically now complete. . . . Eliot I saw 2 nights ago. He is doing his article apace. He also showed me a new long poem (in 4 parts) which I think will be not only very good, but a new departure for him."[23] Lewis, we must infer, had seen part I of *The Waste Land* in its original state ("in four parts"), before it acquired a fifth part, the beginning scene of the drinking binge which was added three months later, sometime in May 1921. If so, Eliot's progress had been rapid at first. Beginning sometime after 23 January, when he completed his "London Letter" ("the first writing of any kind I have done for six months"), he had already completed part I much as we have it today by 5 February, when he showed it to Lewis. Distracted by the two essays he was writing for the *Tyro,* by another on "Prose and Poetry" for Harold Monro's *Chapbook,* by two more substantial ones on "Andrew Marvell" and "John Dryden" for the *Times Literary Supplement,* and by yet another "London Letter" due at the *Dial,* Eliot progressed slowly in writing part II during the period from February to April. With his mother and family due to arrive on June 10, sometime toward mid-May he summarized his progress so far, preparing the typescript of parts I and II and adding a new beginning, the incident of the drinking binge influenced by "Circe," to part I.

RECONNOITERING

Before we address the fifth stratum of materials in the *Waste Land* manuscripts, we must briefly recall the events which engulfed Eliot in mid-1921, and which shaped the conditions of his writing in this period. On 10 June, Eliot's family arrived in London, where they would stay for ten weeks before leaving on 20 August. Eliot's mother and his older sister, Marian, stayed in the Eliots' flat at 9, Clarence Gate Gardens, while Eliot and Vivien moved into some portion of a flat taken by Lucy Thayer, sister of Scofield Thayer (editor of the *Dial*) and a friend of Vivien's since 1915. Eliot's brother Henry, meanwhile, would be lodged in a separate room at 41, Gordon Square.[24] But with Vivien still feeling poorly, as she had been since February, it was decided in early July that she would go out "to a place in the country on Chichester harbour" (*LOTSE,* 459), while Henry would leave Gordon Square and join Eliot in the flat at 12, Wigmore Street.

It was at this moment, however, that Lady Rothermere first broached a plan for publishing a literary and cultural journal, an idea that eventually led to the creation of the *Criterion*. In the short term, it threatened considerable correspondence to work out the terms of her support and Eliot's participation, and by mid-July, Vivien was called back from the country to help. Now Eliot, Vivien, and his brother Henry were "encamped in an attic with a glass roof" (*LOTSE,* 461) at Wigmore Street, as Vivien put it, or in "very confined and uncomfortable quarters for three people" (*LOTSE,* 461), as Eliot put it. There they would stay for the next five weeks until the Eliot family departed. When they left, as we have seen, Henry Eliot took away Eliot's old typewriter, the one he had used since early 1914 at Harvard, and left in its place his own, much newer machine as a present.

The Eliots themselves spent yet another week at Wigmore Street and moved back to Clarence Gate Gardens only on the weekend of 27–28 August. Both Eliot and Vivien were increasingly ill. To Mary Hutchinson he wrote on 1 September: "Also I am feeling completely exhausted—the departure of my family laid us both out—and have had some splitting headaches" (*LOTSE*, 467). And six days later he reported to Richard Aldington: "My wife has been very ill, we have had to have new consultations, and to make matters worse we have been moving from Wigmore Street back here" (*LOTSE*, 468). There were also pressing commitments for journalism. In late August he wrote his regular "London Letter, September 1921" for the *Dial*, his first essay typed on the new 2.10 machine that Henry had left him. On 16 September he "finished an article, unsatisfactory to myself, on the metaphysical poets" (*LOTSE*, 469–470), his review of Herbert J. C. Grierson's anthology, *Metaphysical Lyrics and Poems of the Seventeenth Century: Donne to Butler*, which would appear the next month in the *Times Literary Supplement*.[25] By the end of September, Eliot's condition was so poor that Vivien arranged for him to see a "nerve specialist," who promptly advised Eliot to "go straight away for three months complete rest and change and . . . live according to a strict regimen which he has prescribed" (*LOTSE*, 471). But because plans for the *Criterion* had now crystallized and called for Eliot to produce a first number in January 1922, he took a further ten days to postpone the journal's planned appearance and wrap up affairs in London. It was during this interval, on 10 October, that Ezra Pound arrived in London, where he stayed for eight days with his mother-in-law, Olivia Shakespeare, at 12, Brunswick Gardens in Kensington. Pound met Eliot on the evening of 12 October (Wednesday), went to Oxford to visit Yeats on 13 October, and reported to his wife, Dorothy, on 14 October: "Eliot at last ordered away for 3 months—he seems rejuvinated [*sic*] at prospect."[26]

Finally, on 15 October, Eliot left for Margate, accompanied by Vivien. Vivien stayed with him at the Albemarle Hotel, Cliftonville, until 31 October, then returned to London, leaving him alone. But already by 26 October she had reported to a friend that Eliot was "getting on *amazingly*," looking "younger, and fatter and nicer" (*LOTSE*, 479). Eliot, in the solitude of a seaside resort grown quiet after its high season, stayed for another twelve days, then returned to London late on 12 November.

He stayed for less than a week, from 12 to 18 November, when he departed for Paris, again accompanied by Vivien. In Paris they stayed in the Sixth Arrondissement at the Hotel Pas du Calais, 59 rue des Saints Pères, where Ezra and Dorothy Pound had been residing until only a few weeks before. Pound and Eliot certainly met during the brief period when Eliot was in the city. But it seems unlikely that Pound would have had enough time to go through *The Waste Land*. Eliot departed for Lausanne, on either 21 or 22 November, leaving Vivien behind in Paris.[27] In the weeks ahead she would receive little companionship from the Pounds, who were preoccupied with other matters. On 1 November they had moved into a studio at 70 bis, rue Notre Dame des Champs, and Pound was soon busy painting the walls and constructing furniture. More alarmingly, on 13 December, Dorothy was hospitalized for an abscess on her left forefinger; it required surgery to cut off the tip of the bone, and she remained in the hospital until 27 December.[28] In Pound's extensive correspondence Eliot's visit went almost unnoticed, except for one letter written on 5 December to Scofield Thayer: "Eliot seemed fairly well when I saw him on his way through Paris last week."[29]

In Lausanne, Eliot stayed at the Hotel St. Luce, a quiet pension, from 24 November until 2 January, when he returned to Paris. Lausanne, he wrote on 4 December, was a "very quiet town, except when children come downhill on scooters over the cobbles. Mostly banks and chocolate shops" (*LOTSE*, 490). But it was there, amid "banks and chocolate shops," that Eliot finished his draft of *The Waste Land*. Now, having set out the parameters of Eliot's movements from June through December of 1921, we can turn to the remaining strata of his manuscripts.

MORE PAPER TIGERS

The fifth stratum of materials for *The Waste Land* comprises five documents. The first is a single leaf containing two independent poems, both in autograph, "Elegy" and the first draft of "Dirge" (*TWL:AF*, 116–119). The second is also a single leaf (*TWL:AF*, 48–49), this one containing a section of verse of twenty-six lines, beginning "The river sweats." With very light revisions, this became lines 266–291 of the published poem. The third document is yet another single leaf (*TWL:AF*, 50–51) which contains a section of verse of nineteen lines, beginning "Highbury bore me," a draft for two of the three songs of the Thames-daughters. With the excision of ten lines and some further revisions, these became lines 291–299 of the published poem. The fourth document is another single leaf (*TWL:AF*, 52–53), which contains twelve lines after cancellations, beginning "On Margate Sands." With no revisions at all these became lines 300–311 of the final poem.

The fifth and final document is a single leaf (*TWL:AF*, 36–37) which contains two fragments. One consists of seven lines and begins, "O City, City"; the passage was later lightly revised to become lines 259–265 of the published poem. The other consists of twelve lines and begins, "London the swarming life"; this passage became lines 106–119 in the typescript of part III which Eliot typed up later in London.

These five documents were written on a distinctive type of paper. Each leaf measures 227 × 177 mm and has a thickness of 0.11 mm. The paper is "wove" rather than laid—that is, it has no chainlines—but has a watermark reading "HIERATICA / BOND / BRITISH MAKE / J. S. & C° L^{TD}." The watermark is vertical on the leaf, and measures 45 × 48 mm. Hieratica Bond was a popular brand of paper, and it is hardly surprising that other instances of it should turn up in Eliot's correspondence. The first time is in late 1914, but the size is very different (226–227 × 152 mm), and the paper has a printed letterhead reading "Merton College" (see Table 1, T.19 and T.23; for the sake of clarity we'll call this paper Hieratica Bond [A]).[30] It also turns up for one letter of August 1918 (Table 1, T.143), but once again the size is very different (224 × 151 mm; we can call this paper Hieratica Bond [B]).[31] And it even turns up a third time in 1919 (Table 1, T.218 and T.222), but this time its size differs more sharply still (178 × 114 mm; we'll call this paper Hieratica Bond [C]).[32]

The fourth time that a Hieratica Bond paper appears in Eliot's correspondence (Hieratica Bond [D], see Fig. 6), its size exactly matches that of the five documents we have been discussing. And the dates of its usage are revealing:

DATE	RECIPIENT	NO.
16 November 1921	Harold Monro	U.89
[16? November 1921]	Sydney Schiff	T.382, *LOTSE*, p. 486
17 November 1921	Mary Hutchinson	U.90
17 November 1921	Richard Aldington	T.383, *LOTSE*, p. 487
30 November 1921	Ottoline Morrell	T.385, *LOTSE*, p. 490
6 December 1921	Jacques Rivière	U.92

Eliot, in other words, began to use the Hieratic Bond [D] paper in his correspondence in the first letters that he wrote after his return from Margate to London. Quite plainly, the paper was part of a small supply which

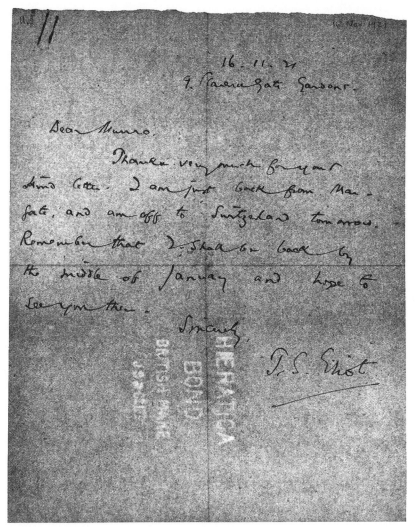

6 Hieratica Bond watermark; letter from T. S. Eliot to Harold Monro, 16 November 1921; courtesy of Donald Gallup.

he had purchased while in Margate, the remainder of which he then proceeded to use up while in London. The Hieratic Bond [D] passages, then, were all composed while Eliot was in Margate, an inference which is confirmed by Eliot himself. For while still in Margate he wrote on [4? November] to Sydney Schiff: "I have done a rough draft of part of part III, but do not know whether it will do, and must wait for Vivien's opinion as to whether it is printable. I have done it while sitting in a shelter on the front—as I am out all day except when taking rest. But I have written only some fifty lines" (*LOTSE*, 484–485). If we now take the passages written on Hieratica Bond [D] and count not the total lines written but only those passages which were not deleted, and correlate them with the published poem, we see a distinct pattern:

HIERATICA BOND [D] PASSAGE	NO. LINES	PUBLISHED POEM
"O City, City" (*TWL:AF*, 36–37)	7 lines	259–265
"The river sweats" (*TWL:AF*, 48–49)	25 lines	266–291
"Highbury bore me" (*TWL:AF*, 50–51)	9 lines	292–299
"On Margate Sands" (*TWL:AF*, 52–53)	12 lines	300–311
Total	53 lines	

These passages, then, were plainly the ones that Eliot had in mind when he wrote to Schiff that he had "written only some fifty lines." They were in good enough shape for Eliot to regard them as an identifiable unit: "a rough draft of part of Part III."

But a word of qualification needs to be entered here. Eliot plainly wrote these passages sometime after Vivien left—either on 30 or 31 October—since she had not yet seen them, and before he wrote to Schiff. But when did he write to Schiff? Eliot's letter to him is dated simply "Friday evening," and the date of [4? November] is Mrs. Eliot's conjecture. But is this the best conjectural date? Eliot's letter to Schiff complains that Vivien "tells me very little about her own health, in spite of my complaints." The plural "complaints" implies *(a)* that Eliot has already received several letters or notes from Vivien, and *(b)* that in reply to them he has already complained at least twice, something it would have been difficult to do in only four days' time. Instead, it seems more likely that the letter to Schiff should be conjecturally dated to Friday, 11 November, and therefore that the passages in question were written between 31 October, when Vivien left, and 11 November, the most likely date when Eliot addressed Schiff.

There are further implications which can be drawn from Eliot's comments to Schiff. We should recall that the four passages that I have listed immediately above do not exhaust the Hieratica Bond [D] documents. Three texts are conspicuously not included in Eliot's account to Schiff: the two independently titled poems, "Dirge" and "Elegy" (both written on one leaf), and the passage beginning "London, the swarming life" (this last written on the same leaf that contains "O City, City," though separated from it by a line that slashes across the middle of the page). Let us deal first with the independently titled poems. Eliot makes no mention of them to Schiff. It is possible, of course, that he makes no mention of them because they were not yet composed—in other words, that they were composed only after he had written to Schiff on 11 November, and before he returned to London on 12 November. But that seems rather unlikely. And if they were not composed after the Schiff letter, if instead they were composed before, then Eliot's decision not to mention them carries the implication that the independent poems "Elegy" and "Dirge" were not viewed as part of the long poem which he had been discussing with Schiff since April, but were conceived as independent works. I suspect that this was the case, and there is further evidence for it in the way that Eliot treats the independent poems. For Eliot never mines them for lines or passages to be inserted into *The Waste Land*. Instead, they are conceived as having their own integrity. And this treatment differs sharply from how he treats the poems and passages contained in the first two strata of materials which date from October 1913 ("After the turning" and "So through the evening"), mid-April 1915 ("The Death of St. Narcissus"), and September 1916 ("The Death of the Duchess"). These, though originally conceived as independent or potentially independent works, were now in 1921 considered simply raw material from which lines and passages might be wrested—quite different from the independent poems which Eliot wrote in the course of 1921, such as "Dirge" and "Elegy," or later "Exequy." Those poems, written contemporaneously with the drafts of *The Waste Land*, were a concession to Eliot's concern that his long poem might not be long enough to make up a book, and they were intended to do just that—make up a book. In effect, their place was later assumed by the notes to the poem.

The third text not mentioned in the letter to Schiff is the twelve-line passage, beginning "London, the swarming life," written on the same leaf that contains "O City, City." Unlike the independent poems, which were neither incorporated into the larger poem nor treated as raw material from which individual lines or passages might be wrested, this passage was incorporated, with alterations, into the typescript draft of part III (and its carbon) that Eliot produced the next week while in London (*TWL:AF*,

30–31 and 42–43, lines 106–119). Why was it not mentioned to Schiff? There are two possible reasons. The first is that Eliot was describing a co-herent "part of Part III," the section that was to become part III's conclusion and stretch across lines 259–311 of the published poem. Since "London, the swarming life" formed no part of that coherent section, there was no need to mention it. At the moment he was writing to Schiff, it was simply a fragment that might or might not be later incorporated into part III, too trifling an affair to announce to a devoted reader and friend. The second possibility is that it simply had not yet been composed. On that hypothesis, it was written still later, sometime during the span of six days when Eliot was back in London (12–18 November), hurriedly preparing the typescripts of part III, hastily packing for Lausanne. Possible, but not very likely. Better to assign it to the period between 31 October and 11 November, with the other Margate or Hieratica Bond [D] materials.[33]

The sixth stratum of manuscript materials for *The Waste Land* con-sists of two typescripts of part III, a top copy and a carbon (each five leaves); one independent poem titled "Exequy" (one leaf), which is also in type-script; and an autograph draft of ten lines, beginning "The rivers tent is broken," which has been written on the verso of leaf one of the typescript part III. For the moment we can set this last text aside and deal with the other three documents. All three documents are preserved on the same kind of paper, which measures 265 × 202 or 203 mm and has a thickness of 0.06 mm. The paper has eight chainlines, which are vertical, at intervals of 25.5 mm. It also has a watermark reading: "VERONA LINEN." It measures 14 × 128 mm.

Dating the typescript copies of part III presents little difficulty. Incorpo-rated into each is the fourteen-line passage beginning "London, the swarm-ing life" (*TWL:AF*, 30–31 and 42–43, lines 106–119) which Eliot had re-cently drafted in Margate, the passage preserved in autograph draft on the same leaf as the "O City, City" passage (*TWL:AF*, 37). The typescripts, therefore, can only have been produced *after* the Margate or Hieratica Bond [D] passage, and can only have been produced when Eliot had access to the new, 2.10 typewriter which Henry Eliot had given to him as a gift when he left England on 20 August. That dovetails with what we already know: that Eliot did not have access to his typewriter when in Margate, since the eight letters and the Hieratica Bond [D] passages and poems which he wrote there were all written by hand. It follows that these typescripts were produced in the brief interval between Eliot's stays in Margate and Lausanne, the period of little less than a week, from 12 to 18 November, when Eliot was in London again and had access to his typewriter. It is most likely that the independent poem "Exequy" was also typed up during the same period.

Having dated these typescripts to the six-day period when Eliot was back in London, or between his stays in Margate and Lausanne, we can also discern the broad arc of Eliot's intentions in producing them. Knowing that he would be away in Lausanne for some six weeks, and planning to make a final effort to bring his long poem to completion, Eliot was assembling a working version of the materials he had so far written, a neatly typed "working draft" which he could consult while in Lausanne. Not that Eliot managed to fulfill his good intentions: he plainly failed to type up the autograph leaves which form the fifth or Margate stratum of materials for *The Waste Land* (apart from the passage "London, the swarming life"), those that correspond to the closing portion of part III of the published poem (lines 259–311). Probably he simply didn't have enough time.

While we can pinpoint the moment when these typescripts were produced, and integrate that knowledge into a coherent account of Eliot's travel and writing plans, we can only speculate about when Eliot first wrote the rough drafts which he must have used (and then jettisoned) as he produced the typescripts of part III and "Exequy." When were they written? Not, plainly, during the Margate period from 15 October to 12 November, when he was writing the autograph drafts ("O City, City," "The river sweats," "Highbury bore me," and "On Margate Sands") and the independent poems ("Dirge," "Elegy") which we have already discussed. The rough drafts that went into making the typescript of part III must date from earlier. In fact, there are really only two periods possible: one, the period from 20 August to 15 October which followed his family's departure for the United States; the other, the period from 10 June to 20 August when his family was visiting and he was staying at Wigmore Street. The later period, 20 August to 15 October, seems less likely. Eliot was busy moving back into his flat from 20 August to 27–28 August, occupied with typing up his "London Letter, September 1921" for the *Dial* in early September, pressed with writing "The Metaphysical Poets" in mid-September, obliged to visit the Woolfs in late September, and worried by his health and hastily planned departure for Margate from 1 to 14 October. It is more likely that he wrote the rough drafts that went into the typescript of part III during the ten weeks when his family was visiting, a lengthy period (10 June to 20 August) when he was wholly free from his regular round of social obligations, the dutiful visits to Mary Hutchinson, the Woolfs, the Schiffs, and Richard Aldington. Though we cannot be certain, this period is the more likely candidate.

Finally, we must turn to the passage that we momentarily set aside, the autograph draft of ten lines beginning "The rivers tent is broken" (*TWL:AF*, 24–25), which is found on the verso side of leaf one in the "Fire Sermon" typescript, the top copy. These lines are, of course, the famous opening to part III of *The Waste Land*. It is possible that they were drafted contemporaneously with the production of the typescript, the period between 12 and 18 November before Eliot left for Lausanne. And if so, they would have been thought of as a fragment awaiting some future destination. But such a scenario defies what little we know of Eliot's compositional practices at this time: if his comments to Sydney Schiff are indicative, he wrote with the idea in mind that a new draft would form part of something already in progress or definitely planned, "a rough draft of part of Part III," for example, rather than just writing for the sake of writing. Yet if that is true, then it is much more likely that he wrote what would later become the beginning of part III only when he was actually in need of a beginning to part III. That was hardly the case when he was back in London from 12 to 18 November. Then he had a firm, perhaps even too firm, beginning for part III:

> Admonished by the sun's inclining ray,
> And swift approaches of the thievish day,
> The white-armed Fresca blinks, and yawns, and gapes,
> Aroused from dreams of love and pleasant rapes.
> (*TWL:AF*, 22–23)

Moreover, Eliot believed that the seventy-two-line passage about Fresca formed the beginning to part III not just when he was briefly in London from 12 to 18 November but during the entire time when he was in Lausanne, from 22 November to 2 January, so much so that while there he even drafted another passage of seventeen lines, "From which, a Venus Anadyomene" (*TWL:AF*, 28–29), that was to be inserted into the Fresca passage between lines 56 and 57. By now, of course, it will be obvious that Eliot needed a beginning for part III only after Pound, in Paris, had repeatedly run his pen downward across the entire Fresca passage, with nine swift gashes, one so deep that it scored the paper and allowed the ink to bleed through to the verso side. Appropriately, it is on that very verso, and literally right on top of the ink left by Pound's pen, that Eliot wrote "The rivers tent is broken." For when in Paris, as we shall see in more detail below, Eliot lacked paper and had to borrow some from Pound. To write a new beginning to part III, then, he used the only paper to hand, the discarded old beginning to part III. In short, Eliot wrote this passage in Paris, probably between 5 and 10 January. It was the last passage that he composed for *The Waste Land,* wedged into the middle of the poem, and preserved in a documentary stratum that antedated its composition by two months.

The challenge posed by the passage beginning "The rivers tent is broken" throws into relief a potential problem which until now has remained only latent, a tension between the poem's documentary stratification and its compositional stratification. That tension surfaces only twice in *Waste Land* manuscripts, both times within the sixth documentary stratum which we have just discussed. It surfaces here, with "The rivers tent is broken," and it surfaces again with the two typescripts for part III, which, though typed between 12 and 18 November in London, were clearly written earlier (between 10 June and 20 August, in my view). For the moment we need not tease at the implications of that tension, since it has no practical consequences for dating the prepublication manuscripts.

The seventh stratum of materials for *The Waste Land* consists of four documents: the autograph fair copies of parts IV and V of the poem (*TWL:AF,* 54–61 and 70–79); an autograph fair copy of the independent poem "Dirge" (*TWL:AF,* 120); and the autograph passage of seventeen lines, beginning "From which, a Venus Anadyomene" (*TWL:AF,* 28–29), which was inserted into the Fresca episode.

All four are written on paper which measures 270–271 × 208 mm and has a thickness of 0.06 mm. The paper is wove, and so without chain-lines. It also lacks a watermark. It has, however, a distinctive pattern of violet quadrules: the horizontal lines, which begin 21 mm from the top edge of the leaf, consist of twenty-seven lines that occupy a block of space that measures 234 mm and come to an end 16 mm from the bottom edge of the leaf (or: 21.234(27).16). The paper is not of the quality which Eliot normally used in his correspondence. It should be no surprise, then, that it appears in only one letter, a note from Eliot to Sydney Schiff, dated 19 December 1921 and written when Eliot was in Lausanne. As scholars have long suspected, these materials were composed between 21–22 November, when Eliot left for Lausanne, and 2 January, when he returned to Paris with the sheaf of manuscripts which Ezra Pound would now edit.

The eighth stratum of materials for *The Waste Land* consists of two documents, the typescripts for parts IV and V of the poem (*TWL:AF*, 62–69 and 82–89). The paper used in each is briefly described in Table 4 (pages 200–201), an account that need not be repeated here. The papers do not match any found in Eliot's letters, and for an obvious reason: we have no surviving letters from Eliot for the period between 25 December 1921 and 20 January 1922, and it is very likely that these papers were simply borrowed from Ezra Pound. The violet typewriter ribbon and the large sized typewriter (its individual characters are 2.54 mm in width) are recognizably those of Ezra Pound. There can be no doubt that these typescripts were prepared in Paris sometime between 2 January 1922, when Eliot arrived from Lausanne, and 16 January, when he left Paris to return to London. It is reasonable to infer that the typescript was made early in the visit, between 2 and 5 January.

Because we are tracing both the compositional and documentary strata of the prepublication materials, we must devise an additional or ninth stratum here to account for the ten-line passage beginning "The rivers tent is broken." Composed by Eliot to serve as a new beginning for part III after Pound had removed the entire Fresca passage, it represents the last stretch of continuous writing that Eliot did for *The Waste Land.*

The tenth and final stratum of the *Waste Land* materials consists of a single typescript leaf that contains the poem's title and an epigraph from Joseph Conrad's *Heart of Darkness*. The paper measures 263 × 203 mm and has a thickness of 0.06 mm. It has eight chainlines, which are vertical, at intervals of 25.5 mm. It also has a watermark ("VERONA LINEN") that measures 14 × 128 mm. The same type of paper appears in two letters by Eliot from January 1922: one, dated 20 January 1922, addressed to Scofield Thayer (T.391, *LOTSE*, 501; see Fig. 7), the other dated [26 January 1922] to Ezra Pound (T.394, *LOTSE*, 504).[34]

The second of these is the more important, for it replies to Pound's comment in a letter written two days earlier on "24 Saturnus," or January (*LOTSE*, 497–499): "I doubt if Conrad is weighty enough to stand the ci-

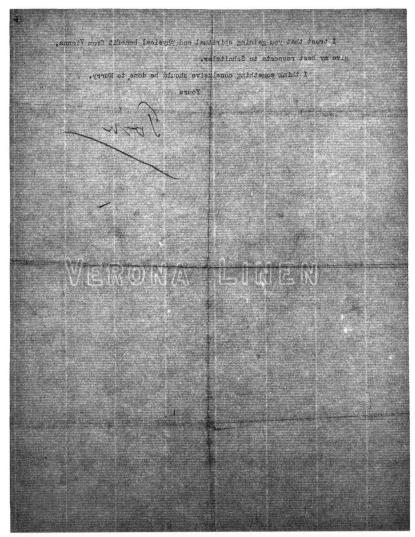

7 Verona Linen watermark; letter of T. S. Eliot to Scofield Thayer, 20 January 1922;
courtesy of the Beinecke Rare Book and Manuscript Library, Yale University.

tation." In his reply of 26 January, Eliot asked: "Do you mean not use Conrad quot. or simply not put Conrad's name to it? It is much the most appropriate I can find, and somewhat elucidative" (*LOTSE*, 504). Though Pound's
response was diffident ("Do as you like . . . re the Conrad; who am I to
grudge him his laurel crown" [*LOTSE*, 505]), Eliot decided to jettison the

epigraph by Conrad and find another. All of which makes clear that the single leaf which we have been discussing, containing the Conrad epigraph and the title of the poem, was the topmost sheet of the nineteen-page manuscript seen by Pound on 24 January, containing the penultimate version of *The Waste Land*. It had never formed part of the materials which Pound saw in Paris between 2 and 15 January 1922, nor was it part of that nebulous entity which recent scholars have called "the 1921 text." It was typed between 16 January 1922, the day Eliot returned to London, and 20 January, the day he probably sent the typescript off to Pound. Sadly, the rest of the famous nineteen-page manuscript has never been found and was probably discarded by Eliot when he made a final draft of the poem sometime after 30 January; but if the missing manuscript ever does turn up, we can be sure that it will have been typed with the same 2.10 machine which Henry Eliot had left behind on 20 August 1921, and that it will be on paper bearing the Verona Linen watermark.

Having completed our tour through the prepublication manuscripts which are reproduced in Valerie Eliot's facsimile edition, we can summarize our conclusions in a synoptic table:

Stratum 1

Dates: 2–10 October 1913, Cambridge, Massachusetts
   "After the turning" (*TWL:AF*, 108–109)
   "So through the evening" (*TWL:AF*, 112–113)
   "I am the Resurrection" (*TWL:AF*, 110–111)

Stratum 2

Date: c. 15 April 1915, Oxford
   "The Death of St. Narcissus," autograph draft (*TWL:AF*, 90–91)
Date: May 1916, London
   "The Death of St. Narcissus," autograph fair copy (*TWL:AF*, 92–93)
Date: September 1916, London
   "The Death of the Duchess" (*TWL:AF*, 104–107)

Stratum 3

Dates: 23–31 January 1921, London
   "Song for the Opherion," autograph draft (*TWL:AF*, 98–99)

Stratum 4

Dates: typed 9–22 May 1921; missing drafts for lines 1–76 of the published
        poem composed between 23 January and 5 February, shown to
        Wyndham Lewis on 5 February; missing drafts for part II composed
        between 6 February and 9 May; missing draft for Boston version
        of "Night-town" incident (*TWL:AF*, 4–5) composed c. 21 May.
        "Those are pearls," autograph draft (*TWL:AF*, 122–123)
        part I, typescript (*TWL:AF*, 4–9)
        part II, typescript (*TWL:AF*, 10–15)
        part II, carbon typescript (*TWL:AF*, 16–21)

Stratum 5

Dates: composed 31 October to 11 November 1921, Margate
        "Elegy" and "Dirge," first draft (*TWL:AF*, 116–119)
        "O City, City," autograph draft (*TWL:AF*, 36–37)
        "The river sweats," autograph draft (*TWL:AF*, 48–49)
        "Highbury bore me," autograph draft (*TWL:AF*, 50–51)
        "On Margate Sands," autograph draft (*TWL:AF*, 52–53)
        "London, the swarming life," autograph draft (*TWL:AF*, 36–37)

Stratum 6

Dates: typed 12–18 November 1921, London; composed 10 June to 20 August
        1921, London
        part III, typescript (*TWL:AF*, 22–23, 26–35)
        part III, carbon typescript (*TWL:AF*, 38–47)
        "Exequy," typescript (*TWL:AF*, 100–101)

Dates: composed 5–10 January 1922, Paris (see also *Stratum 9*)
        "The rivers tent," autograph draft on part III, typescript, leaf 1, verso
        (*TWL:AF*, 24–25)

Stratum 7

Dates: composed 22 November–31 December 1921, Lausanne, Switzerland
        part IV, autograph fair copy (*TWL:AF*, 54–61)
        part V, autograph fair copy (*TWL:AF*, 70–79)
        "Dirge," autograph fair copy (*TWL:AF*, 120–121)
        "From which, a Venus Anadyomene," autograph draft (*TWL:AF*,
        28–29)

Stratum 8

Dates: typed 2–5 January 1922, Paris
        part IV, typescript (*TWL:AF*, 62–69)
        part V, typescript (*TWL:AF*, 82–89)

Stratum 9

Dates: composed 5–10 January 1922, Paris; preserved on document from
        Stratum 6.
        "The rivers tent," autograph draft on part III, typescript, leaf 1, verso
        (*TWL:AF*, 24–25)

Stratum 10

Dates: typed 17–22 January 1922, London
        Title page with epigraph, typescript (*TWL:AF*, 2–3)

The creation of the title page for a penultimate version of the poem marked only a passing moment in the protracted conclusion to the poem's genesis. Even after Eliot returned to London on 16 January, his manuscripts now bearing Pound's editorial interventions, the poem had still not assumed the shape we know today. Writing on 20 January to Scofield Thayer to offer him the poem for publication in the *Dial*, Eliot briefly characterized his new work as "a poem of about four hundred and fifty lines, *in four parts*" (*LOTSE*, 502; italics mine). Remarkable as it seems to us, Eliot was planning to issue the poem without part IV. But evidently he had second thoughts about this plan and reinserted part IV into the poem again within a few days. A few days later, however, Eliot had third thoughts when writing again to Pound on 26 January, asking: "Perhaps better omit Phlebas also???" (*LOTSE*, 504). Pound replied with characteristic vigor: "I DO advise keeping Phlebas. In fact I more'n advise. Phlebas is an integral part of the poem; the card pack introduces him, the drowned phoen. sailor, and he is needed ABSoloootly where he is. Must stay in" (*LOTSE*, 505).

For Eliot, at least, the decision to retain part IV effectively marked the end of his actively composing the poem, a process that had required just over a year of time, from the final days of January 1921, when he had first begun the draft of part I that he soon showed to Wyndham Lewis, to the final days of January 1922, when he was absorbing the last admonitions of Ezra Pound. Indeed, in contemporary letters Eliot repeatedly alluded to the length of time it had taken him to write the poem. When Scofield

Thayer offered him $150 for the poem (sight unseen), Eliot refused be-
cause the sum "did not strike me as good pay for a year's work" (*LOTSE,*
507); he had no intention of accepting such a figure "for a poem which it
has taken me a year to write" (*LOTSE,* 515). The yearlong saga of the poem
had indeed reached its end. But the story of its coda, the composition of
the notes, was just beginning.

Even after he had acceded to Pound's demand that part IV, the ten
lines of "Phlebas," be restored, Eliot still faced a nagging problem which
had intermittently troubled him throughout the time when he had been
composing *The Waste Land.* The poem was too short to make up an independent book. Worse still, Pound had vetoed the idea of including what
Eliot called the "miscellaneous pieces" (three independent poems, "Song,"
"Exequy," and either "Dirge" or "Elegy"), or what Pound termed "Those at
end" (*LOTSE,* 504). Moreover, Eliot's concern over this question had been
exacerbated by that of an eminent authority, the American publisher Horace
Liveright. Back in January 1922, when Eliot had first returned to Paris
from Lausanne, he had been introduced by Pound to Liveright, who was
traveling in France and England in search of new authors. Liveright had
promptly agreed to offer Eliot a $150 advance for the poem and a royalty of
15 percent, largely on Pound's recommendation, as he hadn't yet read the
poem. But already on 11 January, Liveright, by then in London, had written
to Pound about his concern over the poem's length: "I'm disappointed
that Eliot's material is as short. Can't he add anything?" he pleaded with
Pound, who doubtless relayed his worry to Eliot, still in Paris.[35]

It was Liveright's suggestion that Eliot "add anything" which ultimately
led Eliot to furnish the poem with notes. While they might not make the
poem long enough to suit Liveright, they would suffice to make up a small
volume which could be published as a deluxe or limited edition in the
event that Liveright balked. On 16 February, having learned from his friend
Conrad Aiken about Maurice Firuski, a publisher of deluxe editions who
was situated in Cambridge, Massachusetts, Eliot wrote to pursue this
prospect:

> Your name has been given me by Conrad Aiken. . . . I under-
> stand that you issue these books in limited editions, and that
> for the volumes you take in this series you give a sum down
> in advance royalty.

> My poem is of 435 lines; with certain spacings essential to
> the sense, 475 book lines; furthermore, it consists of five parts,
> which would increase the space necessary; and with title pages,
> some notes that I intend to add, etc., I guess that it would run
> to from 28 to 32 pages.[36]

But Firuski was slow to reply, and by 12 March Liveright had confirmed his interest in publishing the poem as a book. When Liveright finally sent a contract in mid-June, however, Eliot was alarmed at the vagueness of its terms and turned to John Quinn, the New York lawyer and cultural patron who had generously handled Eliot's contracts with his previous American publisher, Knopf, without charging a fee. To Quinn, therefore, he wrote describing his new work: "I have written . . . a long poem of about 450 words [lines], which, with notes that I am adding, will make a book of 30 to 40 pages" (*LOTSE*, 530). Even now, four months after his letter to Firuski, Eliot had still not completed the poem's notes, and at best had begun "adding" them. But "with notes that I am adding" may well have been more a pious aspiration than a statement of fact, and as late as mid-June 1922, Eliot may not have written even a portion of the poem's notes.

Meanwhile, the deadline for submission of a final manuscript, if the book was to be included in the autumn list, was fast approaching: "Liveright said he would print it for the autumn if he had the poem by the end of July" (*LOTSE*, 531). When Liveright, around 9 July, sent Eliot a letter suggesting that he was amenable to the revised contract that Quinn had proposed in the interim, Eliot hurriedly addressed the problem of a typescript in a letter to John Quinn, dated 19 July: "As it is now so late I am enclosing the typescript to hand to him when the contract is complete, or to hold if he does not complete. I had wished to type it out fair, but I did not wish to delay it any longer. This will do for him to get on with, and I shall rush forward the notes to go at the end" (*LOTSE*, 547). If Eliot really had begun "adding" the notes in mid-June, he must have proceeded very slowly if he hadn't finished by mid-July. Plainly it was a task he approached with diffidence, even indifference.

When Ezra Pound requested a copy of the poem in order to show it to James Sibley Watson, Jr., the co-owner of the *Dial* who had been entrusted with negotiating for the serial rights to the poem after Eliot had quarreled with his colleague Scofield Thayer, Eliot replied on 28 July: "I will let you have a copy of the Waste Land for confidential use as soon as I can make one. Of the two available copies, one has gone to Quinn to presented to Liveright on completion of the contract, and the other is the only one I possess" (*LOTSE*, 552). If this second copy of the poem was an exact replica of the copy sent to Liveright, it, too, lacked the notes. Though we cannot be entirely certain, it appears that the notes were not completed until early August, and that they were then posted directly to Liveright. Only then was *The Waste Land* completed in the form that we know it today.

By 15 September, Eliot could tell Pound, in a brief postscript to a letter about other matters: "Liveright's proof is excellent" (*LOTSE*, 570). Eliot was much less happy, though, with the printer who produced the *Criterion* version of the poem in London. To Richard Cobden-Sanderson he wrote on 27 September, "I am also sending you the manuscript and the proof of the first part of my poem, so that you may have a record of the undesired alterations made by the printers" (*LOTSE*, 574). And on 3 October, Eliot wrote him again: "You will see that I am enclosing the corrected proof of the rest of *The Waste Land*. I shall ring you up tomorrow morning at about eleven and will explain why I have done so" (*LOTSE*, 576). But at last the long travails of the poem were drawing to a close. Two weeks later, on 16 October, the first number of the *Criterion* appeared, containing the first publication of *The Waste Land*, without notes. Publication of the poem in the *Dial*, an American magazine, took place a few days later. Five weeks after that, about 1 December, the poem appeared for the first time as an independent book, complete with notes, issued by the American firm of Boni and Liveright.[37]

CONNECTING THE DOTS

Most of the prepublication manuscripts for *The Waste Land* are typescript and autograph fair copies rather than drafts, documents which Eliot assembled from extant drafts in anticipation of a turning point in his private life (parts I and II in May before the arrival of his family in June; the typescript of part III between 12 and 18 November, before he left for Lausanne). Drafts, in contrast, can tell us more about the process of composition. If we set aside the materials produced before February 1921, or strata 1 to 3, then we have only seven or eight autograph drafts extant: seven if we think, as Mrs. Eliot does, that "Highbury bore me" and "On Margate Sands" formed a single draft; eight if we think, as I am inclined, that these were separate drafts. If we arrange them in order by their length, from shortest to longest, and then note how many lines from each draft were retained in the final poem, the result would look like this:

PASSAGE	NO. OF LINES	LINES SURVIVING IN PUBLISHED POEM
"Those are pearls" (*TWL:AF*, 122–23)	5	1
"O City, City" (*TWL:AF*, 36–37)	7	7
"Highbury bore me" (*TWL:AF*, 50–51)	8	8
"The river's tent" (*TWL:AF*, 24–25)	10	10
"On Margate Sands" (*TWL:AF*, 52–53)	12	12
"London, the swarming life" (*TWL:AF*, 36–37)	12	0
"From which, a Venus Anadyomene" (*TWL:AF*, 28–29)	17	0
"The river sweats" (*TWL:AF*, 48–49)	25	25
Total	96	63

Whether these figures are the product of seven or eight drafts, it remains remarkable how short was a typical draft by Eliot: 13.7 lines in length if they represent seven drafts, only 12 lines if they represent eight. Moreover, since on average only two-thirds of a draft typically survived into the published text, it is equally remarkable how many drafts it would have required to make a poem of 433 lines. If the 63 lines that have survived into the final poem represent seven drafts, it would have required forty-eight drafts of comparable average length. If they represent eight drafts, the poem would have required fifty-five such drafts. (These calculations suggest that between forty and fifty drafts may have been lost or discarded during composition.) The trick in writing such a long poem, then, was how to stitch together between 48 and 55 separate drafts. Connectedness, plainly, was a pressing problem.

Of the seven drafts that survive (henceforth we shall follow Mrs. Eliot's view that "Highbury bore me" and "On Margate Sands" are a single draft), one went into the making of part I ("Those are pearls"), while the other six went into part III. Of those six, we recall that four were composed in Margate between 31 October and 11 November, and that three were already conceived as forming a "part of Part III" by about 11 November, when Eliot described them to Sydney Schiff—"O City, City" (*TWL:AF*, 36–37), "The

river sweats" (*TWL:AF*, 48–49), and "Highbury bore me" (*TWL:AF*, 50–53).
Together they make up lines 259–311 of the poem as published and form
the conclusion to part III. What unites the three is an associative logic dictated by motifs of music and the river, both fused (after line 266) by the
ghostly echo of Wagner's Rhine-maidens, now the Thames-daughters. For
our purpose, we needn't tease out all the possible implications of these
passages, the subject of considerable debate.[38] Instead we want to stay
close to the surface of the poem, to the associative logic and syntactic patterning which shape the flow of composition. The first of the three passages
starts up just after the loveless coupling of the young man carbuncular
and the unnamed typist, a scene followed by two lines that quote from
The Tempest (already quoted in part I), then surge eastward across the
cityscape of London, as if traveling from the flat of the typist toward the
heart of the financial district, the City (already invoked in part I):

> "This music crept by me upon the waters"
> And along the Strand, up Queen Victoria Street.

Now the poem resumes with a new draft:

> O City, City, I have heard and hear
> The pleasant whining of ~~the~~ a mandoline
> ~~Outside~~/Beside a public bar in lower Thames Street,
> And a clatter and a chatter ~~in the bar~~ from within
> Where fishmen lounge ~~and loafe and spit at noon~~ at noontime
>   ~~out there~~/where the walls
> Of Magnus Martyr stood, and stand, and hold
> ~~Inviolable~~   ⎰ music
> ~~Their joyful~~ ⎱ splendour of Corinthian white and gold
> Inexplicable (*TWL:AF*, 36–37)[39]

What is striking in this draft is the repeated tension among three conflicting imperatives: the ambition to assert connectedness to earlier parts of
the poem (and especially to earlier passages in part III) through either repeated images or syntactic and aural patterning; a countervailing tendency
to turn away or digress into new subject matter that threatens to prove a
dead end; and a discernible worry that the assertion of connectedness will
be too obvious. The phrase "I have heard and hear," for example, resolutely
recalls "But at my back from time to time I hear" (a line that appears twice

in the earlier portions of part III), but is also vexed by the need to be different, to avoid mere repetition.[40] When not working to establish external connectedness to previous portions of the poem, local revisions enhance an assertion of internal relatedness within the draft passage itself: the word "Beside" replaces "Outside" so as to reiterate the plosives of "public bar" and "pleasant," while "there" (in "there the walls of Magnus Martyr") must give way to "where" so as to create exact syntactic repetition ("Where fishmen lounge" and "where the walls"). Yet this way of proceeding also courts the risk of too much repetition, of being rather too obvious in its way of asserting relatedness, a dilemma that is played out in the last line of the "O City, City" passage: the phrase "inviolable music" obviously echoes the "inviolable voice" of the nightingale in part II—much too obviously, we want to say. And so it must be deleted, to be replaced instead with "Inexplicable splendour," a phrase which reinforces aural connectedness with the preceding lines (still three more plosives), but which is no longer too obvious in reinforcing the motif of music. "Inexplicable splendour" now harks back to "inviolable voice," but in a very muted way, having changed the ground of likeness from an auditory to a visual register. So muted, in fact, that the passage effectively reaches an impasse: for if one risk that attended this passage had been the danger that it might become too obvious in emphasizing music ("inviolable music"), the other was that it would simply trail off to nowhere, twist away into a dead end, turning into a "withered stump" of composition, we might say. And so it does. True, a marvelous "withered stump"—but still a "withered stump." And the passage comes to an end. There is no choice now except to begin again, which is precisely what Eliot will do in his next draft.

And just as we see these procedures at work at a micro-level, so they can also be discerned at a macro-level. For when Eliot completes the three drafts that now form the ending to part III, with their insistent stress on music, the river, and nymphs or watery semideities (the Thames-daughters), the conclusion isn't just good, it is too good: it seems strangely unrelated to part III's opening, the seventy-odd lines of acerbic couplets that depict the wealthy socialite Fresca. The only solution is to force the Fresca passage into having more relatedness with the conclusion, and that is just what Eliot does in the draft that he subsequently writes in Lausanne. As before, the point of connection must be water, and so Eliot puts a large asterisk and the command "insert" directly opposite a passage about Fresca's reading habits, her immersion "in a soapy sea / of Symonds-Walter Pater-Vernon Lee." Once more he begins, this time transforming Fresca into a version of Venus rising from the sea:

> From which, a Venus Anadyomene
> She stept ashore to a more varied scene,
> Propelled by Lady Katzegg's guiding hand,
> She knew the wealth and fashion of the land.
> (*TWL:AF,* 28–29)

And so it continues for another thirteen lines, all in what Pound called the "too loose" manner of Eliot's pastiche of Pope (*TWL:AF,* 38–39). (The image of Venus Anadyomene even furnishes a neat echo of the "gilded shell" in which Elizabeth and Leicester sail, in the Thames-daughters' song.) But our concern here is not with the passage's success or failure but with the kind of order which is dictating the composition of the poem: that order is fundamentally contingent and retrospective. It is not, in other words, an order being achieved as the realization of a plan or program, dictated by some predetermined notion of mythic structure or ritual pattern; what *The Waste Land* achieves are always relative and incremental orders of coherence that are local, contingent, and retrospective in nature.

Which brings us to the last of the six drafts written for part III, the one written so late that it is effectively the final extended passage of the poem, penciled in only after Pound had gutted the eighty-seven lines devoted to Fresca. As before, when drafting "From which, a Venus Anadyomene," Eliot starts with the same givens inherited from his earlier composition of the ending to part III, music, the river, and nymphs or watery semideities:

> The rivers tent is broken and the last fingers of leaf
> Clutch and sink into the wet bank. The wind
> Crosses the brown land, unheard. The nymphs are departed.
> (Sweet Thames etc.)
> The river bears no empty bottles, sandwich papers
> ~~Ca~~ Newspapers, cardboard boxes, cigarette ends
> Or other testimony of summer nights. The nymphs are departed.

(And their friends, the loitering heirs of City directors)
Departed, have left no addresses.
By the waters (*TWL:AF*, 24–25)

In one sense, this passage does exactly what it was meant to do: it "anticipates" the City location, the motifs of music and song, and the nymphs
(or Thames-daughters) that appear at part III's end. Its diction resonates
with calculated echoes that extend both backward and forward, with "clutch"
looking back to part I ("What are the roots that clutch?" line 19), or "brown,"
glancing not only back to a line in part I ("Unreal City, / Under the brown
fog . . .," lines 60–61) but also ahead to its repetition in part III ("Unreal
City / Under the brown fog . . .," lines 207–208), and still farther ahead
to the brown tones that dominate the opening of part V ("the sandy road"
[332], "the mountains of rock" [334], the "mudcracked houses" [345], and
"dry grass" [355]) and culminate in the mysterious figure "gliding wrapt
in a brown mantle, hooded" (364). And because this new introduction so
closely "anticipates" the terms of part III's conclusion, part III now acquires
an envelope, circular, or ring structure in which music, nymphs, and City
location appear at both the beginning and the end, a structure that all the
more firmly sets off the little five-line coda which has been excluded from
the circle's interior and so contrasts all the more violently with, and comments all the more damningly on, what has come before it:

To Carthage then I came

Burning burning burning burning
O Lord Thou pluckest me out
O Lord Thou pluckest

burning

Surely it does. Surely the desolating power of the coda has only been en-
hanced by the new introduction to part III. And yet many readers, I think,
may still deem the introduction to part III a bit forced, a tad strained. And
signs of such strain are all too readily detected: why is that we are being
asked to bid farewell to nymphs who, until this point in the poem, have
never appeared? How can we say "good-bye" before we've managed to
mutter "hello"? And doesn't this transparent rupture in logical-causal relatedness work to undermine the very assertion of connectedness which

this passage was meant to achieve through the use of anticipatory repetition? Or is it perhaps the other way around? For isn't it the case that the
factitious use of repetition to intimate connectedness, say at the beginning
and ending of part III, works to disable, to neutralize, to annihilate the
claims to logical and spatiotemporal connectedness which are elsewhere
being asserted, say in the line "and along the Strand, up Queen Victoria
Street" (258), that line which was to transport us from the flat of the typist
to the locale of the City? Such attention to the demands of the cityscape,
and to an implied logic of spatiotemporal coordination, is rendered otiose
by the competing claims of a wholly different kind of order that is organized
around the use of repetition and pattern to suggest symbolic depth, resonance, and development. The outcome is something of a standoff: the incremental moments of coherence which *The Waste Land* fashions are not
only local, contingent, and retrospective in nature, they are also driven by
conflicting imperatives derived from their claim to modes of coherence
—one appealing to repetition and pattern to invoke symbolic depth, resonance, enhancement; the other appealing to the kind of logical, causal,
and spatiotemporal connectedness typical of narrative—that are deeply
contradictory, perhaps even self-canceling.

Yet that self-canceling quality is not solely or strictly an effect of juxtaposition. Consider the tensions at play in one especially notable instance
of repetition and patterning which spins around the phrase "Unreal City"
that turns up with artful symmetry in parts I, III, and V:

> Unreal City
> Under the brown fog of a winter dawn (60–61, part I)

> Unreal City,
> Under the brown fog of a winter noon (207–208, part III)

Readers, by this point, will reasonably expect the next variant to run:

> Unreal City
> Under the brown fog of a winter evening

Or perhaps:

> Unreal City
> Under the brown fog of a winter twilight

But instead the poem offers up:

Falling towers
Jerusalem Athens Alexandria
Vienna London
Unreal (374–377)

Pattern, in this stunning sequence, dissolves into something that resembles patter—the schemata of a list, that lowest of all literary forms, unorganized by any syntax; a bare heap lacking even the fig leaf of a comma. Surely repetition and pattern have been invoked in this sequence of passages; but just as surely they have also been undermined in a histrionics of non-relationship. "Unreal City / Under the brown fog of . . .": that phrase, we are led to infer, has somewhat the same status as the "inviolable music" which flickered into view when Eliot was drafting the "O City, City" passage. It is obvious, the poem seems to say; it is too obvious. And the effect is wickedly corrosive, for it also decomposes the claim to connectedness and resonance advanced by the repetition of "brown"—the "brown land," the "sandy road," or the "brown mantle, hooded." Here are likenesses, the poem murmurs, but likenesses that only turn into illusions. So perhaps the real work of signifying, we reason, is being done somewhere else: perhaps there, in that grim catalogue of toponyms, or in the kind of spatio-temporal connectedness which place names imply, connectedness that is a property both of realistic fiction and of our sense of the world to which such fiction lays claim. But of course, we have already traveled "along the Strand, up Queen Victoria Street" once before, and we have seen where that led.

Consider another example, the verse paragraph that makes up the poem's famous opening, with its surfeit of lexical, syntactic, and thematic gestures toward pattern and cohesion, some of which I have highlighted for emphasis:

April is the cruellest month, *breeding*
Lilacs out of the dead land, *mixing*
Memory and desire, *stirring*
Dull roots with spring rain.
Winter kept *us* warm, *covering*   5
Earth with forgetful snow, *feeding*
A little life with dried tubers.
Summer surprised *us, coming* over the *Starnbergersee*

With a shower of rain; *we* stopped in the colonnade,
And went on in sunlight, into the *Hofgarten*,   10
And drank coffee, *and* talked for an hour.
Bin gar keine Russin, stamm' aus Litauen, echt deutsch.
When *we* were children, *staying* at the *archduke's*,
My cousin's, he took *me* out on a sled,
And I was frightened. He said, Marie,   15
Marie, hold on tight. *And* down *we* went.
In the mountains, there *you* feel free.
I read, much of the night, *and* go south in the winter.

Here is pattern and repetition—and with a vengeance. As sentence after sentence uncoils, new modes of syntactic and lexical patterning spring into shape, creating recognizable if evanescent zones of coherence.[41] No one, after all, can miss the five participial constructions that set off the line endings in lines 1–6, or the insistent use of six adjective-noun pairings ("cruellest month," "dull roots," "spring rain," "forgetful snow," "little life," and "dried tubers"). A second and overlapping zone of coherence springs up at line five with the appearance of the poem's first pronoun, an "us" first echoed and then elaborated in lines eight, nine, and thirteen before giving way to "me" (14) and "I" (15, 18). Still a third zone, overlapping with the second, looms into view at line eight, stretching to at least line thirteen and typified by words that are either German ("Starnbergersee," "Hofgarten") or associated with a German-speaking area, the former Austria-Hungary ("archduke"). While yet a fourth zone, overlapping again with both the second and third, begins to materialize at line ten with the conjunction "and," which is artfully reiterated at lines eleven (two times), fifteen, sixteen, and eighteen. And we might identify still other tonal zones within this verse paragraph—the gnomic sobriety of the opening or the conversational banality of the closing, separated by the uneasy oscillations of the middle—while we would certainly agree that a semantic vein that concerns the seasons flickers across the entire verse paragraph: "April" (1), "spring" (4), "winter" (5), "summer" (8), "winter" (18). Yet one may legitimately wonder why should there be no "autumn" in this catalogue of the seasons, if catalogue it be; or why the catalogue follows no discernible order. And is the winter that occurs in "Winter kept us warm, covering / earth with forgetful snow" really identical with the one that occurs in "I read, much of

the night, and go south in the winter"? The one is oracular, the other in-
sipid. Yet the effect of their conjunction is devastating: for here repetition
functions not to intensify semantic likeness but to eviscerate it. Likeness,
again, is giving way to illusion. And indeed, a similar movement occurs
over the paragraph's entire trajectory, which begins by intoning a pattern
of oracular solemnity but ends by reporting empty patter—those final
spasms of vacant thought, twitching like the limbs of a dying animal.

The problem, then, is not in recognizing the syntactic and lexical repetitions that unfold in the opening verse paragraph. If anything, they are
not just discernible but are too readily discernible. Five participial constructions; six adjective-noun pairings; eight first-person pronouns; six instances of the conjunction "and"—in only eighteen lines? Their obvious-
ness seems to urge their unimportance; it is not here that the poem is
doing the real work of offering an account of the world. And that impression is reinforced by another: the assertions of connectedness may be remarkably insistent, but the connectedness itself isn't really vivid; it remains
inert and extraneous, like so much scaffolding erected around a building
that remains obstinately and mysteriously invisible. (Even today, eighty
years after the poem was first published, critics disagree about that building's shape or how many rooms it contains, still divided over how many
speakers are voicing these lines.) As zones of coherence loom into sight
and recede, like ghosts who beckon us down darkened paths that repeatedly issue in dead ends, they insinuate that the poem's real reckoning
with the world must be happening elsewhere: perhaps in the intersection
and overlap of those evanescent zones; or in the interchange of oracular
solemnity and cosmopolitan banality, in the overall play of opacity and
transparency. Or perhaps somewhere else altogether.

Critics have not, of course, been slow to respond to that insinuation.
After all, one "somewhere else" is quite explicitly indicated in the first
note which immediately follows the poem proper: "Not only the title, but
the plan and a good deal of the incidental symbolism of the poem were
suggested by Jessie Weston's book on the Grail legend: *From Ritual to Romance* . . ." But surely this is just one more dead end, perhaps the deadest
of them all. *The Waste Land* has as much to do with Grail legends and vegetation rituals as *Ulysses* has with the rickety schema that Joyce concocted
as he neared the end of his masterpiece. Both writers, as publication approached, worried that their works might seem too disordered, too struc-

tureless for contemporary readers and critics, and each responded by hinting that his work was governed by an arcane logic that could be reconstructed "by any who think such elucidation of the poem worth the trouble." But the core of *The Waste Land* is not to be found in the turgid speculations of Jessie Weston, or in the pseudo-arcana of vegetation rituals.

Critics have also been fond of turning the poem into a narrative in which there is a "protagonist" or (in more Grail-inflected versions) "quester" who, in some mysterious way, moves through the poem's scenes. And there is a sense in which this responds, however crudely, to one aspect of the poem. Although much attention has been given to Pound's role in cutting out three major narratives from the draft poem (from parts I, III, and IV), not enough has been given to his insistence that the final ten lines of the original part IV be retained as an independent part. Pound was typically laconic when explaining his view, offering a rationale that borders on tautology. "Phlebas is an integral part of the poem; the card pack introduces him, the drowned phoen. sailor, and he is needed ABSoloootly where he is" (*LOTSE*, 505). Yet his appeal to the cards dealt out by Madame Sosostris is suggestive, for it implies that he assigned her and the card pack a certain degree of authority. Threadbare authority, perhaps, but enough for the needs of the poem. "She must," one critic has observed, "provide the dots that the rest of the poem must connect into a semblance of plot."[42] This is a perceptive account, provided we understand that its key word is really "semblance," to be taken in the strong sense as "an assumed or unreal appearance of something; mere show." What *The Waste Land* needed wasn't plot or narrative coherence, but the likeness of a plot, one that would instantly dissolve into illusion. For it requires only a moment to recall that Madame Sosostris is a charlatan, or that the drowned Phoenician sailor isn't even a card in the traditional Tarot pack. And when she discloses the drowned Phoenician card, the text swiftly divorces itself from straightforward narrative, intruding cruelly: "Those are pearls that were his eyes. Look!" Phlebas the Phoenician, whose reappearance (repetition) at first promises narrative connectedness between the first and later parts of the poem, turns out to be another figure in the poem's grim histrionics of nonrelationship. *The Waste Land* doesn't have a narrative; instead, it has the scent of a narrative, hovering in the air like a perfume after someone has left the room.

THE OFFICE BOMBSHELL

Histrionics: an exaggerated, wild quality; and fierceness, a notion comprising wildness and rage, even cruelty—*The Waste Land* thrives on those dark qualities. To say that, admittedly, is to depart sharply from our received notion of Eliot as a neoclassical poet. But depart from it we must. "It has been too tempting for too long," one of Eliot's most astute readers has recently observed, "to assimilate the poem to the events that came later in the decade, even shortly later, to see it as safely predicting the dispositions of the mid- and late twenties: the poem as proto-Anglican, crypto-classical, or neo-monarchist."[43] Indeed, to read the ten essays that Eliot wrote in 1921 while working on *The Waste Land* is to discern the discontinuous but coherent outline of an aesthetics deeply at odds with the notions of decorum, repose, sobriety, and equilibrium typically associated with neoclassicism.[44] One key word in Eliot's critical vocabulary is "surprise," a term he stresses again and again. Writing about Andrew Marvell in February 1921, Eliot notes "the high speed, the succession of concentrated images" in Marvell's "Coy Mistress," then observes that these are the basis for another effect: "When this process has been carried to the end and summed up, the poem turns suddenly with that surprise which has been one of the most important means of poetic effect since Homer." Citing another passage by Marvell, Eliot remarks: "There is here the element of *surprise* . . . the surprise which Poe considered of the highest importance, and also the restraint and quietness of tone which makes the surprise possible."[45] Writing in early April, when now well into work on part II of *The Waste Land,* he praises Dryden's "Mac Flecknoe" because it offers "the most fun . . . the most sustained display of surprise after surprise of wit from line to line. . . . Dryden's method here is something very near to parody"; while in the same essay he dismisses a passage by Abraham Cowley because it lacks "the element of *surprise* so essential to poetry."[46] Writing in mid-June, when at work on the first half of part III, Eliot reformulates his view of "surprise": "The strange, the surprising, is of course essential to art. . . . The craving for the fantastic, for the strange, is legitimate and perpetual; everyone with a sense of beauty has it."[47] The strange, the surprising, the fantastic, something very near to parody . . . these are terms at some remove from the cool sobriety conjured by "Tradition and the Individual Talent." Not that "Tradition and the Individual Talent" doesn't encapsulate certain Eliotic aspirations which will grow more prominent over time, so much so that Eliot himself will eventually enshrine it as the gateway into that vast graveyard known as his *Selected Essays*. But that was much later. In 1921, instead, "Tradition and the Individual Talent" was only one of several options facing Eliot, and in relation to *The Waste Land,* "The Road Not Taken" might be the most appropriate title for it. And the road taken? The strange, the surprising, the fantastic, something very near to parody . . . histrionics.

Similar terms preoccupy Eliot over the course of 1921, among them "ferocity." Praising Marie Lloyd, the music hall star whose death a year later would elicit one of Eliot's finest essays, he praises her for having "wit" that is "mordant, ferocious." Of Nellie Wallace, another music hall star whom he admired, Eliot writes: "The fierce talent of Nellie Wallace . . . holds the most boisterous music hall in complete subjection."[48] He finds some of H. M. Bateman's caricatures compelling because they "continue the best tradition from Rowlandson and Cruikshank. They have some of the old English ferocity." And he adopts with relish Baudelaire's dictum concerning caricature: *"Pour trouver du comique féroce et très-féroce, il faut passer la Manche"* (To find comedy that is ferocious and very ferocious, one has to cross the English Channel).[49] A related if more muted term is "intensity," and the cognate words "intense" and "intensify." They appear twenty-one times in Eliot's essays from the first half of 1921 ("The Romantic Englishman," "The Lesson of Baudelaire," "Andrew Marvell," and "Prose and Verse"). But Eliot also deploys another term far more extreme than "intensity." Quoting Dr. Johnson late in 1921, he praises the metaphysical poets because in their works "the most heterogeneous ideas are yoked by violence together."[50] A few months earlier he praises Baudelaire over Dryden because he "could see profounder possibilities in wit, and in violently joined images."[51] While around the same time he enthusiastically takes up Baudelaire's view on the distinctive trait of English comedy: *"le signe distinctif de ce genre de comique était la violence"* (the distinctive sign of this kind of comedy was violence).[52] Ferocity, intensity, violence, companions to the strange, the surprising, the fantastic, something very near to parody: here is the core of Eliot's aesthetics while he was writing *The Waste Land.* Which is why, of course, his essays of the time also show him so responsive to caricature and music hall, modes of cultural production which thrive on wild exaggeration, hyperbolic repetitions which pivot on the play of likeness and illusion, a grotesque machinery of extremism.

If *The Waste Land* repeatedly engages in a histrionics of nonrelation-ship which effectively undermines the modes of connectedness (repetition, narrative) that the poem elsewhere takes pains to assert, nowhere do the tensions between these assume starker form than in the grisly puppet show staged by the typist and the young man carbuncular at the heart of the poem, the middle of part III. The typist, after all, is repetition personi-fied, her task to repeat someone else's words, whether dictated aloud or transcribed in longhand; while the young man carbuncular is a paradigm of the stranger or intruder whose arrival sets in motion the mechanics of event and plot, sparks narrated activity. Their story is a narrative of repe-tition, in the sense that their loveless coupling is inferred to be but one in a protracted series of similar encounters; while it is also a repetition of narrative, in the sense that it elaborates *topoi* associated with representations of the typist in realist and naturalist fiction of the period 1910–1922. (We shall examine those topoi shortly.) Moreover, a juxtaposition of narrative and repetition serves to structure the presentation of their encounter from beginning to end: a laconic narrative, divided into three scenes or tableaux, is punctuated by the stark repetition (three times) that demarcates the presence of the observing "I Tiresias."

Little wonder that Eliot, in a note which he wrote as much as one year later, should assign this episode exemplary status: "What Tiresias *sees*, in fact, is the substance of the poem." True, that is "a declaration that critics have tended to view rather sceptically," as Carol Christ has noted, and the rationale behind their skepticism has been voiced by another critic: "But it is doubtful . . . whether Tiresias attains within the poem as a whole the importance that Eliot attributes to him in his Note on this passage. . . . The *persona* of Tiresias fails to control the tone of the whole passage and the result is a failure of proper impersonality."[53]

Still, we may harbor suspicions about the standard that is guiding such evaluations. For it assigns "Tradition and the Individual Talent" a normative function epitomized in the phrase "proper impersonality," while that essay presents an aesthetics radically incommensurate with the sort articulated in the essays Eliot wrote while producing *The Waste Land*. We need, in short, to revisit a scene so casually dismissed by Eliot's admirers, a scene which also brings us back—by what arcane logic?—to the subject we first began with, the typewriter. For in the period that ran from Eliot's birth to roughly 1920, the typewriter and the typist were virtually one, designated by the same term, "typewriter." *Confessions of a Type-Writer,* a sensational novel published in 1893, recounted the seduction of a young woman by a caddish swindler, not the fantastic avowals of a machine; just as *Confessions of a Typewriter; or, Merciful Unto Me, a Sinner* (1903, 1910), recounted a similarly lurid tale but culminated in the heroine's discovery of Christian Science. Or consider the play *Miss Robinson,* performed in 1918 and published in 1920: it shows us Lister, horrified by his mother's plan to marry off his brother to the young secretary who has been working for their father, exclaiming, "You can't expect him to marry a typewriter."[54]

It is difficult today to appreciate just how unprecedented it was to make a "typewriter," or typist, a key protagonist within a serious poem. Before *The Waste Land* typists had appeared almost exclusively in light verse that was humorous or satirical in nature.[55] Fiction was the medium which most fully registered the growing presence of typists in offices after 1885, first in short stories and then, after 1893, in novels. Only quite recently have literary scholars and historians taken note of the typist in fiction, in three essays which together assay seven novels (all British) published between 1893 and 1936.[56] In general the typist, as a subject of cultural representation, has been tacitly dismissed as unworthy of serious study, an object of misogynist scorn. For millions of women, however, clerical work offered the first occupational alternative to teaching or nursing and marked a massive change in their range of experience. The phenomenon was at once international, spreading from the United States to Britain, then France and Germany, and irreducibly local, with specific histories in different countries, even cities.

In 1921, when Eliot was writing *The Waste Land,* female office workers were still relatively new, more so in Britain than in the United States. Increasingly employed in nearly all kinds of business, typists were especially concentrated in the insurance and banking sectors, both centered in the City, or financial district, of London. In March 1917 Eliot began to work for Lloyds Bank, already a huge corporation and the second-largest of the "Big Six" British clearing banks which had emerged after decades of merger and acquisition activity that straddled the turn of the century.[57] The process was just drawing to an end during Eliot's early years at the bank, as Lloyds absorbed four last banks during the period 1918–1923. As a result of this horizontal integration process, Lloyds represented an immensely powerful concentration of capital which was now expanding into the international arena. (In 1911 it had purchased Armstrong & Co., with branches in Paris and Le Havre, and in 1917 it entered into a fifty-fifty partnership with National Provincial Bank to create the Lloyds and National Provincial Foreign Bank; by 1938 the firm had twelve branches on the Continent, serving British companies operating in Europe and British nationals abroad.) Indirectly, it was this expansion which led to Eliot's employment. For it was a friend of Vivien's family, L. E. Thomas, then the chief general manager of National Provincial Bank, who gave Eliot his letter of introduction to Lloyds. Eliot was duly assigned to the Colonial and Foreign Department, with its offices at 17 Cornhill Street in the heart of the City, one of several abutting buildings owned by Lloyds.

After two years Eliot was transferred to the Information Department, a much smaller unit reporting directly to the bank's board of directors. Eliot himself was in daily contact with typists. He was one of 7,400 employees engaged by Lloyds, and it was during the First World War that women clerks had first appeared at the firm. By late 1918 they totaled 3,300, nearly 45 percent of the bank's labor force. With the war's end, they were soon being dismissed, and after 1920 women were engaged only for typing or filing. (By 1925 there were still 1,500 left, all of them single, for until 1949 women were obliged to resign upon marriage.) "My typist is in a bad temper now because I gave a couple of letters to do to someone else who happened to have nothing to do at the moment," Eliot laments to his father in 1917 (*LOTSE*, 204). "I have half of a room, two girls, and half of a typist," he told his mother the next year, explaining, "I share a typist with someone else" (*LOTSE*, 232). In September 1919, after completing his move to the new Information Department, Eliot tells his mother that he is awaiting "a French typist for foreign correspondence": "Next week I shall have an assistant and a typist to write my letters and do card indexing, but last week I have had to struggle through chaos myself, receiving hundreds of reports from Branches of the bank, classifying them, picking out the points that needed immediate attention, interviewing other banks and Government Departments, and trying to elucidate knotty points in that appalling document the Peace Treaty" (*LOTSE*, 369).

It may seem a small matter, but it's worth noting that comment about doing "card indexing." Card indexing was a relatively new office procedure, one of many which attended what business historians have increasingly recognized as "a veritable revolution in communication technology" which took place between roughly 1890 and 1910.[58] The epitome of that revolution was the typewriter, first manufactured in 1873 but widely used in offices only after 1890. Another was something as modest as the loose-leaf (ring- or post-bound) ledger system, first marketed in 1894 to replace the bound ledger books which had been used until then.[59] Whereas before a client's growing account had to be continued on the next available page at the end of a bound book, with laborious cross-referencing to connect the two parts of the account, now it was possible to extend or add new accounts as needed. In effect the loose-leaf ledger introduced the idea of interchangeable parts to the office. It was soon followed by the card file ledger, and then by the vertical file such as we still know it today. By roughly 1910 vertical filing was universal among larger firms. The recording of outgoing correspondence was done through carbon copies, another novelty which had also become standard in large firms by 1910, while the reproduction of internal documents for large firms was facilitated by the invention of the rotary mimeograph in 1888, and the creation of new stencil papers. Eliot, in short, worked in a new office culture which had only recently taken form, an interlocking grid of new communications and storage-and-retrieval technologies—typewriters, telephones, Dictaphones, adding machines, duplicators, loose-leaf ledgers, card indexes, and vertical filing systems. The typist was the epitome of that grid—capital concentrated into flesh, flesh turned into a nexus of formal communication flows under the impress of systematic management.

That was one aspect of the typist as a distinctively modern figure. Another was related to it, yet also in contradiction. The typist was one of a family of figures who represented the promise of modern freedom: an allegedly new, autonomous subject whose appetites for pleasure and sensuous fulfillment were legitimated by modernity itself, by its promise that those new technologies, harnessed under systematic management, would ultimately enhance individual agency and create a richer life-world. (More exotic members of this family included the aviator and the automobile racer.) It was this belief which prompted early feminists to embrace the typewriter and its emancipatory potential for women, even as they swiftly noted mounting signs of betrayal (low wages, depressing workplace routines, the raw exploitation). And it was this same thematic which obliquely

informed novels about typists, which often explore the boundaries of legitimate desire through the blunt but pressing question of how far a young
woman should go in sexual relations with men.

But novels about typists did not emerge in a social vacuum. Often they
developed topoi first articulated in contemporary journalism. Consider what
might be called the food or diet debate, a subject taken up in an essay by
"Frances," an otherwise anonymous journalist whose feature "Five O'Clock
Tea Talk" appeared in the popular British newspaper *T.P.'s Weekly*. (The newspaper sold between 120,000 and 175,000 copies a week, reaching "an esti-
mated half a million readers, chiefly among the culturally aspiring urban
working- and lower-middle-classes.")[60] Frances notes widespread agreement
that the lunch food available to typists and secretaries is extremely poor:

> Over the quality of that mid-day meal there need not be any
> contradictions. Goldsmith's inquiring citizen might pursue
> his way from Broad Street to St. Paul's . . . putting his head in
> at the glass door of every tea shop he met, yet have naught to
> report at his journey's end but "coffee or tea and roll," with the
> sometimes addendum of "sandwich," or "sausage," or "pastry,"
> or "jam." Can the girl-worker thrive and be happy on such fare,
> and does it content her?[61]

Frances goes on to give a journalistic history of "the girl-worker of to-day."
The invention of the typewriter has led to the proliferation of typists, "the
crowds of girls who go hurrying through the city's big highways morning
and mid-day and evening." These, in turn, have given rise to another institution: "And as the typewriter was responsible for the girl-worker as she
is to-day, so may she be said to be responsible for the tea shop." But the
proliferation of tea shops has led only to increasingly poor diets for female
office workers. The root of the problem is low salaries, especially for "the
homeless girl":

> For the girl who lives in a comfortable home and goes out to
> business in order to have extra dress and pocket money, the
> tea-shop lunch is well enough—a substantial dinner awaits her
> when the day's work is done. But the girl who has to provide
> food, lodgings, and clothing out of a salary which does not
> always reach a pound a week, and rarely exceeds thirty shil-

lings, more often than not has to make her tea-shop lunch her principal meal. She would die rather than confess it, and I have heard her talk quite bravely of not being able to eat meat or vegetables in the middle of the day, and pretend to look forward to dinner, whilst I knew that it was only by the most exquisite manipulation of her pence that cold meat supper could be managed.

Frances wistfully urges that "a woman's restaurant" be established to meet the needs of these workers, but holds out little prospect for immediate change:

Mark the tone of resignation with which they at last ask for the inevitable roll, or pastry, or sausage, or egg, or any of the other edibles which will not map out beyond the eightpence or ten-pence which forms the lunch allowance. . . . It does not require very strong powers of observation to see that all those girls who throng the tea shops would welcome any change which would give them a chance of getting varied and palatable food. Their sticking to the much-condemned rolls and coffees and pastries is purely and simply a matter of purse—nothing else.

The problem was indeed genuine, and larger firms soon addressed it by building "bars" on site to cater for their employees. One of the first to do so was the Prudential Assurance Company, which, having completed its new headquarters on Holborn in the City in 1906, soon employed more than four hundred young women as office workers.[62] One of them was Ivy Low, an aspiring writer who joined the firm in 1908 and later drew on her experience in creating the setting for *The Questing Beast* (1914), her novel about a typist named Rachel Cohen.[63] At one point the narrator describes the lunchtime routine:

Lunch time was a pleasant break in the day. The directors of the New Insurance Society were too careful of their female employees to allow them to go into the streets and seek their lunch in crowded restaurants. . . . At any rate, whether they admitted it or not, it was a distinct advantage to the girls that they were able to get even an indifferent lunch in the office. Anyone, that is to say any woman, who has attempted to get

lunch at city restaurants of the cheaper kind will realize the
truth of this. . . . Besides, grumble as the clerks might and did
at the quality of the food, it was not worse, and certainly far
cheaper, than that provided by the surrounding restaurants.
(*TQB*, 42–43)

These accounts of typists and food, though dating from 1903 and 1914,
were by no means irrelevant in the immediate aftermath of World War I.
When some 1,100 women who had been secretaries or typists in 1919
were asked to recall their work experiences, they stressed the subject of
food again and again. They recalled eating at Lyons or ABC tea shops and
getting "a boiled egg, ginger pudding with treacle and a cup of tea for
1/3d." Or, since even these cut into the weekly pay packet, "the large ma-
jority" took sandwiches. Some companies even paid their women for over-
time work with food: "Bread, jam and tea for one hour," and "Scrambled
eggs, scones and tea for two hours." Summarizing their recollections, an
unidentified writer commented: "It was not unknown for a girl to faint at
her work from lack of adequate nourishment."[64] And the topic persisted
as a topos in contemporary fiction after the war. Consider the following
scene from *Money Isn't Everything,* a novel published in 1923, which recounts a dialogue between Jim Rogers, who is a clerk at a City legal firm,
and Elizabeth Tudor, a typist who lives alone and shares her daily lunch
with him in the garden of St. Paul's:

This morning, however, as they sat on a bench watching the
sparrows feed on crumbs thrown them by lunchers, he did
venture to ask, when she offered him a chocolate, "Is that all
you've had for lunch?"
"I had a cup of coffee and a bun at an A.B.C."
"That's not enough."
"I don't want more. I have dinner when I get home in the
evening."
He could give a pretty shrewd guess at the kind of dinner it
was—not the substantial appetising meal which, thanks to [his
sister] Letty's skill as a cook, he found awaiting him on his own
return at night from the office.[65]

When novelists took up typists as fictional protagonists, they inherited the topics and topoi of contemporary journalism. Food was one. Lodgings were another, and the small room, scarcely large enough to house a young woman and her belongings, also became a fictional topos. "I had one small room, at the top of a dreary old house, in a small turning off the Tottenham Court Road," says the first-person narrator of Tom Gallon's *The Girl Behind the Keys*.[66] The single small room also presented a practical problem for receiving visitors—the bed. When Fred Norman, a successful New York lawyer in David Graham Phillips's novel *The Grain of Dust* (1911), goes to visit the room of typist Dorothea Hallowell, he immediately notes this feature: "It was a small neat room, arranged comfortably and with some taste. ... The bed was folded away into a couch—for space and for respectability."[67] The room of Rachel Cohen, the typist working in the London office of the New Insurance Society in Ivy Low's *The Questing Beast* (1914), is equally small and Spartan:

> Besides the bed, the room contained a small enamelled washstand, six deal shelves holding a good many books, and a little table-crockery, a round table, two rush-bottomed "bedroom chairs," one fairly comfortable-looking upholstered arm-chair, and a large knee-hole desk, fitted with a great many small drawers and littered, not only with books and papers, but with various articles of clothing, a bunch of bananas and a glass jar half full of potted meat. (*TQB*, 8)

And whether adopting the voice of the narrator or a character, the novels often focus on female sleeping and undergarments, stressing their threadbare quality. In *The Questing Beast*, the narrator tells us: "Rachel Cohen, rising twenty, standing barefooted in her meagre cotton nightgown (they can only be got rather meagre for two and eleven three), looked like a very tired child of thirteen years" (*TQB*, 9). A more elaborate account appears in *The Grain of Dust:* "He went up with her [to her room] and helped her to pack—not a long process, as she had few belongings. He noted that the stockings and underclothes she took from the bureau drawers were in anything but good condition, that the half dozen dresses she took from the closet and folded on the couch were about done for. Presently she said, cheerfully and with no trace of shame: 'You see, I'm pretty nearly in rags.'"[68] *The Grain of Dust* is pertinent because Eliot evidently knew of its author, David Graham Phillips, damning him in an essay he wrote in late January 1921, just before beginning *The Waste Land:* "The conventional literature of America is either wretchedly imitative of European culture, or ignorant of it, or both; and by this standard one easily dispels . . . Mr. David Graham Phillips, with his exploitation of the Noble Fallen Woman who, in England, has vanished into the underworld of romance."[69] Eliot was referring here to Phillips's most recent and posthumously published novel, *Susan Lenox: Her Fall and Rise* (New York: D. Appleton, 1917), which recounts the heroine's plunge to prostitution and her rise as a Broadway star. But at least he was familiar with Phillips, who enjoyed a considerable reputation in the period 1900–1920, and Eliot may well have known his earlier *Grain of Dust*. Likewise, Ivy Low's novel *The Questing Beast* could easily have come to Eliot's attention. Low was a good friend of Katherine Mansfield and John Middleton Murry, and Eliot was in frequent contact with Murry during the two years (1919–1920) when Murry edited the *Athenaeum* and published thirty-three essays and reviews by Eliot.[70] *The Questing Beast* is doubly suggestive because Low uses the disarray of Rachel Cohen's room to index her character's moral confusion, the trait that lets her be seduced by a caddish young clerk named Giles Goodey—treatment which has striking similarities to the narrative trajectory which, it has been urged, Eliot adopts for the typist in *The Waste Land*.

These, then, were topoi of contemporary journalism and realistic fiction which treated typists: a single room with cramped conditions, poor food, a bed that doubles as a couch or divan, references to female garments and undergarments. *The Waste Land* evokes them all in the eight lines of its first tableau:

> At the violet hour, the evening hour that strives
> Homeward, and brings the sailor home from sea,
> The typist home at teatime, clears her breakfast, lights
> Her stove, and lays out food in tins.
> Out of the window perilously spread
> Her drying combinations touched by the sun's last rays,
> On the divan are piled (at night her bed)
> Stockings, slippers, camisoles, and stays.

Subject matter is being stressed here: details of setting, the props of the realist and naturalist novel, are being summoned. And the voice of the poem itself, Tiresias, directs our attention to this fact: "I Tiresias, old man with wrinkled dugs / Perceived *the scene . . .*" (italics mine). We are, in short, in a play or novel about a typist, and the plot line is predictable (". . . and foretold the rest").

But that is not all. For our novel or play about a typist also does something else here: it invokes poetry. Beginning at the midpoint of this passage a quatrain slowly emerges into view, and by its end it lies spread before us as neatly as "Stockings, slippers, camisoles, and stays." Well, perhaps not quite so neatly: for the meter of this passage is marked by deep uncertainty, shifting uneasily between four and five stresses per line, ranging from nine to thirteen syllables, uncertainty that turns it into a sign of poetry's flimsiness, its fragility in the face of the modern world, or that tacitly asks a question about whether poetry's traditional resources, rhythm and rhyme, suffice for what the modern world can throw in its path—a typist, her room, a scene of urban squalor. But at least now we have the rudiments of our story laid out before us: we have a typist, subject matter of the contemporary novel; we have a "scene," set with the props of realism and naturalism; we have signs of poetry's resources, or resourcefulness, to be tested against the matter of modernity; and we have our more or less predictable plotline.

But "predictable" in what sense? What expectations about plot or genre conventions would contemporary readers have brought to a scene that turns around a typist? The answer to that question is more complicated than we might expect, chiefly because of changes in the constellation of popular genres that took up the typist as subject matter over the long period that extends from 1890 to roughly 1925.[71] In the earlier decades, 1890 to 1910, typists were depicted chiefly in two kinds of novel. One was overtly melodramatic, drawing on conventions and plotlines derived from late Victorian melodrama. In these the heroine was typically threatened by the predatory desires of an unscrupulous employer, a villain who resorted to deception and violence to attain his end, and she was invariably saved from danger by her beloved, the hero whom she would eventually marry.[72] The other kind of novel was broadly realistic and was written by such British authors as George Gissing, whose *The Odd Women* (London: Lawrence and Bullen, 1893) is one of the earliest explorations of "the New Woman," or Ménie Muriel Dowie, a "New Woman" writer whose novel *The Crook of the Bough* (London: Methuen, 1898) probes the contradictory expectations faced by women entering the new world of work. Their American counterpart was Henry Blake Fuller, whose novel *The Cliff Dwellers* (New York: Harper, 1893) addressed the life forms in the new skyscrapers being built in Chicago.

But in subsequent years, a period running from roughly 1910 to 1925, the melodramatic novel vanished, its place gradually assumed by a new, still-emerging genre, women's romance, the genre that would later produce Barbara Cartland and Catherine Cookson. In such novels the heroine typically experienced a series of temptations and tribulations, often precipitated by an older and wealthier man, and ended by marrying another man of considerable wealth—or, what comes to the same thing, her employer.[73] Realism, meanwhile, continued to serve as a counterweight. Less driven by plot conventions than by protocols of treatment, it was an elastic mode perpetually in search of subject matter which could not be represented within the conventions of other genres, and increasingly it was turning to that controversial topic, sexual activity outside or prior to marriage. It was epitomized by such British authors as Arnold Bennett, Rebecca West, and Ivy Low; or by American authors following in the tracks of Theodore Dreiser and Upton Sinclair, writers like Sinclair Lewis, or the muckraking journalist David Graham Phillips, or Winston Churchill, now forgotten but from 1900 to 1920 "the author most widely read by the American middle class."[74] Between 1911 and 1922 each of the six authors published a novel about a typist or stenographer, four of which portray a heroine who engages in consensual sex before marriage—depictions which explicitly transgress the convention which had made the preservation of the heroine's chastity a governing device of melodrama and romance.[75] (One of the novels, Ivy Low's *Questing Beast,* was banned by W. H. Smith and Son, which refused to handle it.)[76] Yet it is precisely at this point that all four novels encounter serious difficulties with plotting. For in the real world an unmarried and pregnant woman of limited financial resources faced only one prospect, the certainty of social ostracism, and most likely the necessity of putting an illegitimate child up for adoption. But for novelists bent on affirming the dignity of protagonists who engaged in consensual sex before marriage, that outcome could only validate the social prejudice they hoped to question. The result was an impasse. Consider *The Questing Beast.* The heroine Rachel Cohen is first seduced by a caddish clerk named Giles Goodey, then engages in consensual sex with a young actuary named Noel Young and becomes pregnant. Low resolves the impasse by resorting to what can only be called a fairy-tale ending: the heroine's landlady miraculously possesses enough money to support her throughout her pregnancy, and meanwhile her former colleagues at the office type up the novel she has been working on, which is soon published to critical acclaim and commercial success. The final chapter jumps forward, leaping over seven years and all potential complications: Rachel, still accompanied by the benevolent landlady, is now a successful novelist living in an isolated village by the sea, where she is successfully raising her child. Winston Churchill resolves the dilemma by having the pregnant heroine, Janet Bumpus, be taken in by two friends; the child's father is soon murdered, and when the heroine-mother dies only a few months after childbirth, the child is adopted by her benevolent friends. Rebecca West, in a daring strategy, leaves the future of the mother and child radically open and unresolved: the novel ends just at the moment when the heroine reaches her decision to sleep with the protagonist, even though she knows that he has killed his mother only a few hours earlier, that he will soon be apprehended by the police, and that she and he will never have a life together. Arnold Bennett depicts a heroine who frankly acknowledges her innate propensity to give pleasure to a man (a woman's true nature, it is implied): she freely accepts her employer's offer to lead a life of pleasure on the Continent; but when it is learned that he is gravely ill, he hastily organizes a wedding, carefully arranges his will in her favor, and conveniently dies within days, leaving her the proprietor of the typing agency in London where she had been employed. After childbirth she returns to London, admired and envied by all her former colleagues. Bennett is out to subvert the melodramatic and romance convention which makes the seductive employer into a villainous cad; but to do so he resorts to turns of plot as improbable and unmotivated as those of the genres he is subverting. Yet his dilemma was highly representative, shared by all the realistic novelists who wanted to shape a sympathetic account of a young woman who, having engaged in consensual sex before marriage, became pregnant: the consequences in the real world were unspeakable, ineffable in the most literal sense, and could be evaded only through recourse to a deus ex machina, a magical or fairy-tale ending. In effect, the contradictory impulses at work in the realist novel's depiction of the typist turned her into something strange and paradoxical: a figure for what was resistant to figuration, a sign of what could not be signified but had to be circumvented.

Which brings us back to the typist in *The Waste Land,* whose appearance in the first tableau has been accompanied by a "scene," set with the props of realism and naturalism; signs of poetry's resources or resourcefulness; and the promise of a fairly predictable plot (". . . and foretold the rest"). These elements, in turn, have been juxtaposed with two others. One is the way in which the poem takes pains to assert an identity between the typist and the figure for its own activity: "I *too* awaited the expected guest," says Tiresias in the brief interlude that separates the first tableau from the second; *"And I* Tiresias have foresuffered all" (243), he will reiterate at the next interlude (italics mine). Both comments merely reinforce an earlier identification drawn between the typist, Tiresias, and the modern machine, all three connected through reiteration of the word "throbbing" in the passage which brings the typist onstage:

> At the violet hour when the eyes and back
> Turn upward from the desk, when the human engine waits
> Like a taxi throbbing waiting,
> I Tiresias, though blind, throbbing between two lives (215–218)

But that identification is further complicated by another element, the poem's oblique recognition that the typist exceeds the capacity of conventional representation.[77] For which perspective is it that enables us to see, at the same time, "the eyes and back" of that "human engine"?

All these elements make what happens next only the more startling. For when the curtain next opens on the scene, the principal actress is abruptly whisked off the stage:

> He, the young man carbuncular, arrives,
> A small house agent's clerk, with one bold stare,
> One of the low on whom assurance sits
> As a silk hat on a Bradford millionaire.
> The time is now propitious, as he guesses,
> The meal is ended, she is bored and tired,
> Endeavours to engage her in caresses
> Which still are unreproved if undesired.
> Flushed and decided, he assaults at once;
> Exploring hands encounter no defence;
> His vanity requires no response,

And makes a welcome of indifference.

. . . .

Bestows one final patronising kiss,
And gropes his way, finding the stairs unlit . . .
(231–242, 247–248)

In the second tableau the typist vanishes entirely as an autonomous agent. She exists only through the thoughts of the young man carbuncular, a present-tense variant of free indirect discourse ("as he guesses, / . . . she is bored and tired"), or as a pronominal object of his gropings ("Endeavours to engage her . . ."). And as the passage goes on, she dissolves into a ghastly/ghostly series of negations: "unreproved," "undesired," "no defence," "no response," "indifference," their horror amplified because four of them are placed in the emphatic position of ending a line of verse, reverberating with each other ("no defence"/"indifference") and other rhyme words ("tired"/"undesired" and "at once"/"no response"). The privative prefixes ("un-," "in-," "no,") throbbing across the desolate syntax sequester the typist in a region of inexplicable, unbearable privation.

Nor is it just the typist who disappears in the course of the central tableau. The young man carbuncular, as soon as he "assaults at once," is displaced with synechdoche ("Exploring hands encounter . . .") and then vanishes under personification ("His vanity requires . . ."). Even his "final patronising kiss" has nobody and nothing that serves as a grammatical subject to bestow it; we must infer that "bestows" is governed—but is anything being "governed" here?—by the subject of the preceding clause, "His vanity." Vanishing and vanity, both stemming from the Latin *vanus*, meaning "empty," or to cite a fuller definition: "I, *that contains nothing, empty, void, vacant;* 2, *empty* as to purport or result, *idle, null, groundless, unmeaning, fruitless, vain.*"[78] Void and vacant; groundless and unmeaning: stark terms, but they seem to be all that this conjuncture of repetition and narrative leaves us. Yet is that all there is to "the substance of the poem," if we may borrow the language of the much-discussed note which Eliot later provided for this passage?

That withering final kiss is horrific. It toys with a convention, of course, one in which the novel makes a kiss into the climax of a scene, a chapter, or even a whole work. And lodged within that convention is another, those martial metaphors which crop up in the central tableau: "Flushed and decided, he *assaults* at once; / Exploring hands encounter *no defence*" (italics mine). No doubt the lover as soldier has a venerable pedigree in lyric poetry, one that reaches back to Propertius and Ovid and flourishes anew in sixteenth- and seventeenth-century poetry.[79] But by the early twentieth century it has become fossilized language in the novel. Ivy Low adopts it at the moment when Giles Goodey begins to seduce Rachel, a climactic moment in the book. He has been reading aloud a manuscript in her room, which she is typing up as extra work on a freelance basis, and during a pause they both step to the room's window:

> Then Rachel turned and faced him, her eyes a little ghastly, her cheeks suddenly flushed, her mouth almost imperceptibly trembling. The little bells over their heads chimed ever so faintly. Giles took a step towards her, and she suddenly shrank back against the window, never taking her eyes off his face. The sudden movement touched Giles. He stooped and kissed her wrist.
>
> "Are you afraid of me, little girl?" he said.
>
> "Oh, no, Giles, not of *you*," said Rachel, looking at her wrist with a quaint air of surprise. "Of *me*!" she continued, and looked up at him with a crooked smile.
>
> The appeal was double-edged. There was an invitation to his chivalry and subtler invitation to his desire in it. "Poor little girl, I must help her," suggested one voice, and "The fortress is not impregnable. It *wants* to be stormed!" clamoured another.
>
> Another short step forward and Rachel was in his arms, timid, unresponsive, but submissive. He kissed her dark head several times, then bent it back and tried to quench a long thirst at that traitorous mouth of hers. She remained cold and bewildered—a girl under her first kiss. . . . Her acquiescence, coupled with such a truly virginal quality of coldness, was maddening, intolerable, adorable! (*TQB*, 150–151; ellipsis in original)

Eliot's use of the kiss could hardly be more different. It comes not as a climax, but as willfully gratuitous anticlimax. What had promised to be a narrative has given way to a world in which characters vanish, actions are reduced to random flailings ("exploring hands"), and the conventions of a seduction scene evoke only a grisly pantomime of nonrelationship.

The final tableau concludes with a ferocious coda, a savage travesty of the novelistic scene where the typist, in the aftermath of her sexual encounter, finds herself alone and reflects on her deed. When Rachel Cohen wakes up the next morning:

> She wondered if she had not plumbed the limits of disgust.
> She could not believe that life would ever hold zest for her
> again. A very plain person, who had never seen his face in
> a glass and had had to form an opinion of his features from
> his natural vanity and the features of other people, might have
> felt, on being suddenly presented with a mirror, something
> of the shock and horror that Rachel now felt. Exactly the ques-
> tion that this person would most naturally ask was constantly
> in Rachel's mind: "Am I like *that*? *I*?" . . . Rachel, hitherto
> triumphant over other people's weakness, now thought, in her
> bitter humiliation, that none was so fallen that she was not
> sister to. Again and again the memory of her pride in being
> "not that sort of girl" stung her to fresh writhings. (*TQB*, 157;
> ellipsis mine)

A similar moment occurs in *Chickie,* a popular novel by Elenore Meherin that was serialized in newspapers in 1923 and turned into a successful film in 1925. Here the protagonist, Helen Bryce, or "Chickie" (aged twenty), has not been seduced by a caddish villain but has simply made love with her fiancé, a twenty-five-year-old lawyer named Barry Dunne:

> In her mind was a black sport of terror. It grew large—a stark
> live thing, shaking her pulse with dread. It was the memory
> of the night.
>   She shrank from it. It pressed down and seized her heart.
> It was a dark, heavy beast crouching on her chest. She tried to
> beat it off. It came nearer and blew warm, sickening breaths
> in her nostrils. Fighting, she had to draw them down. Again
> and again. . . . She hid from it—oh she would get away—push
> off this thing of horror weighing so heavily on her breast. Be
> free—be light again. . . .

She hated herself. Turning on the pillow, her hair fell across her face. With a violent revulsion she flung it back. Oh, this sickening contact with herself. If she could only get away from her breath, from her own hands, from her feet that were so cold they ached! If she could fly out of this body that held her fast to the immutable yesterday.[80]

Disgust, shock, horror, bitter humiliation, terror, dread, memories that sting, seize the heart, or weigh heavily . . . here is the lexicon of the contemporary novel when treating a postseduction or postcoital scene. And here is *The Waste Land:*

She turns and looks a moment in the glass,
Hardly aware of her departed lover;
Her brain allows one half-formed thought to pass:
"Well now that's done: and I'm glad it's over."
When lovely woman stoops to folly and
Paces about her room again, alone,
She smoothes her hair with automatic hand,
And puts a record on the gramophone. (249–256)

Horror and terror: they are the more powerfully present for being inscribed in silence.

But it is the "automatic hand" that is most arresting here, riveting the reader's attention. For in Western philosophy from Aristotle to Heidegger, the hand has been invoked to signal the critical difference between the human and the animal, at once the instrument of reason and its material counterpart.[81] Yet the typist's gesture erases precisely that boundary between willful human action and the helplessness of automatism. Paradoxically, at the same time it also invokes what might be called a lyrical temporality and effect: for it interrupts, shocks, and freezes the scene. Gesture, here, is being summoned to substitute for speech, assigned a total expressivity that rests upon the ineffability of what is to be expressed. It becomes the consummate figure for what cannot be figured, a sign of what resists, exceeds, or dwarfs signification. Connoisseurs of art history will inevitably be reminded of how the hand was used in early Byzantine churches to substitute for a representation of God at a time when it was deemed blasphemous to depict him on the assumption that divine form exceeded the limits of human representation.[82] Tellingly, Eliot himself urges that the hand performs an analogous function in the Jacobean play *The Duchess of Malfi*. Reviewing a recent performance of it in 1920, he singles out the notorious scene in which the Duchess, trapped in a darkened chamber, is deceived into kissing a severed hand, one which she is told is that of her lover Antonio. It was "extraordinarily fine," Eliot says, for "here the actors were held in check by violent situations which nothing in their previous repertory could teach them to distort." "The scene of the severed hand," as Eliot calls it, has an uncanny effect: it prevents the actors from acting, prohibits the presenters from representing. Frozen and contracted in the clutch of rigor mortis, the dead hand dispenses with all mediation, which can only "distort," and is transformed into an eerie paradox: it is a trope of not troping and, at the same time, is pure, unmediated communication. "Here," writes Eliot in summarizing his view of the scene, "the play itself got through, magnificently, unique."[83]

What is it, then, that "gets through" the typist's "automatic hand," that hand momentarily and yet forever contracted in a gesture charged with communicating what is otherwise ineffable, unspeakable? Doubtless there are many answers to that question, and ours can be only a tentative one, a provisional extrapolation from two phrases perhaps insignificant in themselves. One is a note that Eliot probably wrote in December 1921, when in Lausanne under the care of the Swiss psychiatrist Dr. Roger Vittoz. It is found in the margin of Eliot's own copy of Vittoz's book, *The Treatment of Neurasthenia by Means of Brain Control*. Opposite a sentence by Vittoz which reads, "The muscles are at first more or less contracted and sometimes painful," Eliot has penciled a single word: "handwriting" (*LOTSE*, 480 n. 1). The other phrase, somewhat strangely, is found in the final words of *The Waste Land*. By that I do not mean the famous "Shantih shantih shantih" which closes the published poem of 1922 but rather the last passage of text proper which Eliot composed, the passage that he wrote in Paris in January 1922, after Pound had deleted the entire passage about Fresca which had originally opened part III, leaving Eliot no choice but to find a new beginning. Oddly, it too begins with the image of a hand contracted:

> The rivers tent is broken and the last fingers of leaf
> Clutch and sink into the wet bank. . . .

Yet it ends not with a phrase or even an image intended to suggest the ineffable, but with ineffability itself, with speechlessness:

By the waters

What is unbearable, what cannot be written even when concluding the poem, is the rest of that line: ". . . I sat down and wept." The ineffable is that sense of immense commiseration, at once a profound pity at the lacerating horrors of modernity and an unspeakable sorrow that there is no language, whether in narrative or lyric (epitomized by repetition), adequate to the terror which the poem wishes to account for. Fictively situated beside the heart of modernity which is the financial district of London, the poem offers only speechless weeping, a wild pathos at once unutterable and irredeemable, over the conditions that have governed its production. Perhaps that truly is "the substance of the poem."

CHAPTER TWO

The Price of Modernism

PUBLISHING *THE WASTE LAND*

"HISTORY IS A NIGHTMARE," wrote James Joyce. "History has many cunning passages, contrived corridors / And issues," murmured T. S. Eliot. It distinguishes the epic, declared Ezra Pound, in a transparent reference to his own life's work, *The Cantos*.[1] The modernists were obsessed with history. They mourned it and damned it, contested it as tenaciously as Jacob wrestling with the image of God: "I will not let thee go, except thou bless me." Yet if the deity of history had ever deigned to reply to them, it might have said: "Behold, I set before you this day a blessing and a curse." Modernism, scholars announced in 1965, had "passed into history."[2] The comment appeared in the preface to a textbook; it was in part a historical description and in part a speech act enacting the event that it appeared to describe, modernism's passage to academic respectability. Today, of course, we live on the other side of that moment. We take for granted modernism's place in the canon or even equate its progress among the professors with its trajectory through history. Yet in doing so, we forget that modernism flourished long before 1965, that it had erupted into the public consciousness at least forty years earlier, and that its status as a cultural resource had been secured by an array of institutions at some remove from the academy. The event that epitomized this process was the publication of *The Waste Land* in late 1922, which announced modernism's unprecedented arrival on the scene of public debate. It generated a substantial amount of publicity and media attention and marked a crucial moment in its critical fortunes, establishing the poem as a reference point for a wider public. Long before textbooks about it were written, popular and critical understanding of modernism had already been shaped by the publication dynamics that characterized modernism's productive processes, dynamics at once volatile and contradictory. It may prove worthwhile, then, to reconsider that earlier and more fractured moment, to reconnoiter the murky terrain that is vaguely mapped out by the preposition "into" in the phrase "into history." For "into" evokes transition, a liminal moment attended by the possibility of failure, a risk that modernism's passage through the "contrived corridors" might have miscarried.

A core of basic facts about the publication of *The Waste Land* has long been known. In October 1922 it was simultaneously published in two journals: the *Criterion* in England, on 16 October, and the *Dial* in the United States, around 20 October (though in the November issue). In December it appeared a third time, now an independent book that for the first time included line numbers and Eliot's explanatory notes, published by the American firm of Boni and Liveright.[3] Ten months later, in September 1923, it appeared a fourth time, once more as an independent book that included Eliot's explanatory notes, now published by the Hogarth Press, a British firm run by Leonard and Virginia Woolf. Together these constituted an event that has acquired almost mythical status, a legend that recounts the story of modernism's troubled or difficult emergence, its initial repudiation by a purblind critical establishment and a benighted public, and its slow but irreversible triumph. "Eliot," writes one critic when surveying the transition *From Modern to Contemporary American Poetry, 1945–1965,* "had been reviled in the twenties as a drunken Bolshevik," but by 1945 he "had ascended . . . to the status of a kind of grandfatherly literary institution." True, the author concedes, it might be difficult to pinpoint the author of that epithet "drunken Bolshevik"; but "even if the story is apocryphal, it accurately evokes the public reception of 'The Waste Land.'"[4] But does it?

To reexamine that complex event, we might begin by exploring not where the poem was ultimately published but where it was *not* published —in the witty and sophisticated pages of *Vanity Fair,* or in the intransigent leaves of that avant-garde journal the *Little Review.* For both were considered as potential publishers at various points in 1922 as negotiations for the poem followed their unpredictable course. And together these possibilities, with the stories that lie behind them, set out a spectrum of modernist publishing practices—the halting steps that modernism took as it groped its way through the darkened corridors of its own production.

One might begin by examining an unnoticed occasion in early August 1922, when John Peale Bishop visited the Paris studio of Ezra Pound. Two weeks earlier Bishop had resigned his post as managing editor of *Vanity Fair,* and ostensibly he was traveling on an extended honeymoon after his recent marriage. Unofficially, however, Bishop had come to visit the savage god of modern experimentalism—and to talk business.[5] The topic was the publication of *The Waste Land,* a work that Bishop had never read but whose vicissitudes he had been following for five months. In early March, while still in New York and laboring for *Vanity Fair,* he had received an essay from Aldous Huxley that reported the poem's composition and announced—mistakenly, it turned out—its imminent publication in the *Dial.* An astute and conscientious editor, Bishop had phoned to confirm the report with his colleague and counterpart at the *Dial,* Gilbert Seldes. Seldes was puzzled, having heard nothing about the poem; on 6 March he cabled *Dial* co-owner and chief editor Scofield Thayer, who was then residing in Vienna: CABLE WHETHER ELIOT POETRY COMING SELDES. Three days later Thayer replied in French: ELIOT REFUSA THAYER. Seldes immediately contacted Bishop and urged him to alter Huxley's article to indicate that the poem's appearance in the *Dial* was, as Seldes expressed it, "problematical but probable."[6] More important, Bishop had now glimpsed the growing rift between Eliot and the *Dial.*

By late April 1922, in fact, relations between Eliot and Thayer had completely broken down, and in the wake of their collapse Pound had begun to intervene actively in the search for a publisher. On 6 May 1922 he wrote to Jeanne Foster, who was the beloved companion of the New York lawyer and cultural patron John Quinn, but also an occasional contributor to *Vanity Fair* and a friend of Bishop's.[7] Pound was soliciting an offer of publication for the poem in the bluntest possible terms: "What wd. Vanity Fair pay Eliot for 'Waste Land.' Cd. yr. friend there [Bishop] get in touch with T. S. E., address 12 Wigmore St., London W.1." By August, when he visited Pound, Bishop was clearly apprised of the situation—indeed, was responding to a suggestion advanced by Pound himself. The two met on 3 August, and two days later Bishop reported their conversation to Edmund

Wilson, his closest friend and his successor as managing editor at *Vanity Fair:*

> Pound I met the other afternoon. I found him extended on
> a bright green couch, swathed in a hieratic bathrobe made of
> a maiden aunt's shit-brown blanket. His head is quite fine,
> but his voice is offensively soft, almost effeminate and [illegible
> word], and his body is rather disagreeably soft. However, he
> was quite gracious, and the twinkle of his eyes whenever he
> makes a point is worth something. He held forth for two hours
> on the intellectual moribundity of England—the old stuff.
> Here's the thing however—Eliot is starting a quarterly review:
> he is to run 'Waste Land,' the new series of lyrics in the first
> number: he and Thayer have split and the *Dial* will not publish
> it. Perhaps you might want to arrange for the American publi-
> cation. Pound says they are as fine as anything written in En-
> glish since 1900. I'm lunching with EP tomorrow [6 August]
> and will report further.

Whether Bishop wrote again to Wilson as he promised is unknown. On 7 August he left for Vienna, and by the time his letter could have reached Wilson in New York (around 16 August) and Wilson could have replied, his proposal had already been overtaken by events previously set in motion.[8] Yet the seriousness with which it was advanced by both Bishop and Pound should indicate that *Vanity Fair* was considered a serious contender to publish the poem. How serious, indeed, we shall see later.

Bishop's meeting in August also indicates the centrality of Pound's role in prompting and facilitating this abortive plan, recapitulating a story that grows increasingly familiar: Pound was the cultural impresario who, precisely by virtue of this role, occupied a critical position at the heart of modernism.[9] It is this position, in fact, that informs the rhetoric in which he articulated his advocacy of *The Waste Land*'s publication: "Pound says they are as fine as anything written in English since 1900," wrote Bishop, evidently quoting him verbatim. A month earlier Pound had written to Felix Schelling, his former professor at the University of Pennsylvania: "Eliot's *Waste Land* is I think the justification of the 'movement,' of our modern experiment, since 1900."[10] Bishop had clearly been subjected to a variant of that argument: the poem was important precisely for its representative quality, and to publish it did not require that one appreciate its aesthetic qualities or sympathize with its contents—however one defined those terms—but that one be eager to stake out a position as the spokesperson for a field of cultural production, the voice of an array of institutions ("the justification of the 'movement,' of our modern experiment, since 1900"). How much this animated Bishop's interest in the poem is underscored by a curious anomaly in the nature of his enthusiasm, for Bishop was praising a poem that he had yet to read—indeed, whose exact title was still a bit obscure to him ("'Waste Land,' the new series of lyrics").[11]

Bishop's imperfect knowledge was not unique. Indeed, insofar as he knew the title of the poem at all, he knew more than Horace Liveright had known when he first advanced his own offer of publication for the poem on 3 January 1922—the date being notable because it was before the poem had been completed, before it had even acquired its present title. Liveright's interest, like Bishop's, was the consequence not of an aesthetic encounter with a work he had read and admired but of an eagerness to buy a product that promised to meet a series of minimum conditions. Yet what were these conditions?

Like Bishop's, Liveright's access to Eliot's poem had been mediated by Pound. It was he who assumed the function of stage director cuing the characters in their parts: the reserved and diffident poet played by T. S. Eliot, the brash young publisher acted by Horace Liveright. Eliot had arrived in Paris on 2 January 1922 and was to stay for two weeks, until 16 January. He had come from Lausanne, bearing the disorderly sheaf of manuscripts that he and Pound began to edit and revise, producing a quasi-final version of *The Waste Land*.[12] His arrival coincided with the visit of Liveright, the partner who was guiding editorial policy at Boni and Liveright. Liveright was touring Europe to acquire new works of literature, and his visit to Pound was designed to set their relations on firmer ground. In 1919 he had published Pound's *Instigations*; in 1920 he had undertaken *Poems, 1918–1921*, a volume released only three weeks before his arrival in Paris; and in the summer of 1921 he had paid Pound for a translation of Remy de Gourmont's *Physique de l'amour*, an engagement that had rescued Pound from dire financial straits. Now Liveright hoped to establish more stable relations; he trusted Pound's capacity to recognize new talent, saw him as a valuable link to other authors whose work interested him, and even entertained the idea that Pound's work might prove commercially viable at some point in the future.[13] In turn, Pound thought that he might make Liveright into the principal publisher of modernism and hoped to secure a long-term agreement guaranteeing financial security and time for work.

Poet and publisher courted one another actively. During the six days of Liveright's stay in Paris (30 December 1921–4 January 1922), they saw each other daily.[14] Pound treated Liveright to visits with Paul Morand and Constantin Brancusi, and the young publisher left "a good impression" on Pound, who felt that he was "going toward the light[,] not from it." He was "much more of a man than publishers usually are," and indeed "perhaps the only man in the business."[15] He was "a pearl among publishers."[16] The pearly and masculine publisher had arrived at an opportune moment. Joyce was seeking an American publisher for *Ulysses,* and Eliot would need a publisher for his unfinished poem. On 3 January 1922, Liveright had an extraordinary dinner with Joyce, Eliot, and Pound to discuss a milestone publishing program. The encounter was productive. With Joyce he agreed to publish *Ulysses* and to give $1,000 against royalties. To Pound he offered a contract guaranteeing $500 annually for two years in addition to translator's fees for any work from French agreed upon by both parties. To Eliot he offered $150 advance against 15 percent royalties and promised publication in the fall list. Liveright was nervous only about length; in a brief note dated 11 January, a week before Eliot had even left Paris, he worried that the poem might not be long enough. "I'm disappointed that Eliot's material is as short. Can't he add anything?" he pleaded with Pound.[17]

Pound, it is clear, was eager to gather under one roof the principal authors and works of modernism, including Yeats, whom he encouraged to abandon a long-standing contract with Macmillan in favor of Liveright.[18] At stake in these efforts was an attempt to present modernist writings as the articulation of an idiom, a serviceable language that was shared (and in this sense collective in character), yet also amenable to a high degree of individuation: the voice of a "'movement,' of our modern experiment since 1900." In short, his activity was characterized by programmatic ambitions and a coherent sense of their interaction with market conditions.

The same traits surface in his dealings with Scofield Thayer, the editor of the *Dial* who was eventually to purchase *The Waste Land.* Pound lobbied forcefully for the poem's publication from the outset, invoking a rhetoric by now familiar. On 18 February 1922, when Thayer and Eliot were still at a preliminary stage of discussion, Pound wrote to Thayer: "Eliot's poem is very important, almost enough to make everyone else shut up shop." When Thayer replied (5 March) that he could not comment on the poem's merits, since Eliot had not yet sent him the text, Pound persisted: "His poem is as good in its way as Ulysses in its way, and there is so DAMN little genius, so DAMN little work that one can take hold of and say, 'This at any rate stands, makes a definite part of literature.'" *The Waste Land* was represented as a verse equivalent of *Ulysses,* a work that epitomized not just the experiences of an individual, whether author or protagonist, but the modernist claim to a preeminent position in the institution of "literature," an ambiguous entity that was both distinct and yet inseparable from the commercial production of reading matter. Its merits resided not just in a specific set of words or text but in its capacity to articulate this collective aspiration of a small but influential group.

Pound's letter of 9–10 March also outlined practical suggestions that would prove pivotal both for *The Waste Land* and for subsequent literature: "I wish to Christ he had had the December award," he hinted, referring to the influential prize which the *Dial* had recently founded, the annual Dial Award. But other solutions were also available. Eliot might be granted "a professorship," as Robert Frost had recently been. Or he might be given a job on the *Century* or the *Atlantic,* since "he is not an alarming revolutionary, and he don't, as I at moments, get mistaken for a labour-leader or bolshy bomb-thrower."[19] Yet it was his suggestion of "the December award," the Dial Award for services in the cause of letters, that would ultimately bear fruit both for Eliot and for modernism.

Pound's suggestions were advanced just when communications between Eliot and Thayer were breaking down. On 8 March, Eliot had telegraphed Thayer that he could not accept less than £50 ($250). Unfortunately, the message was distorted in transmission, and Thayer had received a shocking request for an unprecedented sum: "cannot accept under !8!56 pounds = eliot + [sic]." In reply, on 12 March, Thayer reiterated his offer of $150 for the poem, a figure that was advanced without sight of the manuscript and was 25 percent higher than the $110 to $120 he normally would have paid.[20] (One should recall that income per capita in the United States at this time was about $750 per annum; income per capita in the United States in 2003 stood at $30,941, so if Thayer's offer were scaled up as a percentage of income per capita in 2003 dollars, it would be the equivalent of roughly $6,200.)[21] Not unreasonably, Thayer also asked to receive a copy of the manuscript. In addition, he pointed out the staggering deficits the *Dial* was incurring and argued that it could not alter its policy of "pay[ing] all contributors famous and unknown at the same rates." In reply Eliot was curt and frankly insulting, and he proceeded to withdraw the poem entirely:

> Please excuse my not replying sooner to your letter, except by my wire; but I have had a good deal of trouble over letting my flat furnished and moving here, where I shall be till the 20th June. In addition, there have been engrossing personal affairs, and I have been prevented from dealing with any correspondence.
>
> I also took some days to think about your offer, during which time I happened to hear on good authority that you paid £.100 to George Moore for a short story, and I must confess that this influenced me in declining $150 [£30] for a poem which has taken me a year to write and which is my biggest work. To have it published in a journal was not in any case the way I should choose for bringing it out; and certainly if I am to be offered only 30 to 35 pounds for such a publication it is out of the question.
>
> I have written to Ezra Pound to explain my reasons for refusing to dispose of the poem to the Dial at that price and he concurs with me. . . .
>
> You have asked me several times to give you the right of first refusal of any new work of mine, and I gave you the first refusal of this poem.

When Thayer received Eliot's letter, he wrote in pencil on the margin, opposite Eliot's charge about George Moore: "novellette length / serially." At the bottom of the letter he also noted: "Seen Moore work[,] exception for him[;] and because review had offended[,] Moore had already sacrificed several hundred dollars." True, the *Dial* had paid Moore a higher than usual fee, but in part this was because of the work's length, in part because the *Dial* had been remiss in fulfilling earlier obligations to Moore ("had offended"), thereby forcing him to sacrifice "several hundred dollars," for which the larger payment had been a form of compensation. But more important was Thayer's remark opposite Eliot's last sentence withdrawing the offer to publish. Thayer vented his tart indignation: "Not submitted."[22]

Eliot's allegations about Moore appeared to invoke a principle of equal pay for all contributors. In fact, it was precisely the opposite principle that interested him, as he had explained a few days earlier to Pound: "I think these people should learn to recognize Merit instead of Senility, and I think it is an outrage that we should be paid less merely because Thayer thinks we will take less and be thankful for it, and I thought that somebody ought to take steps to point this out."[23] At first sight Eliot's argument may strike us as sympathetic, if only because it seems so familiar. But the issues were rather more complicated: in an important sense the question of aesthetic value is inseparable from commercial success in a market economy, a difficulty that beset every argument for the intrinsic merit of literary modernism. By 1922 literary modernism desperately required a financial-critical success that would seem comparable to the stunning achievement of modernist painting; yet every step in this direction was hampered by market constraints less amenable to the kinds of pressure from elite patronage and investment that had secured the fortunes of Cubism and modern painting. The legal definition of intellectual property—which continued to belong to the author after its purchase by the consumer, in contrast to a painting or a statue, which became the property of the purchaser—posed a series of intractable dilemmas. Patronage could nurture literary modernism only to the threshold of its confrontation with a wider public; beyond that point, however, only commercial success could ratify its viability as a significant idiom. That was the question that permeated discussion about publication of *The Waste Land:* assuming that the poem epitomized the investment of twenty years in the creation of a collective idiom—"our modern experiment, since 1900"—the protagonists were obliged to find a return on their investment in modernity.

Thayer was shocked and insulted by Eliot's letter of 16 March and refused to engage in further communications with him. Instead he turned to Pound, who was more vulnerable to the threat of losing his job with the *Dial* and might be reproached for having encouraged Eliot's intransigence. On 10 April, Thayer demanded that he explain himself: "Perhaps you will be able to enlighten me as to why you concur with Eliot in his refusal to let The Dial have his poem."[24] In reply Pound rehearsed the same charge (which Eliot had communicated to him), that George Moore was "getting special rates from *The Dial* (also Sherwood Anderson)," and he concluded: "That being the case I can hardly reprove Eliot—if you have put the thing on a commercial basis, for holding out for as high a price as he can get. [Added in autograph in margin:] (i.e. if The Dial is a business house, it gets business treatment. If The Dial is a patron of literature T. contends it should not pay extra rates for 'mere senility,' all of which is extreme theory-ism, perhaps, on his part.)" But in passing, Pound added another point. While he could hardly attest to the veracity of Eliot's or Thayer's claims, in general he preferred that the poem be published in the *Dial:* "I shd. perhaps prefer one good review to several less good ones. I have, as I think you know, always wanted to see a concentration of the authors I believe in, in one review. The Dial perhaps looks better to me than it does to Eliot. (Life in general does.)"[25] As always, Pound displayed a keen understanding of the nexus between cultural ambitions and their institutional actualization. Implicit in his remarks to Thayer was his view that literary modernism could best present itself as a shared language through a centralization suggesting the coherence of its ambitions—the same project that animated his endeavor to unite the works of Joyce, Eliot, Yeats, and himself under the umbrella of a single publisher. Such a project would facilitate the perception of modernism as an idiom both collective and capable of individuation: an identifiable, distinctive, and serviceable language. Yet with equal acuteness Pound also articulated a central dilemma that characterized the *Dial* and the role it might play in any such project. Was the *Dial* a form of patronage, or was it a commercial venture? Unlike traditional journals that were the organs of publishing houses, the *Dial* could shun the diversity and heterogeneity that increasingly typified a literary journal, presenting itself as a patron of letters that was benign and "disinterested." Its owners, Scofield Thayer and James Sibley Watson, Jr., however, were also active purchasers of modern painting and sculpture, and in this sense were investors in a market commodity whose value was rapidly rising, in part through the efforts of the publicity apparatus that they themselves owned and controlled. Literary modernism, by analogy, was now courting the risk of becoming "smart art," an investment that would pay and pay big if successful in an expanding market. But pay whom?

The contradictions were irreconcilable. Driven by conflicting imperatives, the participants muddled through the summer of 1922. On 30 April, Thayer summarized the state of his relations with Eliot: "We now correspond only through Pound with whom my relations are also strained, but who seems to desire to keep his job." Pound himself was more cavalier. On 6 May, while traveling through Italy, he paused to send Thayer a post-card: "My present impression of the case is 'Oh you two Bostonians.'"[26] The surface gaiety, however, was a pose. The same day he also posted his letter to Jeanne Foster, inquiring about the price that *Vanity Fair* might be willing to pay for *The Waste Land.*

Discussions remained stalled throughout the rest of May and June as the participants reconsidered their strategies. On 2 June, Pound and Eliot met in Verona, a meeting recorded a few weeks later by Pound in a series of drafts and draft fragments suggesting the substance of their con-versations. One of these (later incorporated into *The Cantos*) makes clear that they considered the editorial program of Eliot's new review (still un-titled, but soon to be named the *Criterion*) a topic that probably led to an-other: where to publish *The Waste Land.*[27] From the outset of his under-taking the *Criterion,* Eliot had entertained the idea that it might collaborate with American reviews in simultaneous publication; his first letter an-nouncing the new journal to Pound, written on 12 March, had proposed exactly this: "I also see no reason why some things should not appear in this and in the Little Review concurrently."[28] The timing of this suggestion should be noted: it was four days after Eliot had sent his provocative tele-gram to Thayer and four days before he withdrew his offer of publication to the *Dial.* It was a curious proposal: Eliot had not published in the *Little Review* since 1918 and had never evinced particular interest in its fortunes. Yet if Eliot was already assuming that *The Waste Land* would be published by his own journal in England, then his 12 March reference to the *Little Review*—addressed to Pound, a force behind its current editorial activity —was probably an effort to suggest a replacement for the *Dial.* The same idea, we may suppose, arose in their discussions at Verona. And quite naturally so, since the editors of the *Little Review* were now in Paris and often in touch with Pound, who had recently assembled a special Brancusi issue for them. Like *Vanity Fair,* the *Little Review* was also a possible candi-date for what had now become a project of simultaneous publication.

In the wake of the Verona meeting, the decisive episodes in the story unfolded quickly. Pound returned to Paris on 2 July 1922 and two weeks later received a personal visit from James Sibley Watson, Jr., the co-owner and co-editor of the *Dial* and the partner of Thayer. Two days later Pound reported the meeting to his wife, Dorothy, who was away in London: "Usual flood [of people visiting]: Lunch with Watson of Dial, on Wed. [19 July], amiable . . . wants T's poem for Dial, etc." The report leaves no doubt about the purpose of Watson's visit: he had come to purchase *The Waste Land*.[29] Presumably he was treated to a variant of Pound's argument that the poem was "as good in its way as Ulysses in its way"—resonant, even haunting terms to Watson now that he was in Paris. For when Watson had gone to Sylvia Beach's bookstore to pick up his own copy of *Ulysses* (number 33, at 350 francs), he had learned that the last of the 150-franc copies had already soared in value to 500 francs. Watson and Thayer, after all, had ordered nine copies of the first edition for themselves, the *Dial*, and various staff members (Thayer had purchased copy number 73). And Thayer understood the kind of publicity such a work could generate: he had been called as a witness at the *Little Review* trial and seen at first hand its sensational newspaper coverage. Influenced by these events and the assumption that the poem vindicated the project of modern experimentalism, Watson was seized with anxiety that the *Dial* would suffer an ignominious defeat in its effort to position itself as *the* representative of advanced cultural life. What if the poem were published in the *Little Review* or even *Vanity Fair*? The day after his meeting with Pound, Watson flew to Berlin and met with Thayer.[30]

The chief subject of discussion in Berlin was *The Waste Land* and the *Dial*'s prospects for publishing it. Increasingly fearful and excited, the two editors reached an unprecedented decision: they would offer Eliot the second annual Dial Award with its $2,000 prize as payment for the poem, in confidence, while officially they would pay only the $150 that had been their original offer.[31] Literary history records few spectacles so curious or so bizarre as this: two editors of a major review offering a figure nearly three times the national income per capita—in 2003 dollars, the payment would exceed $83,000—for a poem that neither of them had seen or read. What they had decided to purchase was less a specific poem, more a bid for a preeminent position in the field of cultural production. Moreover, their strategy for reaching that goal was exquisitely self-fulfilling: since news of the Dial Award would attract media attention, it would augment the sales of the work and further redound to the credit of the *Dial*.

Seven days after his encounter with Thayer, Watson returned to Paris and met with Pound a second time. Two accounts of the meeting survive, one by Pound addressed to Dorothy: "Watson in Thursday [27 July] with Cummings. . . . Wat. troubled at not having T. S.'s poem for Dial."[32] More revealing is Watson's account, addressed to Thayer:

> Pound has written a [autograph addition: *very*] veiled hint to
> Eliot. He took me to see Brancusi, who [illegible word] appears
> very anxious not to be reproduced anymore. I gather this is
> mostly a pose. Such chittering and apologizing and kowtowing
> as Pound indulged in I have never before seen. It was disgust-
> ing. I pointed out several things I thought you would like, but
> no, I must take what the master will give. "You win the victory,"
> says Brancusi, as though I had been beseeching him for a
> week. A dam' Pyrrhic victory, by me! . . . He will, of course, be
> furious if we don't take any; and Pound will say that we have
> destroyed his only remaining Parisian friendship. I hope you
> will write Brancusi rather than have me go to see him again;
> if I go, I shan't take Pound, that's sure. . . . Pound looks pretty
> unhealthy. He handed me two lemons which he recommends
> very highly and which I send to you on the [canceled: hope]
> chance you may like one of them.[33]

Pound's letter to Eliot, which has not survived, was written immediately after Watson's visit on 27 July. And though his "hint" had been "*very* veiled" when issued from Paris, a certain rending evidently took place as it crossed the channel. Eliot understood fully the implications of his request for a typescript: "I will let you have a copy of the Waste Land for confidential use as soon as I can make one. . . . I infer from your remarks that Watson is at present in Paris. I have no objection to either his or Thayer's seeing the manuscript."[34] Evidently it took Eliot some two weeks to arrange (or type himself) a copy of the typescript, and it was not until 12 or 13 August that he sent it to Watson in Paris. When it arrived, Watson hastily read it and reported the news to Thayer in Vienna:

> In response to Pound's letter Eliot has assumed a more con-
> ciliatory attitude and has sent on a copy of Wasteland for our
> perusal. I am forwarding it to you. . . . Anyway I wrote him
> more plainly about the prize and await his answer. I found the
> poem disappointing on first reading but after a third shot I

think it up to his usual—all the styles are there, somewhat toned down in language [autograph addition: *adjectives!*] and theatricalized in sentiment—at least I thought.[35]

Here again, one is struck by the discrepancy between Watson's initial assessment of the poem and views of it enshrined in later criticism. "On first reading" Watson found the poem "disappointing," and after perusing it three times he considered it merely "up to [Eliot's] usual." In some respects, his letter implies, it was perhaps below his usual: the diction seemed flat ("somewhat toned down"), while the tone was overdone ("theatricalized"). Yet all this makes only more remarkable Watson's decision to advance a publication proposal that entailed an unprecedented scale of payment, which he presented to Eliot in a letter of 13 or 14 August.

Eliot responded on 15 August: "Subject to Mr. Liveright's consent, I would let the *Dial* publish the poem for $150, not before November 1st. In this event I would forego the $150 advance from Mr. Liveright, and he would delay publication as a book until the new year. Possibly he would be glad to do this, on the possibility of the book's getting the prize, which might increase the sales."[36] His proposal reached Watson late in the afternoon of 16 August. The next day, however, he was seized with panic at the audacity of his proposal and sent a telegram reporting that he could not make up his mind. On 19 August, Watson reported both events to Thayer:

Got a letter from Eliot [received 16 August] regretting his haste in thinking we were trying to rob him, and offering us the right of publishing his poem simultaneously in Dial with its pub. in the Criterion. I find from Pound that Bel Esprit hasn't enough yet for one year, that it goes to Eliot only when he leaves his bank and engages in writing exclusively. He gets only a nominal salary from Lady Rothermere. In other words I don't see why we shouldn't be doing something moderately popular in giving him the award. But the next day [17 August] I got a [canceled: cable] telegram saying "don't act till you receive a second letter." Haven't received it yet, though it may come on board tonight when we touch at Plymouth. So the matter is still in the air. Please don't do anything definitive without letting me know first. I reach New York probably August 26, and there is also the telegraphie sans fil.[37]

Pound, clearly, had informed him about the difficult state of Eliot's personal finances. Watson, in turn, hoped these circumstances might be exploited to the advantage of the *Dial*, that it might be viewed as "doing something moderately popular in giving him the award." Eliot's actual services to letters (the ostensible justification for the award) and the merits of *The Waste Land* were issues that never appeared in his discussion of the Dial Award. Instead, Watson cheerily admitted his view that the proposal was a device intended to garner goodwill for the *Dial,* a tactic in its struggle to consolidate its position as the dominant journal of advanced culture.

Meanwhile, on 21 August, Eliot sent his own letter to Quinn, apprising him of the recent developments and leaving open the possibility for action: "A few days ago I had an attractive proposal from Mr. Watson of the *Dial* who are very anxious to publish the poem. . . . They suggested getting Liveright to say postpone the date of publication as a book, but I have written to them to say that it seemed to me too late to be proper to make any change now and that I should not care to trouble either Mr. Liveright or yourself with any questions of alterations in the contract."[38] Nine days later Eliot wrote to Pound and reported his letters to Watson and Quinn:

> I received a letter from your friend Watson most amiable in
> tone . . . offering $150 for the "Waste Land" (not "Waste Land,"
> please, but "*The* Waste Land," and (in the strictest confidence)
> the award for virtue also. Unfortunately, it seemed considerably
> too late, as I had the preceding day [14 August] got contract,
> signed by Liveright and Quinn, book to be out by Nov. 1st, etc.)
> I can't bother Quinn any more about it, I don't see why Liveright should find it to his advantage to postpone publication in
> order to let the Dial kill the sale by printing it first, and there
> has been so much fluster and business about this contract that
> I don't want to start the whole thing up again, so I see nothing
> but to hope that the Dial will be more businesslike with other
> people. Watson's manner was charming, if Thayer had behaved
> in the same way the Dial might have published it long ago,
> instead of pretending that I had given him the lie as if he was
> *ehrenfähig* anyhow. Anyway, it's my loss, I suppose; if Watson
> wants to try to fix it up with Liveright I suppose he can,
> that's his affair. I suppose the move was entirely due to your

beneficent and pacific efforts, which are appreciated. Dam but why don't they give the prize to you? More presently.[39]

Notwithstanding the disingenuous demurral by Eliot, the issue was already all but settled. The suggestion he had advanced—that the *Dial* undertake to arrange terms with Liveright—was rapidly realized through the agency of Watson. On 29 August his ship arrived in New York; the next day he received Eliot's letter of 21 August broaching the new arrangement. He set to work immediately, as Gilbert Seldes duly reported to Thayer: "Watson has just come back and the Eliot affair is taking up much of our time."[40] A week later he and Seldes met with Liveright in the New York office of the lawyer John Quinn, and there the deal was concluded. Liveright required that the *Dial* purchase 350 copies of the volume at standard discounts, assuring himself an advance sale and adding $315 to the *Dial*'s costs for procuring the poem. But the *Dial* had achieved its victory, and the outcome would be a remarkable success.

Liveright reported on these later events in a letter to Pound written on 5 February 1923, eleven weeks after the poem's publication in the *Dial*, seven weeks after his own release of the book-cum-notes: "God bless you and Cantos IX to XII. If we can get as much publicity from them as The Waste Land has received, you will be a millionaire. The Waste Land has sold 1000 copies to date and who knows, it may go up to 2000 or 3000 copies. Just think, Eliot may make almost $500 on the book rights of this poem. And Gene Stratton Porter makes $40,000.00 to $60,000 a year out of her books. Well, it's all in a life time, so who cares."[41]

Liveright's estimate of the poem's sales was too low, according to his biographer, for in fact "more than 5,000 copies were . . . sold."[42] More important, though, was the tenor of his comments, insofar as it tended to echo Watson's rationale in urging Thayer to take on the poem: the argument that the *Dial* would "be doing something moderately popular in giving him the award." Liveright's stress on how much publicity the award-and-publication package received is telling. For by now it should be clear that the publication of *The Waste Land* marked the crucial moment in the transition of modernism from a minority culture to one supported by an important institutional and financial apparatus.

The contours of this transition can best be understood by a rapid survey of the three journals that were considered for simultaneous publication in the United States—the *Little Review*, the *Dial*, and *Vanity Fair*. Each represented a moment in the growth and triumph of modernism. When Eliot suggested in March 1922 that the *Criterion* engage in simultaneous publication with the *Little Review*, his proposal looked back to the world of modernism's past, to its origins in a *littérature de cénacle*, to the heady days of 1917–1918 when his own poems and articles had appeared in the rebellious journal. When Pound suggested in May and August that the poem be published by *Vanity Fair*, his proposal looked forward to modernism's future, to the ease and speed with which a market economy could purchase, assimilate, commodify, and reclaim as its own the works of a literature whose ideological premises were bitterly inimical toward its ethos and cultural operations. These distinct moments were mediated by what, in the early 1920s, was modernism's present: the sensibility epitomized by the *Dial*, a form of production supported by massive and unprecedented patronage that facilitated modernism's transition from a literature of an exiguous elite to a position of prestigious dominance.

The velocity of this process is illustrated by the fate of Eliot's own work shortly after the publication of *The Waste Land*. Only seven months later, in June 1923, *Vanity Fair* devoted an entire page to reprinting earlier poems by Eliot; among them were "Sweeney Among the Nightingales" (first published in the *Little Review* in 1918), "A Cooking Egg" (first published in a tiny journal named *Coterie* in 1919), and "Burbank with a Baedeker" (first published in the short-lived *Art and Letters* in 1919). Linking the poems was an editorial box in the center of the page, presumably composed by managing editor Edmund Wilson, that lucidly articulated the magazine's assumptions: "Since the publication of *The Waste Land*, Mr. T. S. Eliot has become the most hotly contested issue in American poetry. He has been frequently attacked for his unconventional form and what many readers consider his obscurity. But if one has read Mr. Eliot's earlier poems . . . from which the present selection is made, one gets the key to both his technique and his ideas." In subsequent months of 1923–1924 *Vanity Fair* conducted an intense campaign, printing essays by Eliot in July, November, and February and a study of Eliot's work by Clive Bell in September 1923. Eliot had indeed become "the most hotly contested issue in American poetry"—in part because the *Dial* and *Vanity Fair* had said so themselves.[43]

It was a long way from the world of the *Little Review*, a distance that can be measured more accurately if we recall some of the journal's principal features. (Because information on the *Little Review* is notoriously sparse, I shall also use data from the *Egoist,* which Eliot edited during 1918 and which occupied a similar position within the economic structure of modernism.)[44] The *Little Review* had existed in a special space that was insulated from the direct demands of larger market structures by the beneficent hand of a modest yet influential patronage (such as the syndicate organized by Quinn or Harriet Weaver's support of the *Egoist*). The scale of such operations was tiny; circulation of the *Little Review* was roughly three thousand, and for the *Egoist* it typically hovered near two hundred.[45] Both maintained a low ratio of advertising to circulation revenues, something like 1:10, indicating that they survived by a direct rapport with a restricted group of readers.[46] They rejected the strategy of the mass-circulation journals that had been the dominant market force since the late 1890s and instead returned to the kind of direct relationship with readers that had typified literary magazines in the genteel tradition. This relationship was also reflected in their form of sales: neither enjoyed newsstand sales (distributing agencies were not interested), and both were associated with a meager set of specific retail outlets (the Washington Square Bookshop, the Sunwise Turn, and Brentano's in New York for the *Little Review;* the stores of Friedrich Neumaier, Elkin Mathews, and Harold Monro in London for the *Egoist;* and Sylvia Beach's Shakespeare and Company in Paris for both). At its height the *Egoist* sold only 132 copies to readers who were not already subscribers, the *Little Review* only 600 (19.4 percent of total circulation). Advertising, too, played a minimal role in the *Little Review.* Its issue for September 1918 contained sixty-four pages and three covers (inside front, inside back, and back) that could potentially carry ads; but in practice ads actually occupied only one and a half of those pages (2.2 percent). In its issue for spring 1922, which was exactly the same length, paid ads more than doubled to three and a quarter pages—but that still amounted to only 4.9 percent of the journal. Advertising, following a convention of the genteel tradition, was segregated at the beginning and end of an issue.

The *Dial* operated quite differently. Its subscription list was some two and a half times as large as the *Little Review*'s: 6,374 in 1922 (compared with the average of 2,500 for the *Little Review* in 1917). Its ratio of advertising to circulation revenues was not 1:10 but something closer to 1:3 (specifically, $9,100 to $31,400)—much lower than those of more commercial journals, to be sure, but much higher than those of the *Little Re-*

view or the *Egoist*. But above all, the *Dial* was supported by massive patronage: its deficits for the three years from 1920 to 1922 were, respectively, $100,000; $54,000; and $65,000, a cumulative deficit of nearly $220,000 that was paid for directly by Thayer and Watson at the rate of a little more than $3,000 per month from each.[47] Nothing is more revealing than comparable figures for the *Little Review*, which in 1918 was supported by a syndicate of four donors whose contributions totaled $2,350 per year, or for the *Egoist*, which from 1917 to 1920 was supported by donations from Harriet Weaver averaging £253 ($1,265) per year.[48]

How the *Dial* mediated a transition between the *Little Review* and *Vanity Fair* is also apparent in its editorial practices. The *Dial*, for example, repeatedly published materials that had previously appeared in the *Little Review*, such as Wyndham Lewis's "Starry Sky" or a photo of Ossip Zadkine's sculpture "Holy Family."[49] Indeed, at times all three journals were publishing the same material: the spring 1922 issue of the *Little Review* was devoted to works by Brancusi, the May number of *Vanity Fair* showed photographs of the same works, and the November issue of the *Dial* reproduced Brancusi's *Golden Bird* for a third time in the same year. Its mediating role was also apparent in editorial policy. The *Little Review* boasted its intransigent aestheticism on the masthead: it would brook "no compromise with the public taste." But the *Dial* was more cautious; in a letter of November 1922 Thayer told his managing editor that he wished to publish works that "have *aesthetic value* and are not *commercially suicidal*."[50] The litotes "not commercially suicidal" is noteworthy, and translated into ordinary prose it means *might be successful*. The journal's official policy was also a compromise; it invoked an uneasy translation of Crocean idealism to justify eclectic aestheticism, a tone of patrician urbanity, and the conviction that "one must confine one's self to works of art" independent of social or moral considerations.[51] The *Dial*, in other words, differed from the *Little Review* and *Vanity Fair* in its tone of high seriousness and gravity, not in substantive ideology.

Yet the *Dial* did not borrow only from the *Little Review*; in many respects it strove to imitate *Vanity Fair*. Editorially it copied *Vanity Fair*'s practice of offering a regular "London Letter" and "Paris Letter," and it imitated *Vanity Fair*'s institution of so-called service departments that offered advice and arrangements for the purchase of books and travel. Its layout and design were also conspicuously similar, and by 1922 the two magazines were even using the same printing operations. The *Dial* also attempted to integrate editorial and advertising functions in ways reminiscent of *Vanity Fair:* its monthly listing of gallery exhibitions took pains to praise its own advertisers. And like *Vanity Fair,* too, its management stressed publicity, advertising revenues, and street sales (as opposed to subscriptions). It developed displays to be set up at newsstands, and it aggressively cultivated a larger metropolitan public. When its editors contemplated penetrating the British market in 1921, Eliot urged them to pursue the same course abroad: "You must have your future manager here arrange for the paper to be visible and handy on every bookstall, at every tube station."[52] When the *Dial* published *The Waste Land* and announced its award, Thayer ordered the staff to keep a minute record of every reference to these events in the press—an early form of market testing.[53] Above all, the *Dial* imitated the central principle behind the success of *Vanity Fair* and its sister journal *Vogue:* in an era when most publishers were attempting to produce magazines aimed at a mass market, Thayer, like Condé Nast, publisher of *Vanity Fair* and *Vogue,* deliberately appealed to a select, restricted audience.[54]

The *Dial* was acutely conscious of its competition with *Vanity Fair,* a theme that recurs in letter after letter by Thayer. On 16 December 1922 he complained to his mother that contributors and staff members of the *Dial* were frequently writing for *Vanity Fair.* Ten days later he lamented to Seldes: "If we have no aesthetic standards whatever in what respect are we superior to Vanity Fair which in other respects gives more for the money?" A month later he urged Seldes to hasten the printing of a new photograph "lest 'Vanity Fair' get ahead of us on this point too." And four months later he ordered him to secure rights to a new painting by Pablo Picasso: "Otherwise Vanity Fair will be getting it." How closely the market for the two journals overlapped became clear when the *Dial* issued its special art folio in June 1923. Desperate to stimulate sales, Thayer begged Seldes to intervene: "Cannot you get Rosenfeld to write the thing up for Vanity Fair, which is our most important selling possibility?"[55]

To be sure, the *Dial* and *Vanity Fair* were not twins. By comparison the *Dial* was a modest operation. Its $9,100 in advertising revenue was tiny compared with the $500,000 per annum generated by *Vanity Fair.* Paid advertising occupied less space; in the November 1922 issue of the *Dial* that included *The Waste Land,* 27.5 of 156 pages (or 18 percent) were taken up by advertising. Compare this with the July 1923 issue of *Vanity Fair,* which contained Eliot's poems: of 140 pages, 76 were devoted to paid advertising (54 percent), and many articles offered fashion and automobile reviews that were advertising thinly disguised. The *Dial,* like the *Little Review,* segregated its paid ads in sections placed only at the beginning and end of the journal; most of its ads came from publishers, all were printed in black and white, and few made conspicuous use of visual imagery. *Vanity Fair,* in contrast, handsomely displayed its arresting ads, many in color and set among the editorial contents. In 1922 the *Dial's* circulation stood at 9,500 copies per month; in the same year *Vanity Fair's* reached 96,500 (see table).[56] (Other monthlies boasted much larger circulations, such as *McClure's Magazine* [365,000] or *National Geographic* [734,000]; and monthlies classed as "women's publications" had the largest circulations: *McCall's,* 1,340,000, and *Woman's Home Companion,* 1,468,000.)

Journal Circulation and Revenues, 1922

	LITTLE REVIEW	DIAL	VANITY FAIR
Total circulation	3,100	9,500	96,500
Subscriptions	2,500	6,374	n/a
Retail sales	600	3,100	n/a
Advertising revenue	$500	$9,100	$500,000
Circulation revenue	$5,000	$31,400	$357,000*
Ratio, ad revenue: circulation revenue	1:10	1:3.5	1:0.7
Paid ads (% of pages)	4.8	18	54
Yearly patronage	$2,350	$73,300	0
Price per copy	$1.00	$0.50	$0.35
Subscription per year	$4.00	$5.00	$3.50

*Based on assumption of 66,000 subscribers and 30,000 street sales

Despite their diversity, one set of interests did bind together the *Little Review,* the *Dial,* and *Vanity Fair*—their involvement with the visual arts. All three journals published many photographs of contemporary painting and sculpture. More important, however, was another affiliation that this signaled, one with the world of contemporary art collecting. John Quinn, who was patron of the *Little Review,* Scofield Thayer, who was co-owner, patron, and editor of the *Dial,* and Frank Crowninshield, who was the editor of *Vanity Fair,* were all major buyers of contemporary art. Quinn's purchases in 1920 alone totaled $24,000. In 1923 he purchased Paul Cézanne's portrait of the artist's father; a huge still-life interior by Henri Matisse, six by eight feet; *The Jungle* by Henri Rousseau; five Picassos, including the magnificent *Portrait of William Uhde;* two small works by Georges Braque; and three major works by Brancusi.[57] Thayer was almost as active: after residing in Paris, Vienna, and Berlin, and acting under the influence of Herwarth Walden, owner of the famous Der Sturm gallery, Thayer gathered a well-considered collection of pre–World War I German Expressionists, including Oskar Kokoschka, along with a substantial number of works by Picasso, Matisse, and others, and at his instigation the *Dial* published a lavish collection of contemporary art reproductions titled *Living Art.*[58] Frank Crowninshield was also a collector: his penthouse flat housed eighteen paintings by André Segonzac, five by Amedeo Modigliani, seven by Jules Pascin, a large collection of African art, and at least one work by virtually every major painter in Paris.[59] Often he drew upon his own collection for works to be reproduced in the magazine, and at times he wrote captions for photographic art features. In 1929 he became one of the original seven members of the board of the Museum of Modern Art, and when Alfred Barr first announced the formation of the museum in 1929, he did so with an essay in *Vanity Fair.*[60] Quinn also published two essays in *Vanity Fair,* one on the sculptor Jacob Epstein and another on Joyce, a pairing that suggests the extent to which contemporary art and literature might be counterpoised. And when Quinn held a private party in 1923 to unveil his new Georges Seurat painting, the great *Le Cirque,* he invited only his immediate family and Frederick James Gregg, the lead writer on art for *Vanity Fair* and an old friend.[61]

Much can be learned from the interaction among the three journals and their common role as potential publishers of *The Waste Land.* For these journals, it is clear, are best viewed not as antagonists that represented alien or incompatible ideologies but as protagonists that shared a common terrain, whose fields of activity overlapped and converged at crucial points within a shared spectrum of marketing and consumption. Their activity suggests that there was no single or essential feature that distinguished the avant-garde from modernism. These were not irreconcilable poles of a dichotomy, as has been argued by such scholars as Peter Bürger, Andreas Huyssen, or Marjorie Perloff, who have urged that a set of formal devices (montage, for example) constituted a vague yet potent ideology that challenged dominant cultural norms, assaulted the bourgeois concept of art, or anticipated the concerns of postmodernism.[62] Such arguments are sustained only by confining one's attention to formal values viewed in isolation from their social actualization. When seen in institutional terms, the avant-garde was neither more nor less than a structural feature in the institutional configuration of modernism. It played no special role by virtue solely of its form, and it possessed no ideological privilege; instead it was constituted by a constellation of marketing and publicity structures that were integrated in varying degrees with the larger economy of its time. Its typical endeavor was to develop an idiom, and that, indeed, is how the editors who purchased *The Waste Land* perceived it: they were buying "the justification of the 'movement,' of our modern experiment, since 1900." They were purchasing a work whose scope and pretensions could vindicate an emerging idiom —vindication that could, in a market economy, be ratified only in the conspicuous expenditure of money: whence the Dial Award with its lavish expenditure for a single poem; whence Liveright's decision to double his normal per copy expenditure on advertising for *The Waste Land;*[63] whence Thayer's concern to register every reference to the *Dial*'s announcement of the award and publication of the poem. They were organizing an event that might be "moderately popular" (Watson), an occasion to generate "much publicity" (Liveright)—itself the surest commodity of the modernist economy.

The three journals that were considered as candidates to publish *The Waste Land* formed a tripartite structure within the productive apparatus of modernism. But a similar structure, with analogous kinds of relations, also informed modernism's larger productive economy. In particular, a modernist work was typically published in three forms: first, in a little review or journal; second, in a limited edition of recently collected poems (or as an individual volume if the work was large enough); and third, in a more frankly commercial or public edition issued by a mainstream publisher and addressed to a wider audience. Especially important were the two forms of book publication, the limited and the public editions. These were part of a protocol that had become normative in the course of a complex fusion of heterogeneous and to some degree conflicting traditions of publishing. On one hand, there was the program of multiple publication itself, with its origins in practices that had been developed by Alfred, Lord Tennyson as part of his effort to be a truly national poet: in 1878, to cite only one instance, Tennyson had issued his collected works in both a thirteen-volume Shilling Edition and a single-volume Crown Edition printed in three bindings (plain, gilt, and Roxburgh), a program that effectively addressed a diverse and heterogeneous audience (first-year sales of roughly thirty thousand and sixty thousand, respectively).[64] On the other hand, there was the limited edition, with its origins in the publishing practices of William Morris and the Kelmscott Press. Originally the limited edition had realized a programmatic rejection of the capitalist production of texts. In its production, for example, the role of the publisher was minimized and authorial control was maximized, the standardized design and formatting that had become publishing norms were replaced with special typography and layout, and the altered author-publisher relations were embodied in differing contractual arrangements: instead of a small advance against 15 percent royalties, the author usually received a guaranteed advance against 50 percent profits and a right to republish in another (more commercial) form within a specified amount of time. But the rebellious impulses of the Morris enterprise were Janus-faced: though Morris had at first intended to produce books solely for his own interest, the sheer cost of his experiments had obliged him to issue them as limited editions that might recoup at least a share of the expenses. The limited editions, in turn, had been rapidly assimilated by the rare and antiquarian book markets that had matured in the nineteenth century, turning them into commodities and potential investments. Thus, while the book increasingly resembled the work of art, as indeed its producers hoped, the work of art itself had already become subject to a commodity economy. Inevitably the limited edition was rapidly appropriated by other constituencies that were not merely indifferent but even hostile to the socialist impulses that had animated Morris.

One constituency was represented by William Butler Yeats, whose sisters founded the Dun Emer (later the Cuala) Press in 1902 with advice and help in typographical design from Emery Walker, a close associate of Morris at the Kelmscott Press.[65] Beginning with *In the Seven Woods* in 1903, all of Yeats's works were published first in a limited edition at the Dun Emer/Cuala, then in a public-commercial edition with Macmillan.

In turn, through Yeats's influence on his young admirer Ezra Pound, the practice of publishing books in two forms was adopted by the emerging English avant-garde, for which it became an indispensable instrument. The limited edition established a kind of special productive space insulated from the harsh exigencies of the larger marketplace. It bypassed a broad public receptive to standardized products (such as the six-shilling novel) and suspicious of novelty, and instead addressed a prosperous minority with a luxury good that emphasized innovation and was produced in small quantities (though with high profit margins per sale). It enacted, in other words, a return to an essentially precapitalist economic structure, an artisanal economy producing luxury goods in limited quantities for aristocratic consumption. By the early 1920s it had become a routine step in a tripartite publishing program—journal, limited edition, and public or commercial edition—that was now normative for the avant-garde.

Yeats represented only one of the constituencies that could appropriate and adapt the ways of Morris. In the United States, similar forms of book production were soon adopted by the ensemble of figures and institutions often labeled "the genteel tradition" and associated with Boston and with Harvard University. The process is epitomized in the career of the typographer Bruce Rogers.[66] After working briefly in Indianapolis for a journal called *Modern Art,* Rogers moved to Boston in 1895, where he was soon frequenting circles that evinced a growing interest in fine books and the experiments of Morris. Among them were the Grolier Club, a society founded in 1884 to promote the collecting of fine books; *The Knight Errant,* a review that devoted extensive discussion to William Morris, established in 1892; and the Tavern Club, founded the same year (headed by Professor Charles Eliot Norton) and devoted to fine books. From 1895 to 1912 Rogers worked for the Riverside Press, which acted as Harvard's printer, a period during which he assimilated Morris's interest in the well-made book to his own anachronistic, more classicizing style of typography. After several other jobs, Rogers settled down. Between 1920 and 1928 he was serving as typographical adviser to Harvard University Press and working for the printing firm of William Edwin Rudge, for which he issued a series of limited editions published by Maurice Firuski, owner of a bookstore known as Dunster House in Cambridge, Massachusetts. Which, strangely, brings us back to T. S. Eliot.

The Waste Land, we recall, was not published in book form solely by

Horace Liveright; nearly ten months later (12 September 1923) it appeared a second time, issued by Virginia Woolf's Hogarth Press in a limited edition of about 460 copies. The date suggests that the publication was an afterthought, as if Eliot had been seeking to retrace a missed step in the normal process of avant-garde publishing. Yet the idea of a limited edition was anything but tardy. Eliot had begun to worry about the precarious implications of his agreement with Liveright almost immediately after their encounter in January 1922. It was a precipitous move that bypassed the normal rhythms of avant-garde production, in which a work was transmitted from a small elite to an ever wider yet presumably less discriminating audience, and therefore a move that threatened the status of his work. Like anyone who works within a specific institution, Eliot had internalized an array of unwritten protocols considered normal and appropriate. No sooner had he completed the poem in its final version (probably in the first week of February 1922) than he began to seek a publisher who would issue a limited edition. On 14 February he lunched with Conrad Aiken and discussed his dilemma. Aiken, the next day, reported their conversation to Maurice Firuski, the Cambridge bookseller and publisher who was issuing Aiken's own book of poetry *The Pool of Priapus:*

> Brief is this note, and chiefly occasioned by a talk with Tom
> Eliot at lunch yesterday. He has a poem, 450 lines long, wh.
> I haven't seen. He seeks a publisher who will produce it nicely,
> and in America, and in a small edition. Firuski! cried I, and
> there you are. When I elucidated, mentioning [Bruce] Rogers
> and 450 copies and two years exclusive right and a possible
> hundred dollars and a beautifully produced book, his eyes
> glowed with a tawny golden light like fierce doubloons, his
> hands took on singularly the aspect of claws, his nails tore
> the table-cloth, and he took your address. . . . As I say, I have
> not seen the poem. It may or may not be good, or intelligible.
> But, reflect: Eliot has a real reputation; a poem of that length
> by him will be a real curiosity, even perhaps an event; and he
> assumes that you will have of course, the English as well as
> the American market. He may have to get Knopf's permission,
> as I did, to make the arrangement: he doesn't remember how
> his contract stands. But that, I fancy, will present no difficulty,

for the book is too small for Knopf, and besides Knopf doesn't
regard Eliot as a golconda . . . Address: 9 Clarence Gate Gardens, London, W.W.1.[67]

Eleven days later, on 26 February, Eliot himself wrote to Firuski, pur-
suing the same question more fully:

> Your name has been given me by Mr. Conrad Aiken, who has
> also shown me a volume of poems by Mr. John Freeman, re-
> cently published by you, with the appearance of which I was
> very much pleased.
>
> I have now ready a poem for which that form of publication
> seems to me the most suitable. I understand that you issue
> these books in limited editions, and that for the volumes you
> take in this series you give a sum down in advance royalty.
>
> My poem is of 435 lines; with certain spacings essential to
> the sense, 475 book lines; furthermore, it consists of five parts,
> which would increase the space necessary; and with title pages,
> some notes that I intend to add, etc., I guess that it would
> run to from 28 to 32 pages.
>
> I have had a good offer for the publication of it in a periodi-
> cal. But it is, I think, much the best poem I have ever written,
> and I think it would make a much more distinct impression
> and attract much more attention if published as a book.
>
> If you are interested in this, I should be glad to hear from
> you what terms you would be prepared to offer for it, at your
> earliest convenience, as the other offers for it cannot be held
> in suspence very long.[68]

Eliot's letter, of course, is fascinating. Most important for our purpose,
it demonstrates how fully Eliot understood the protocols of avant-garde
publishing, as well as how easily those procedures could be assimilated
to features already long established in a genteel tradition of private and
limited editions. The book of poems by John Freeman (1880–1919) that
Eliot had admired was *The Red Path, a Narrative, and the Wounded Bird,* a
slender volume of poems issued in 425 copies that were printed for Firuski's
Dunster House at the press of William Edwin Rudge, its design executed
by Bruce Rogers. The volume was handsome and, like all of Rogers's work,

inspired by classical models of typography and design; it suggested a tone of genteel decorum, a distinctly Harvardian note, and yet it sounded that note with even greater subtlety, as if to hint at an elite within the elite, a more reflective minority with discriminating taste, one opposed to that of a broader elite that unreflectively assumed its privileges solely on the basis of class, money, and inherited status.

Despite having already received "a good offer" of $150 for the poem from Thayer and the *Dial* and despite his preliminary agreement with Liveright in Paris, Eliot preferred to see the work issued in a limited edition: "I think it would make a much more distinct impression and attract much more attention if published as a book." To be sure, Liveright had also offered to publish the poem as a book, but a different kind of book: a public and more commercial edition that would directly address a wider audience and not be preceded by the limited edition typical of the avant-garde. That proposal violated the institutional logic of avant-garde production, so much so that Eliot instinctively sought a form of publication that would set matters right. Firuski, however, was slow to respond. Moreover, by 12 March (only two weeks after his letter to Firuski), Eliot had received another note from Liveright reaffirming his interest in publishing the poem. As Eliot promptly informed Pound: "Liveright wrote to say he wanted it, and I have written asking what he wants to give and telling him the exact length," adding cryptically, "and I have other plans also if Thayer doesn't cough out."[69] The other plans, of course, were those with Firuski, plans presented as an acceptable alternative to publication in the *Dial*. The plans underscore a common procedure of publication: just as the *Dial* occupied the middle position in the tripartite structure of journal publication (between the *Little Review* and *Vanity Fair*), so the limited edition occupied the middle position within the larger tripartite structure of avant-garde and modernist publishing (between journal and commercial edition). Indeed, it was the violation of this logic that distinguished the actual publication of *The Waste Land*, its first appearance in book form being the commercial edition by Liveright, and it was a late and retrospective effort to "correct" this anomaly that prompted Eliot to issue a limited edition with the Hogarth Press in 1923.

Eliot, it is clear, wanted his poem to be successful, yet not too successful. For the prospect of immediate publication by a commercial firm raised prospects that were largely unimaginable within the logic of modernism.

And similar considerations must also have influenced the discussions concerning *Vanity Fair* as a possible venue for the poem. Pound, after first raising the issue on 6 May 1922, presumably reported his action to Eliot during their meeting in Verona a month later, though how they viewed this prospect cannot be stated with any degree of certainty. Still, it is clear enough not only that Pound and Eliot considered *Vanity Fair* a potential publisher, but also that *Vanity Fair* considered itself a serious candidate. The journal not only sent John Peale Bishop to discuss the project with Pound in Paris, it even advanced an explicit offer of publication. The proposal appeared in a letter written by Edmund Wilson to Eliot on 1 August 1922. Eliot, in another letter that has not been previously published, replied on 14 August: "Thank you for your letter of the 1st inst., I should be very glad to do for you such an article as you suggest. For the next two months I shall be far too busy to attempt such a thing, but I think that I should be able to provide one during October or November if that is satisfactory to you. As for a poem, I am afraid that is quite impossible at present as I have only one for which I have already contracted."[70] Eliot, plainly, was not being straightforward; as yet he had not "contracted" for *The Waste Land* in a journal at all. Only a day or two before his letter to Wilson, in fact, Eliot had sent off the typescript of *The Waste Land* to Pound and James Sibley Watson, Jr., in Paris, and only the day *after* his letter to Wilson did he write to Watson announcing his terms for the poem: the Dial Award plus $150, provided he publish the poem not much before the book issued by Liveright. Eliot, it is clear, rejected the offer from *Vanity Fair* not because he had "already contracted" for its serial publication but because *Vanity Fair* represented a degree of commercial success and popular acceptance that would have undermined the status that he was trying to establish for the work. That status, however, was not simply intrinsic or implanted in the poem's text; it was a function of the institutional structures that had informed its production at every step in the poem's life.

In retrospect, we can see that the proposal for a limited edition by Firuski looked not only back to the Cambridge and Harvard environment of Eliot's college days but also forward to modernism's future, to the moment when Eliot would make his triumphant return to Harvard in 1932 and seal the fateful association between modernism and the academy. Yet that association, which has been so much commented on, did not occur naturally or without relations to other changes in the wider culture. By the early 1930s, in fact, all the magazines that Eliot had once considered for *The Waste Land* were dead or dying. The *Little Review* and the *Dial* had both closed in 1929, and *Vanity Fair* was to expire in 1936. The Great Depression effectively eliminated the structures of private patronage that had sustained modernism's growth and its emergence as a significant idiom within the family of twentieth-century languages. Thereafter, modernism would be slowly but inexorably absorbed into the university, as it had also been appropriated by the marketing and publicity apparatus of *Vanity Fair.*

The price of modernism, in this sense, was a double one. In part, it was a specific and concrete figure epitomized in the sums paid to Eliot for publication of *The Waste Land:* $150 as the price of the poem proper, $2,000 for the Dial Award, a subsequent $580 in royalties on the sales of the Liveright edition, and perhaps another $100 from the Hogarth Press edition—altogether about $2,800, a figure that in modern terms would be somewhere around $115,000. (It was almost two and a half times the $1,150 earned annually by the executive secretary to the editor of *Vanity Fair.*)[71] But hidden among such figures was another, more important price: an obscuring of a determinate productive space, the elision of boundaries between specific institutions and wider zones of cultural activity, the illusion that "art" or "the poem" or "the text" had been the central concern of participants whose decisions were consistently made when as yet they had not read a word of the work in question. And not without reason, for the text was largely irrelevant. *The Waste Land* was transmitted not through a conduit that received and reproduced a neutral image of its original but through a multiplicity of social structures driven by conflicting imperatives: it became part of a social event in a discontinuous yet coherent process, an effort to affirm the output of a specific marketing-publicity apparatus through the enactment of a triumphal and triumphant occasion. It was not simply the institutions that were the vehicle of the poem; the poem also became the vehicle of the institutions—inseparable, finally, from the contradictory network of uses in which it had been historically constituted.

It would be easy, perhaps too easy, to cluck over the kind of "not reading" that was practiced by the editors of the *Dial,* or Horace Liveright, or John Peale Bishop. Yet on some occasions, at least, not reading a work may turn out to be an oblique yet perceptive way of achieving a very good reading. For it is certainly true that the "not reading" which the *Dial* edi-

tors performed was a trenchant reading of the poem's place in the unfold-
ing structural logic of modernism. Perhaps, after all, we can learn from
them. For reading as we do—rummaging among vegetation rituals and
Grail legends, fretting over the arcana of Tarot cards, or more recently
scrutinizing Eliot's biography to uncover a hidden psychodrama of latent
homoeroticism—instead of as they did, we leave the ambiguous heritage
of modernism in history just as desocialized and impervious to understanding as it was before. History may well be a nightmare, as the modernists
so often claimed; but when they entered the "contrived corridors" of its
making, at least they never failed (in a phrase from Eliot's "Gerontion")
to "protract the profit of their chilled delirium."

CHAPTER THREE

IMMENSE. MAGNIFICENT. TERRIBLE.

READING *THE WASTE LAND*

TO BE YOUNG, TO BE RICH, and to be in Paris—perhaps enough to
turn anyone's head. Certainly it had some such effect on John Peale Bishop
(1892–1944), an aspiring poet who had graduated in 1917 from Princeton
University, where his best friends had included F. Scott Fitzgerald and
the soon-to-be distinguished critic Edmund Wilson. After a brief stint of
service in the armed forces, Bishop had become the managing editor of
Vanity Fair, a job he gave up in early 1922 when he married Margaret
Hutchins, a young woman of independent wealth. Having turned over
his position at *Vanity Fair* to Wilson, Bishop set off on his honeymoon in
Europe. It was while there, in Paris, that he had briefly met Ezra Pound
in August 1922 to discuss the possibility of *Vanity Fair's* publishing *The
Waste Land,* a last service on behalf of his erstwhile employer. Bishop, of
course, had never read the poem and knew about it only through the rumors then circulating in the New York publishing world, rumors that
Pound himself had helped set in motion. But nothing came of their discussion, and Bishop soon left to resume his honeymoon.

It was late October when he returned to Paris. He was settling in for
a year to undertake some serious writing. His first book, a collection of
poems and prose pieces that was titled *The Undertaker's Garland,* had been
published only a few weeks earlier, and he was eager to begin on new

work. On 3 November, Bishop wrote to Wilson, known to good friends as "Bunny," describing his circumstances:

> Dear Bunny:
>
> Well here we are installed in an apartment neatly placed
> between the Opera and the wild wild joints of Montmartre;
> the location has, so to say, a symbolic significance. The place
> belongs to two decayed members of the French gentility who,
> being much fallen in estate and finance have been obliged to
> let half their formerly enormous quarters. . . . We have then,
> one large salon furnished quite chastely with a touch of the
> grand manner; a smaller salon which we are using as a dining
> room and likewise as the chief living room, it being the warm-
> est room. M[argaret] has her own bedroom and mine is large,
> light and sufficiently remote to make it a very excellent place
> to work. Imagine me then pecking zestfully at my newly
> repaired typewriter beside a wood fire in silence and solitude.

But in the midst of "pecking zestfully," Bishop found that something was haunting all his attempts at writing. It was *The Waste Land*. In Paris, Bishop had picked up a copy of the first issue of the *Criterion*, published only two weeks earlier and containing Eliot's poem (though without the notes, in-cluded only later when the poem was issued as an independent book).

> I am trying to work out an elaborate form which will be partly
> lyrical, partly descriptive, partly dramatic. . . . I need not say
> that the chief difficulty is to eradicate T. S. Eliot from all future
> work. . . . I have read *The Waste Land* about five times a
> day since the copy of the *Criterion* came into my hands. It is
> IMMENSE. MAGNIFICENT. TERRIBLE. I have not yet been able
> to figure it all out; especially the fortune telling episode, the
> king my brother and the king my father, and the strange words
> that look like a Hindu puzzle to me. I have not of course had
> the advantage of the notes which you say the book version will
> contain. Perhaps you can enlighten me on the following points:
> Mr. Eugenides (his significance), Magnus Martyr, Phlebas
> the Phoenician. The red rock is I take it the modern world both
> intellectual and mechanical. But the cock crowing, presaging

the dawn and rain? And what is the experience referred to
in the last section with all the DAs in it? Do you recognize
Le Prince d'Aquitaine de la tour abolie or *shantih?*

I don't think he has ever used his stolen lines to such terrifying effect as in this poem. And the HURRY UP PLEASE IT'S TIME
makes my flesh creep.

Bishop had no time to write further but pledged to communicate again
as soon as he learned anything more about *The Waste Land.*

To his surprise, he would soon learn far more than he ever expected—
and from a source with remarkable authority. He hastened to notify Wilson:

Dear Bunny,

Ezra and Mrs. Pound came to dinner last night and I wished
many times that you might have been here to see the great
Amurricn Poet work out. There's a lot of his past that came out
after he had begun to get into his cups, which was fairly soon,
as well as a few points about Tears Eliot (as some Paris wit has
recently christened him); the latter I feel I should at once communicate to you.

TSE came abroad with the idea of working up his PhD, presumably in philosophy though of this I'm not sure, and turned
up one day on Pound's doorstep. Ezra had heard of him from
Harvard and at once, upon hearing that he had some poems,
suggested getting out the *Catholic Anthology,* which P[ound]
afterward did, just to publish Eliot whose work at that time
EP had not seen. Then he advised him against vers libre.

Eliot is tubercular and disposed toward epilepsy; on one occasion he decided to kill himself in Pound's house but funked
at the final moment. "The Psychological Hour" in *Lustra* gives
EP's reactions to TSE's wedding, which was substituted on the
spur of the moment for a tea engagement at Pound's. It seems
that Thomas and Vivien arrived in the hallway and then turned
back, went to the registrar's and were wed, to everybody's subsequent pain and misery. She is an English lady, daughter of
a member of the Royal Academy and sister of an officer in the
Guards. She likewise is an invalid and according to Muriel
Draper very weary and washed out. Eliot's version of her is

contained in "the Chair she sat in like a burnished throne" etc.
passage. By the way do you know that the HURRY UP PLEASE
IT'S TIME is what the bartenders say when the English pubs
are about to close? The conversation is evidently gleaned from
one of the ten o'clock, just-before-closing bickers in a pub, and
according to EP reflects the atmosphere immediately outside
their first flat in London. Eliot, it seems, is hopelessly caught in
his own prudent temperament. As EP says, "I am too low for
any steamroller to flatten me out; I can always creep out of the
way. But Eliot is incapable of taking the least chance." As one
would have surmised.

Mr. Eugenides actually turned up at Lloyds with his pocket
full of currants and asked Eliot to spend a weekend with him
for no nice reasons. His place in the poem is, I believe, as a
projection of Eliot, however. That is, all the men are in some
way deprived of their life-giving, generative forces. Phlebas is
simply dead, like the Knight in the Gawain version of the Grail
(also like Attis and the Attis dummy, see Miss Weston); the
Fisher King is castrated; the one-eyed merchant a homosexual.
I do not of course mean to imply that Thomas is that any more
than that he is physically nutted.

Bishop went on to summarize his new understanding of Eliot's poem:

> Please disregard any queries I made before about *The Waste
> Land;* I think I've cleared up the meaning of the poem as far
> as it is possible. From Pound's account, it was originally twice
> as long and included Bleistein and all the old familiar faces.
> It's my present opinion that the poem is not so logically con-
> structed as I had at first supposed and that it is a mistake to
> seek for more than a suggestion of personal emotion in a num-
> ber of passages. The nightingale passage is, I believe, impor-
> tant. Eliot being Tereus, and Mrs. E. Philomel; that is to say
> that through unbalanced passion everybody is in a hell of a
> fix, Tereus being changed to a hoopoo and TSE a bank clerk.
> Thomas's sexual troubles are undoubtedly extreme.

But, as if to hint that Bishop's complacent reading of *The Waste Land* barely

concealed a lingering dissatisfaction and preoccupation, he added a concluding note on the progress of his own poems: "I have written quantities or
half-written them to destroy them later. I don't seem to be able to get the
direction right. And am much discouraged and would give a great deal
for your counsel."[1] Bishop, in fact, would never quite get over *The Waste
Land* or Eliot's accumulating oeuvre. The four volumes of poetry that he
wrote over the course of his lifetime bear witness to a poet struggling desperately to escape the shackles of a compulsive fascination with Eliotic
motifs and devices.

Bishop's two letters, neither of them published until now, are important. For apart from a brief paragraph written by James Sibley Watson,
Jr., a co-editor of the *Dial* who first read *The Waste Land* in August 1922
(see pp. 84–85), they are the only record we have of how Eliot's work was
first experienced by that hypothetical beast that has haunted so many literary discussions, the well-educated general reader. And plainly that experience, as registered in Bishop's first letter, was something close to terrifying
("such terrifying effect"), terror accompanied by a sense of the poem's
compulsive and uncanny power ("I have read [it] five times a day since
the copy of the *Criterion* came into my hands") and its overwhelming horror (". . . makes my flesh creep"). These experiences accumulate in a pal-
pable sense of confusion, patent in Bishop's bewildered attempt to orient
himself, to identify the nature or status of entities that are named in the
poem: "Mr. Eugenides (his significance), Magnus Martyr, Phlebas the
Phoenician."

Part of his confusion, of course, is cultural. An innocent abroad, Bishop
doesn't yet know that "HURRY UP PLEASE IT'S TIME" is simply the closing-
time call of a barman in British pubs. Likewise, he evidently assumes that
"Magnus Martyr," a real church, designed by Christopher Wren in the late
seventeenth century and located near the northern end of London Bridge,
is on the same plane as "Phlebas the Phoenician," a wholly fictional character invented by Eliot. And he is clearly entertaining two different, perhaps
incompatible readings of the poem: he is convinced that it represents a
certain reckoning with the modern world (a view implicit in his comment
about "the red rock"), but is also predisposed to view it in very traditional
terms that regard lyrical poetry as a form of autobiography, a rehearsal of
personal experience (evident in his query: "And what is the experience referred to in the last section with all the DAs in it?").

But part of Bishop's confusion has deeper roots, some of them discernible in his throw-away comment: "And the HURRY UP PLEASE IT'S TIME makes my flesh creep." When he writes his first letter, this line reverberates so much for Bishop precisely because it is uttered by a voice that lacks any clear or obvious origin; it violates our acquired habit of assigning sound to an identifiable source, or voice to an identifiable speaker. Repeated five times toward the close of part II, the last two in direct succession, it acquires an accelerating, frightening urgency, made all the more unbearable because it also has no discernible effect on the speech of that other voice which it cuts into, that of the nameless neighbor of Lil whose Cockney monologue rattles on unheeding, dementedly. For Bishop, plainly, these words become a literary counterpart to the experience of overloaded sound, a phonic order of the sort that we associate with the auditory hallucinations that afflict the psychotic and the ecstatic, or those seemingly possessed by spirits, or that we typically ascribe to divine annunciation and oracular utterance. A voice without any source or origin, such as the one that utters (to Bishop, at least) "HURRY UP PLEASE IT'S TIME," is often one that exhorts ("HURRY UP") or warns ("IT'S TIME") and acquires a note of menace that threatens subjection to an overwhelming power.[2] And it is precisely that sense of overwhelming menace, of terror, that Bishop experiences in this line ("makes my flesh creep").

Bishop, however inadvertently, has also stumbled across one of the major sources of the poem's uncanny power, our extreme uncertainty over just who is speaking at any particular moment in *The Waste Land*. That note of mysterious and oracular utterance which attends the poem's famous opening passage owes much to our bewilderment, our baffled inability to assign its voice to a speaker. And our disorientation about voice and identity only deepens when the first pronoun to appear in the poem ("Winter kept us warm . . .") ends up having a perceptibly different referent when it reappears just three lines later ("Summer surprised us, coming over the Starnbergersee"). Throughout the poem there is a deep, perennial ambiguity about the identity of that intermittent "I" who begins with commands ("Come in under the shadow of this red rock") or promises of enigmatic instruction ("I will show you fear in a handful of dust"), yet concludes with increasingly helpless questions ("Who is the third who walks . . . But who is that on the other side . . . What is that sound . . . Who are those hooded hordes . . . What is the city over the mountains," or even "Shall I at least set my lands in order?"). And is that final, perplexed, and plaintive "I" really the same individual who, when Madame Sosostris hands out Tarot cards to an unidentified recipient

> Here, said she,
> Is your card, the drowned Phoenician sailor

offers the cruel and knowing interjection:

(Those are pearls that were his eyes. Look!)

(And if so, what has happened to transform him by the poem's end, to change him from a fierce and canny commentator into a bewildered, self-ignorant questioner?) Bishop, no doubt mistakenly and yet also insightfully, ascribes the voice who speaks HURRY UP PLEASE IT'S TIME to a recurrent order of oracular interjection (after all, it repeatedly issues commands: "Come in under the shadow . . ." "Look!" "HURRY UP"), an order fraught with uncertainty that is deeply disturbing.

Bishop's observation can be extended. For identity in *The Waste Land* is always enigmatic, shrouded in mystery. Characters rarely have names: the middle-class woman who speaks at the beginning of part II remains as nameless as the working-class neighbor of Lil and Albert. The hyacinth girl, the house-agent's clerk, the typist, the Thames-daughters—all lack names. They also lack any of the features that typically signal individual identity: eyes or hair of a certain color, bodies of a certain height or build. (Only the young man carbuncular is . . . well, carbuncular, and has "one bold stare"; the ghoulish woman in part IV has "long black hair," but it makes "whisper music"; more weirdly, only the "bats with baby faces" have human features.) They may be agents, but they seldom act. Instead, action is either delegated to dissevered body parts via synechdoche or inanimate things via personification, or else it mysteriously transpires through the passive voice: footsteps shuffle, hair spreads and glows in fiery points, the eyes and back turn upward, exploring hands encounter no defense, faces sneer and snarl; there are months that breed and mix and stir, seasons that cover, feed, and surprise, snow that is forgetful, shadows that stride behind you or rise to meet you, the evening hour that strives homeward, the human engine that waits like a taxi throbbing waiting, the currents that pick bones in whispers, dry grass that sings, towers that toll, a door that swings, limp leaves that wait for rain, a jungle that crouches; vanity requires no response, while death undoes so many; sighs are exhaled, while stockings, slippers, camisoles, and stays are piled. This is oneiric syntax, wild and Gothic, eerie and menacing because it severs that basic connection between agent and action, eerier still when punctuated by oracular mumbles uttered by uncertain voices:

> Twit twit twit
> Jug jug jug jug jug jug

or sinister sounds that issue from hollow places:

> And voices singing out of empty cisterns and exhausted wells.

Bishop, in short, was right when he detected apocalyptic menace in "HURRY UP PLEASE IT'S TIME." Alas, not for very long. For when Bishop writes his second letter to Edmund Wilson, perhaps ten days later, he has learned to attach identity to that previously mysterious voice: "By the way do you know that HURRY UP PLEASE IT'S TIME is what the bartenders say when the English pubs are about to close?" The experience of that voice is no longer an unbearable enigma; it has a source that can be situated in space and time: "The conversation is evidently gleaned from one of the ten o'clock, just-before-closing bickers in a pub, and according to EP reflects the atmosphere immediately outside their first flat in London." It even has a precise address, directly opposite 18, Crawford Mansions. The change is now complete. HURRY UP PLEASE IT'S TIME has been transformed from apocalyptic warning to everyday routine, and terrifying uncertainty has been replaced with contented calm: "Please disregard any queries I made before about *The Waste Land;* I think I've cleared up the meaning of the poem as far as it is possible. . . . It's my present opinion that the poem is not so logically constructed as I had at first supposed and that it is a mistake to seek for more than a suggestion of personal emotion in a number of passages."

Two last points should be noted about Bishop's first letter, written just after reading the poem in a version that did not contain the notes. Tellingly, it never occurs to Bishop to assess the poem in light of the Grail legends, and phrases such as "vegetation gods" or "fertility rituals" never appear in his account. Fertility may well be an intermittent concern in the poem; but the Grail materials are so peripheral to the poem's texture that a discerning, well-educated reader such as Bishop could overlook them entirely.

Not so a reader who would read the poem accompanied by the notes. The other point is that even without the notes Bishop is convinced from the first that the poem is "highly constructed." All those repetitions hinting at symbolic density and development, all those insinuations of spatio-temporal connectedness of the sort found in narrative—surely they urged that the poem was "highly constructed," didn't they? That was precisely the question that would preoccupy the poem's earliest reviewers.

Consider the case of Burton Rascoe (1892–1957), then a thirty-year-old journalist whose weekly feature "A Bookman's Day Book," a diary of his week in the world of books, appeared in Sunday editions of the *New York Tribune*. Under an entry for "Thursday, October 26," Rascoe registered his receipt of "the November issue of *The Dial*," the one containing "The Waste Land." Rascoe immediately hailed it as "perhaps the finest poem of this generation," then went on:

> At all events it is the most significant in that it gives voice to the universal despair or resignation arising from the spiritual and economic consequences of the war, the cross purposes of modern civilization, the cul-de-sac into which both science and philosophy seem to have got themselves and the break-down of all great directive purposes which give joy and zest to the business of living. It is an erudite despair. . . . His method is highly elliptical, based on the curious formula of Tristan Corbière, wherein reverential and blasphemous ideas are juxta-posed in amazing antitheses, and there are mingled all the shining verbal toys, impressions and catch lines of a poet who has read voraciously and who possesses an insatiable curiosity about life. . . . The final intellectual impression I have of the poem is that it is extremely clever (by which I do not mean to disparage it; on the contrary): it is a rictus which masks a hurt romantic with sentiments plagued by crass reality; and it is faulty structurally for the reason that, even with the copious (mock and serious) notes he supplies in elucidation, it is so idiosyncratic a statement of ideas that I, for one, cannot follow the narrative with complete comprehension. The poem, how-ever, contains enough sheer verbal loveliness, enough ecstasy, enough psychological verisimilitude, and enough even of

a readily understandable etching of modern life, to justify
Mr. Eliot in his idiosyncracies.[3]

Rascoe's reference to "the copious . . . notes" shows that he has been
reading Liveright's edition (not the November issue of the *Dial* which he
is ostensibly reviewing). But more important is the way he juxtaposes "the
copious . . . notes" to his charge that the poem was "faulty structurally"
and his confession that he "cannot follow the narrative with complete
comprehension." Contained within that juxtaposition were points of critical
debate that would recur again and again in discussion of the poem. To
Rascoe, as to many later readers and critics, the notes hinted at levels of
narrative and/or structural coherence which jarred with his experience of
the poem. To read the poem was to plummet through a series of broken
sketches, antic turns, and fitful moments of oracular solemnity and lyrical
intensity—a dreamworld experience that startled and disturbed. To read
the notes was to find reference to "the plan," an arcane but ultimately
identifiable logic that was dictating the poem's entangled movements, or
perhaps even a narrative structure detectable behind its unruly opacity.

Moreover, that tension led into two other questions. One concerned
The Waste Land's nature, or genre. Was it "a statement of ideas," a medita-
tive poem advancing an argument with claims on public attention, or was
it some sort of "narrative"? (Rascoe used both terms within a single sentence.) Or was it perhaps something more private, an expression of some
personal feelings? That question led on to another about the nature of
poetry, a point that more than any other divides us from Eliot's contempo-
raries. For us today, a poem is an artifact of language; for them it was axiom-
atic that a poem communicated "emotion," perhaps not the "emotion
recollected in tranquility" of Wordsworth, but "emotion" nevertheless.
Consider Edmund Wilson (1890–1972), whose review of the poem appeared in the same December issue of the *Dial* which announced Eliot's
receipt of the Dial Award. Yes, Wilson conceded, the poem showed that
its author had a "constricted emotional experience," but his acute self-
awareness of this limitation was ultimately redemptive, for it generated
"intense emotion" or "strange poignancy."

> But it is the very acuteness of his suffering from this starvation
> which gives such poignancy to his art. And, as I say, Mr. Eliot
> is a poet—that is, he feels intensely and with distinction and

speaks naturally in beautiful verse. . . . His verse is sometimes much too scrappy—he does not dwell long enough upon one idea to give it its proportionate value before passing on to the next—but these drops, though they be wrung from flint, are none the less authentic crystals. . . . The poem is—in spite of its lack of structural unity—simply one triumph after another. . . . That is also why, for all its complicated correspondences and its recondite references and quotations, *The Waste Land* is intelligible at first reading. It is not necessary to know anything about the Grail Legend or any but the most obvious of Mr. Eliot's allusions to feel the force of the intense emotion which the poem is intended to convey. . . . In Eliot the very images and the sound of the words—even when we do not know precisely why he has chosen them—are charged with a strange poignancy which seems to bring us into the heart of the singer.

Wilson seems to have intuited, however, the danger that shadowed this emphasis on "intense emotion." For why should anyone's "intense emotion" be thought to have a claim on public attention, let alone receive a significant prize? He hastily added: "And sometimes we feel that he is speaking not only for a personal distress, but for the starvation of a whole civilization —for people grinding at barren office-routine in the cells of gigantic cities, drying up their souls in eternal toil whose products never bring them profit, where their pleasures are so vulgar and so feeble that they are almost sadder than their pains. It is our whole world of strained nerves and shattered institutions."[4]

While Rascoe detected a tension between the intellectual clarity that was seemingly proclaimed by the notes and the poem's genuine opacity, and Edmund Wilson had dismissed the Grail legend as peripheral to experiencing the poem itself, Gilbert Seldes (1893–1970) sketched the outlines of a wholly different view. Seldes began his review of *The Waste Land* with an overview of Eliot's critical writings—and he was uniquely placed to do so. As managing editor of the *Dial* during 1921, he had published four of the ten essays that Eliot wrote while composing *The Waste Land* ("London Letters," which commented on the literary scene in London).[5] He himself had read Eliot's meditations on music hall and caricature; had noted Eliot's celebration of music-hall "wit" that was "mordant, ferocious, and personal," or his praise for the performer Ethel Levey, with her "fascinating inhuman *grotesquerie*" and "element of *bizarrerie*"; had observed Eliot's predilection for the extremism of the great caricaturists Rowlandson and Cruikshank, artists who possessed "some of the old English ferocity"; had witnessed Eliot's "sense of relief" at "hearing the indecencies of Elizabethan and Restoration drama"; had savored Eliot's vindication of Stravinsky's *Sacre du printemps,* a work that had transformed "the rhythms of the steppes into the scream of the motor horn, the rattle of machinery, the grind of wheels, the beating of iron and steel, the roar of the underground railway, and the other barbaric cries of modern life."[6] Moreover, the discontinuous yet coherent outline of an aesthetics of the histrionic which Eliot drew in these essays could hardly have reached a more receptive observer: Seldes had already written trenchant essays examining jazz and popular film, and one month after writing his review of Eliot he began his own landmark work, *The 7 Lively Arts,* a survey of vaudeville, popular song, the cartoon strip, slapstick film, and other forms of vernacular culture. But when he took up Eliot's critical writings, he disregarded all the Eliot essays that he himself had shepherded through the editorial process. Instead he turned directly to *The Sacred Wood* and promptly fastened on "Tradition and the Individual Talent."

Read in the light of that essay, *The Waste Land* might well seem a bit odd, a little unruly—only for a moment, though.

> It seems at first sight remarkably disconnected, confused, the
> emotion seems to disengage itself in spite of the objects and
> events chosen by the poet as their vehicle. . . . A closer view of
> the poem does more than illuminate the difficulties; it reveals
> the hidden form of the work, indicates how each thing falls
> into place, and to the reader's surprise shows that the emotion
> which at first seemed to come in spite of the framework and
> the detail could not otherwise have been communicated.[7]

By "framework," of course, Seldes meant the Grail legends as interpreted by Jessie Weston's *From Ritual to Romance,* the work which had informed "the plan" of Eliot's poem—or so its notes said. If only one scrutinized the poem long and diligently enough, "the hidden form" that bound together the dichotomy of text and notes would be disclosed. (Curiously,

Seldes himself did not further describe this "hidden form," which remained "hidden" to his readers.)

More directly than any other critic of the time, Conrad Aiken (1890–1972) addressed the dilemmas posed by the notes. Aiken, of course, had known Eliot since his student days at Harvard, knowledge which placed him in a unique position vis-à-vis other critics. For he also knew that passages of *The Waste Land* had existed as poems or independent drafts years before the poem's publication, and years before the publication of Jessie Weston's book. But he felt that it would be unfair somehow to reveal that knowledge, as he later recalled: "How could I mention that I had long been familiar with such passages as 'A woman drew her long black hair out tight,' which I had seen as poems, or part-poems, in themselves? And now saw inserted into *The Waste Land* as into a mosaic. This would be to make use of private knowledge, a betrayal."[8] Having ruled out a more historical reckoning with the poem, Aiken proceeded to a more formal one that stressed the disparity between the poem's wild variety and the claims to extreme coherence implied by the reference to "the plan" made in the notes.

> If we leave aside for the moment all other considerations and
> read the poem solely with the intention of understanding,
> with the aid of the notes, the symbolism; of making out what
> it is that is symbolized, and how these symbolized feelings are
> brought into relation with each other and with other matters
> in the poem; I think we must, with reservations, and with
> no invidiousness, conclude that the poem is not, in any formal
> sense, coherent.

With great prescience, Aiken foresaw the trajectory of critical discussion of the poem: "It is perhaps important to note that Mr. Eliot, with his comment on the 'plan,' and several critics, with their admiration of the poem's woven complexity, minister to the idea that *The Waste Land* is, precisely, a kind of epic in a walnut shell: elaborate, ordered, unfolded with a logic at every joint discernible; but it is also important to note that this idea is false." Aiken, instead, placed emphasis elsewhere: "Thus the poem has an emotional value far clearer and richer than its arbitrary and rather unworkable logical value. One might assume that it originally consisted of a number of separate poems which have been telescoped—given a kind of forced unity." His sense of the poem's factitiousness even included a rudimentary account of what he called "arbitrary repetitions": "We are aware of a superficial 'binding'—we observe the anticipation and repetition of themes, motifs; 'Fear death by water' anticipates the episode of Phlebas, the cry of the nightingale is repeated, but these are pretty flimsy links, and do not genuinely bind because they do not reappear naturally, but arbitrarily." True, critics of today would not accept the easy distinction drawn between "naturally" and "arbitrarily," and Aiken's account of repetition is one that vastly oversimplifies. But Aiken astutely perceived the strains and stresses in the poem, and he fretted over what kind of unity of tone or genre might encompass them: "Could one not wholly rely for one's unity,—as Mr. Eliot *has* largely relied—simply on the dim unity of 'personality' which would underlie the retailed contents of a single consciousness?"

Yet he had no doubt about the poem's success or significance: "the poem succeeds—as it brilliantly does—by virtue of its incoherence, not of its plan; by virtue of its ambiguities, not of its explanations." It was, he concluded, "one of the most moving and original poems of our time. It captures us."[9]

Taken together, Rascoe, Wilson, Seldes, and Aiken had outlined the spectrum of possible responses to a perceived disparity between their experience of the poem and the kind of experience that seemed to be suggested by its notes. At one extreme of the spectrum was Gilbert Seldes, who conceded that parts of the poem at first seemed "remarkably disconnected" and "confused," but who was convinced that these difficulties would evaporate with "a closer view" that disclosed a "hidden form" in which "each thing falls into place." At the other extreme was Conrad Aiken. For him, opacity wasn't an obstacle, but the condition that informed the poem's achievement ("the poem succeeds . . . by virtue of its incoherence"). In the middle of the spectrum were Rascoe and Wilson. For them the poem, whether judged against the expectations raised by the notes or those of competent readers, was "faulty structurally" (Rascoe) or exhibited "a lack of structural unity" (Wilson). And for both there was a tension between the poem's raw beauty, its "sheer verbal loveliness" (Rascoe) or "the very images and the sound of the words" (Wilson), and its obdurate opacity, its many "idiosyncrasies" (Rascoe) or unmotivated tangles: "We do not know why he has chosen them" (Wilson). For both these, too, the poem possessed a recognizable claim on public attention: it was "a readily understandable etching of modern life" (Rascoe), or it was "speaking not only for a personal distress, but for the starvation of a whole civilization" (Wilson).

Rascoe, Wilson, Seldes, and Aiken were not, of course, the only critics to review *The Waste Land* shortly after its publication; but their views and arguments laid out the fault lines that would reappear in subsequent debate. Tellingly, too, all four were American. Elevated by the Dial Award, Eliot's poem tacitly acquired a claim that it was a matter of public significance, a literary work of compelling importance. The debate that followed was a logical consequence of the institutional structures that had shaped its publication. And the contrast with the situation in England could not have been starker. Because the poem was first published there (without the notes) in the *Criterion,* a new journal struggling to find an audience, and then eleven months later was issued in the Hogarth Press edition that was limited to 460 copies, it received very little media attention: three reviews in the wake of the *Criterion* publication, a further six after the Hogarth edition—and all but one of the nine were hostile. In the United States, in contrast, there were more than fifty reviews and notices of the poem, more or less equally divided between negative and positive evaluations.[10]

When subsequent debate was taken up, it took place in the shadow of another event, at first glance one wholly unrelated to *The Waste Land:* T. S. Eliot's religious conversion. In 1928, only six years after he had published *The Waste Land,* Eliot issued *For Lancelot Andrewes,* a collection of eight recent essays preceded by a preface in which Eliot announced that he was now a "classicist in literature, a royalist in politics, and anglo-catholic in religion."[11] It was a deliberately provocative statement, and since then it has often been quoted as if it sufficed to characterize the whole of Eliot's work and life. It was an impression that Eliot himself did much to foster in subsequent years. In 1932 he published his *Selected Essays, 1917–1932,* a compilation of book reviews and essays that he had been writing. The first piece in the book was "Tradition and the Individual Talent," an essay from 1919 in which Eliot had urged that the personality of the individual artist be submerged or expunged in his work, submitting to the imperatives of a vague tradition. Perhaps innocently, Eliot even misdated the essay, assigning it to 1917 and so making it stand as the gateway to all his subsequent work, including *The Waste Land.*[12] Of the ten essays that Eliot wrote while composing *The Waste Land,* only three were included in the *Selected*

Essays—all pieces which reinforced the impression that Eliot had always been a "classicist in literature." Suppressed were the other seven essays from the same period, which only recently have been reprinted for the first time (after eighty-three years).[13] The suppressed essays, which reveled in the vernacular pleasures of British music hall and caricature, had sketched an aesthetics that could be called "classicist" only by a remarkable extension of the term. But that was all in the past. Similarly, the *Selected Essays* gave special prominence to a piece which Eliot had recently written on Baudelaire, one in which he damned the French poet for "having an imperfect, vague romantic conception of Good."[14] This theological estimate of the French poet jarred against the unstinting admiration which Eliot had shown for him in 1921. Eliot's conversion to Christianity, his growing allegiance to conservative political and social views, his concern with the aesthetic and ethical force of classicism—these constituted a profound change in his thought. But it was a change that was masked by the *Selected Essays*, which instead suggested that Eliot had always been a classicist, had always had moral concerns that had only deepened with his conversion, had always viewed modernity (and so secularism) with a skeptical eye.

In the new climate of taste, one that Eliot himself did much to usher in, there was no longer a tension between the text of *The Waste Land* and the claims to coherence implied by the notes' reference to "the plan." The problem that had preoccupied the poem's early reviewers vanished from sight. The most influential critic in erasing that tension was Cleanth Brooks (1907–1994), an American critic and a devout Christian from the conservative South. In 1937 he published "*The Waste Land:* A Critique of the Myth," an essay that profoundly shaped the course of criticism on the poem for the next forty years.[15] Brooks set out to show that the poem was "a unified whole" (136), that every detail in it contributed to a work of extraordinary structural, thematic, and poetic integrity. Characteristically, his starting point was the first of the poem's notes, the one which urged: "Not only the title, but the plan and a good deal of the incidental symbolism of the poem were suggested by Miss Jessie L. Weston's book . . ." No less characteristically, Brooks urged that the theme of the poem could best be reconstructed from Eliot's 1930 essay on Baudelaire, the one in which he had repudiated Baudelaire's "imperfect, vague romantic conception of Good." (That a term such as "Good" appears nowhere in Eliot's writings from the period when he was composing *The Waste Land* deterred Brooks

not a moment.) As for critics who had earlier described a poem more entangled and disquieting than the one delineated by Brooks, they were
merely victims of "the myth" that had quickly gathered around the poem.

Brooks had grown up in the American South at a time when it could
still be viewed, through a haze of ahistorical nostalgia, as the last outpost
of a preindustrial order, one rooted in the land and agriculture. His disdain
for industry, science, popular culture, and every other index of modernity
was summarized in a single word: secularization. And by a form of logic
which is all too human, it turned out that secularization was damned by
passage after passage in *The Waste Land.* When the poem cites a passage
from Dante's description of Limbo, in canto III of the *Inferno,* Brooks
notes that these "characters exemplify almost perfectly the secular attitude
which dominates the modern world" (143–144). He saw no anachronism
in this claim. Those depicted in Dante's canto IV are the unbaptized: "They
form the second of the two classes of people who inhabit the modern
waste land: those who are secularized and those who have no knowledge
of the faith" (144). When the poem seemingly touches on the violation of
a woman, Brooks comments drily: "The violation of a woman makes a
very good symbol of the process of secularization" (147). If one had to summarize the poem one might say: "Our contemporary waste land is in large
part the result of our scientific attitude—of our complete secularization"
(148). And in passing he observed that "secularization has destroyed, or
is likely to destroy, modern civilization" (163–164). The fishmen relaxing
in a pub near St. Magnus Martyr are significant because "they have a meaningful life which has been largely lost to the secularized upper and middle
classes" (170). *The Waste Land,* in short, was being beaten into shape,
forced to accord with a simplistic and schematic view of history that saw
the world before the industrial revolution as a coherent unity organized
around religious faith, the world after it as one long, unremitting, ever-
worsening horror. And Eliot himself, it must be conceded, was wont to
indulge in such thinking during the 1930s—for example, "What I do wish
to affirm is that the whole of modern literature is corrupted by what I call
Secularism."[16] But damning secularization, for Brooks, was not quite
enough. By the end of his essay he claimed: "The Christian material is at
the center [of the poem]," conceding only that "the poet never deals with
it directly" (171).

No less important, Brooks profoundly transformed the poem's nature.

Consider his comment on the verse paragraph that makes up the poem's famous opening, with its ferocious excess of lexical, syntactic, and thematic gestures toward pattern, its uneasy progress through evanescent zones of tonal cohesion, its mercurial swing from oracular solemnity to conversational banality, from insistent pattern to empty patter. Brooks, after announcing that the poem's theme was "death-in-life," turned to its famous beginning: "The first part of 'The Burial of the Dead' introduces this theme through a sort of reverie on the part of the protagonist—a reverie in which speculation on life glides off into memory of an actual conversation in the Hofgarten and back into speculation again. The function of the conversation is to establish the class and character of the protagonist" (139). That was one way to deal with troublesome details of tone and texture: to liquidate them in the name of theme, to quash them under the impress of a new entity who appears onstage here for the first time—"the protagonist." It was also the first step in transforming the poem into a narrative.

For Brooks "the protagonist" was a very busy figure, but one whose mental states were instantly accessible to the discerning critic. When a snatch of song abruptly appears in part I, it is "perhaps another item in the reverie of the protagonist" (141). But the song has an immediate effect: "It brings to the mind of the protagonist an experience of love" (141). Elsewhere we learn:

> But the protagonist, after this reflection . . . remembers a death
> that was transformed into something rich and strange, the
> death described in the song from *The Tempest*—"Those are
> pearls that were his eyes." . . . The description of a death which
> is a portal into a realm of the rich and strange . . . assumes
> in the mind of the protagonist an association with that of the
> drowned god whose effigy was thrown into the water as a
> symbol of the death of the fruitful powers of nature but which
> was taken out of the water as a symbol of the revivified god.
> (See *From Ritual to Romance*.) (149–150)

True, the source and identity of any particular voice in the poem might sometimes seem mysterious. "But to the reader who knows the Weston references, the reference is to that of the Fisher King of the Grail legends. The protagonist is the maimed and impotent king of the legends" (151). (And if the protagonist's "class and identity" were established in the poem's opening verse-paragraph, were they not undergoing a remarkable change at this point—a change so pronounced as to put the notion of "identity" in question, or even in crisis?)

But to be a narrative, it was necessary for the poem to mark progression. Yet no less an authority than the English critic F. R. Leavis, then at the height of his reputation, had already noted the poem's static character: "It exhibits no progression: 'I sat upon the shore / Fishing, with the arid plain behind me'—the thunder brings no rain to revive the Waste Land, and the poem ends where it began."[17] Brooks was determined to set that right:

> I cannot accept Mr. Leavis' interpretation of the passage, "I sat upon the shore / Fishing, with the arid plain behind me," as meaning that the poem "exhibits no progression." The comment upon what the thunder says would indicate, if other passages did not, that the poem does "not end where it began."
> It is true that the protagonist does not witness a revival of the waste land; but there are two important relationships involved in his case: a personal one as well as a general one. If secularization has destroyed, or is likely to destroy modern civilization, the protagonist still has a personal obligation to fulfill. Even if the civilization is breaking up—London Bridge is falling down falling down falling down—there remains the personal obligation: "Shall I at least set my lands in order?" (163–164)

It was a curious non sequitur, for demonstrating that "the protagonist" possessed a "personal obligation" was hardly tantamount to demonstrating narrative progression. Brooks returned to the charge, however, now bent on showing that "the protagonist" exhibited change and development, those features so indispensable to narrative, and he located these in an unlikely place, that final, antic swirl of quotations at the poem's end:

> London Bridge is falling down falling down falling down
> *Poi s'ascose nel foco che gli affina*
> *Quando fiam ceu chelidon*—O swallow swallow
> *Le Prince d'Aquitaine à la tour abolie*
> These fragments I have shored against my ruins
> Why then Ile fit you. Hieronymo's mad againe.

Datta. Dayadhvam. Damyata.
　　Shantih　　shantih　　shantih

Brooks seized on the fourth of these eight lines (*Le Prince d'Aquitaine à la tour abolie*), which is a quotation from a famous sonnet, "El Desdichado" (Spanish for "The Unhappy Man"), by the French poet Gérard de Nerval (1808–1855). In the French original, the immediately preceding line reads, "Je suis le ténébreux,—la veuf,—l'inconsolé," and together the two lines can be translated:

> I am the man of gloom,—the widower,—the unconsoled,
> The Prince of Aquitania, his tower in ruins.

Brooks commented: "The quotation from 'El Desdichado,' as Edmund Wilson has pointed out, indicates that the protagonist of the poem has been disinherited, robbed of his tradition. The ruined tower is perhaps also the Perilous Chapel, 'only the wind's home,' and it is also the whole tradition in decay. The protagonist resolves to claim his tradition and rehabilitate it." Brooks, by a species of logic which I have never been able to follow, could now specify not only the poem's "protagonist" but also his progress as discerned through a resolution that he reaches just before the poem's end. Yes, some aspects of the poem might seem enigmatic or disturbing; but beneath the surface there were traces of a narrative largely compatible with our everyday notions of realism. The poem gave "the effect of chaotic experience ordered into a new whole, though the realistic surface of experience is faithfully retained" (167).

　　Perhaps we can better understand this remark about "the realistic surface of experience" by situating it within a context much broader than that of *The Waste Land* or the critical tradition that first attended it, a context that stretches all the way back to Aristotle's *Poetics,* that seminal essay of literary theory which has exerted such a profound sway over Western cultural thought. Aristotle, we recall, was bent on refuting Plato's charge that poetry and fiction (one and the same in ancient Greece) were mendacious, and hence to be banned from a well ordered republic. Instead, he wished to assert that fiction or drama sparked a process of inference and deduction which was fundamentally the same as that of philosophy, and therefore that it issued in a form of knowledge that was different, but of equal status. The key term in prompting this process, whether in philosophy or imaginative writing, was "wonder." For wonder, he wrote in the *Metaphysics,* lay at the heart of all philosophy:

> It is through wonder that men now begin and originally
> began to philosophize; wondering in the first place at obvious
> perplexities, and then by gradual progression raising questions
> about the greater matters too, e.g., about the changes of the
> moon and of the sun, about the stars and about the origin
> of the universe. Now he who wonders and is perplexed feels
> that he is ignorant (thus the myth-lover [for "myth" here,
> read "fiction"] is in a sense a philosopher, since myths are
> composed of wonders).[18]

A similar process, he urges in the *Poetics* (chapter 9), is set in motion by the complex plot of a tragedy:

> Since tragic mimesis portrays not just a whole action, but
> events which are fearful and pitiful, this can best be achieved
> when things occur contrary to expectation yet still on account
> of one another. A sense of wonder will be more likely to be
> aroused in this way than as a result of the arbitrary or fortui-
> tous, since even chance events make the greatest impact of
> wonder when they appear to have a purpose.[19]

A tragic plot should include actions or events that surprise us ("things [that] occur contrary to expectation"), for that sense of surprise will prompt us to wonder how the events have come about; at the same time, however, those events must exhibit spatiotemporal and logical-causal interconnected-ness, for if they do not, then the process of reasoning that attempts to dis-cern such connectedness will be in vain. The opacity of the wonderful is indispensable to tragedy, but it must always be only momentary opacity that is ultimately redeemed by reason's discernment of sequential intelli-gibility. Oedipus cannot be blinded just because the gods are spiteful or capricious; it must be an outcome of his earlier actions.

Later in the *Poetics* (chapter 24), however, when comparing the different characteristics of tragedy and epic, Aristotle situates the wonderful (or "the marvelous": both words translate the same term in Aristotle's Greek) in a more ambiguous context:

While the marvellous is called for in tragedy, it is epic which
gives greater scope for the irrational (which is the chief cause
of the marvellous), because we do not actually see the agents
[onstage]. The circumstances of the pursuit of Hector would
be patently absurd if put on the stage, with the men standing
and refraining from pursuit, and Achilles forbidding them; but
in epic the effect is not noticed. The marvellous gives pleasure:
this can be seen from the way in which everyone exaggerates
in order to gratify when recounting events.

Yet only one paragraph later, when Aristotle once more takes up the topic
of plot structure, he indirectly returns to the question of the marvelous
via a comment on the irrational, a comment with startling implications:
"Events which are impossible but plausible should be preferred to those
which are possible but implausible. Plots should not consist of parts which
are irrational. So far as possible, there should be no irrational component."[20] This last comment plainly contradicts the preceding one. For if
every irrational (or unmotivated) component is to be excluded from a plot,
and if at the same time the irrational is "the chief cause of the marvellous,"
then it follows that Aristotle has also excluded the marvelous from all plot
construction—despite his having earlier deemed it indispensable to tragedy.
Stephen Halliwell, the distinguished contemporary commentator on the
Poetics, urges that for Aristotle wonder "lies on the boundary of the expli-
cable and the inexplicable, and so can slip into the latter (and hence become
the irrational), or, properly used, may stimulate and challenge understanding."[21] Still, it is hard to avoid the impression that the wonderful entails
more vexing conundrums: we want opacity, but we also fear it; we relish
transgression, but we also crave order. The wonderful marks the uneasy
borderline between these contradictory desires. Tellingly, the passage from
the *Iliad* that Aristotle dislikes is one of the most famous of antiquity. It
occurs in book 22, when Hector and Achilles at last come together for
what promises to be the climactic encounter which the work has been
building toward for all the previous books. What happens, bizarrely, is
nothing. Achilles chases Hector round and round before the walls of Troy,
while everyone else watches, frozen in place. The forward movement of
narrative is utterly suspended. It elicits a famous simile from Homer, the
only simile in ancient epic which invokes a dream:

> As in a dream a man is not able to follow one who runs
> from him, nor can the runner escape, nor the other pursue
>   him,
> So he [Achilles] could not turn him down in his speed, nor
>   the other get clear.[22]

One can only guess what Aristotle would have made of *The Waste Land*'s oneiric syntax and its grim refusal of narrative connectedness.

If Brooks profoundly misread the kind of work that *The Waste Land* was, he did so partly because an Aristotelian poetics of narrative has become so pervasive in our culture that we scarcely notice its presence. But that pervasiveness may also testify to some deeper human need. Tracts of time or sound, even textual time or sound, unpunctuated by the prospect of their being integrated into meaningful networks, are unbearable. Confronted with inexplicable patterns and mazes of contradiction, we seek a hidden shapeliness that will enable us to accommodate them. Fortuity is insufferable. As Steven Connor has recently observed in a comment that has obvious relevance to a reading of "What the Thunder Said":

> The power of a voice without a visible source is the power of
> a less-than-presence which is also a more-than-presence. The
> voice that is heard in the thunder, the eruption, or the whirl-
> wind, is a kind of compromise formation. In that it is ascribed
> to a god, or simply to God, the voice transcends human powers
> of understanding and control; but the very fact that it is so as-
> cribed also makes it possible to begin exercising control, in the
> very considerable form of conferring a name. To hear the thun-
> der as a voice is to experience awe and terror; but to hear the
> voice in the thunder is also to have begun to limit the powers
> of that voice.[23]

To hear the voice in the thunder, we might add, is to undertake a rudimentary form of spatiotemporal and logical-causal coordination of the sort that makes everyday experience comprehensible, if not bearable, and of the same sort that informs narrative. We are programmed to do this, it seems. Steven Connor ascribes our programming to various aspects of neonatal experience, Frank Kermode to our experience of learning to speak a language.[24] Whatever its source, it seems to be an indelible feature of the human mind. Brooks, though plainly a man who had a clear agenda, was also simply human.

Eliot himself, in his later years, evidently felt a need to revisit the two issues that had so decisively shaped discussion about *The Waste Land*—the status of the notes and the question of the poem's structure. In a lecture that he delivered in 1956 to an audience of 14,000 assembled in a basketball arena at the University of Minnesota, he pondered the various ways in which literary critics might be misled:

> Here I must admit that I am, on one conspicuous occasion, not guiltless of having led critics into temptation. The notes to *The Waste Land* I had at first intended to put down all the references for my quotations, with a view to spiking the guns of critics of my earlier poems who had accused me of plagiarism. Then, when it came to print *The Waste Land* as a little book—for the poem on its first appearance in *The Dial* and *The Criterion* had no notes whatever—it was discovered that the poem was inconveniently short, so I set to work to expand the notes, in order to provide a few more pages of printed matter, with the result that they became the remarkable exposition of bogus scholarship that is still on view to-day. I have sometimes thought of getting rid of these notes; but now they can never be unstuck. They have had almost greater popularity than the poem itself—anyone who bought my book of poems, and found that the notes to *The Waste Land* were not in it, would demand his money back. . . . No, it is not because of my bad example to other poets that I am penitent; it is because my notes stimulated the wrong kind of interest among the seekers of sources. It was just, no doubt, that I should pay my tribute to the work of Miss Jessie Weston; but I regret having sent so many enquirers off on a wild goose chase after Tarot cards and the Holy Grail.[25]

Eliot's occasional regret at having included the notes was balanced by his wan recognition that the deed was irreversible: the notes, as Stephen Dedalus might have put it, "were lodged in the room of the infinite possibilities they have ousted."

Three years later, in 1959, Eliot looked back at the much-debated question of the poem's structure. When one interviewer asked him whether Pound's excisions had changed "the intellectual structure of the poem," Eliot answered: "No. I think it was just as structureless, only in a more futile way, in the longer version." The implicit acknowledgment that the "shorter version," the published text of *The Waste Land* as we have it, was "structureless," was a long way from the claim that it was governed by a "plan." And tangled in the sidelong syntax of Eliot's response was another, more striking implication: a work might be structureless, but it could be so in ways that were "more futile" or "less futile." If we put pressure on "less futile," it might almost be thought to imply "useful" in some way, productive for literary thought and practice, provided only that a culture could find some use for it.

"In *The Waste Land*," Eliot went on in the same interview, "I wasn't even bothering whether I understood what I was saying." But that hardly mattered, he now thought. "These things, however, become easier to people with time. You get used to having *The Waste Land*, or *Ulysses*, about."[26] For a man who could be scathing about whiggish narratives of cultural progress, it was a surprisingly whiggish account of the human capacity to assimilate fortuity and disorder. The cognitive threshold for accommodating opacity, in this view, is as mutable and changeable as (let us say) our threshold for velocity (we chuckle condescendingly at the accounts of travelers who experienced vertigo when speeding along at ten miles per hour on early railroads). *The Waste Land* and *Ulysses* had indeed put unprecedented pressure on our expectations about the kinds and degrees of order that characterize a literary work; but it is a legitimate question whether we have really got "used to" the stringent indeterminacy that these works embodied. The human desire to detect pattern and reduce fortuity may be far more tenacious than Eliot imagined. Literary realism, after all, has survived the course of the twentieth century and even enjoyed a conspicuous revival in recent years. And as anybody knows who has ever taught either work to undergraduates, the struggle against easy expectations of narrative cohesion is not a battle that has been permanently won but one that is annually renewed.

For the most part, Eliot's remarks of 1956 and 1959 were politely ignored by his admirers, still laboring in the long shadow cast by Cleanth Brooks's major essay. But when Valerie Eliot published her edition of *The Waste Land* manuscripts in 1971, critical consensus began to dissolve. If nothing else, the manuscripts showed beyond doubt that *The Waste Land* had been potentially a very different poem right up to the last minute in early January 1922, when Ezra Pound had deleted some 240 lines. While there was still uncertainty about precisely when or in what sequence the various parts had been composed, it was clear that none had been produced in straightforward accordance with a "plan." The notes were beginning to recede in importance, but their recession would also prove extraordinarily slow and protracted.

At the same time, the dominance of the New Criticism, epitomized by Cleanth Brooks, was drawing to a close and already one could detect beginnings of the turn to structuralism that was to be signaled by the publication of Jonathan Culler's book *Structuralist Poetics* (1975).[27] The later 1970s and 1980s would see structuralism rapidly displaced by poststructuralism and deconstruction, then by several varieties of feminism and the rise of New Historicism, critical paradigms that stressed not the wholeness and unity of the text but its dividedness, the contradictory impulses at work beneath the surface of all language. But for the most part, criticism of *The Waste Land* has taken an increasingly biographical turn. In that respect, at least, criticism has retraced the trajectory first outlined by John Peale Bishop's two letters from November 1922, which moved from intoxicating and anxious uncertainty to a complacent preoccupation with glimpses of Eliot's private life. At the same time, the New Critical reading of the poem has never entirely vanished and continues to hold sway over the imagination of many critics. One sees its tenacious hold at work in the writing of one recent scholar who repeatedly notes "the poem's marmoreal reserve" and "monumental impregnability."[28] The notion of a neoclassical monument, so alien to the experience of the poem which its earliest readers described, still exerts a compelling power.

We cannot, of course, return to an imaginary state of pristine innocence in which the critical history of the last eighty years has been miraculously effaced. Generations of students encountered *The Waste Land* for the first time under aegis of the New Criticism, and many scholars who had that experience are to be found in English departments throughout the world, still active and still performing that invaluable task of transmitting the poem to new generations. But if the free play of attention that we ideally bring to the reading of any work is genuinely to retain its freedom, it will do so not by denying but by probing the intangible pressures exerted by a highly distinctive critical tradition, one repeatedly molded by historical contingencies as varied and intricate as those that also informed the poem's composition. Doing so, we can remain open to the pleasure of amazement and the sense of wonder that a reading of *The Waste Land* inevitably brings, attentive to the poem's vertiginous twists and turns of language, responsive to its richly varied ironic and climactic moments, receptive to its lacerating wildness and stubborn refusal to accommodate our expectations.

"IMMENSE. MAGNIFICENT. TERRIBLE." Yes, that will do as a starting point.

NOTES

1. WITH AUTOMATIC HAND

1. Valerie Eliot, ed., *The Waste Land: A Facsimile and Transcript of the Original Drafts Including the Annotations of Ezra Pound* (New York: Harcourt Brace, 1971), hereafter cited as *TWL:AF*.

2. Hugh Kenner, "The Urban Apocalypse," in A. Walton Litz, ed., *Eliot in His Time: Essays on the Occasion of the Fiftieth Anniversary of "The Waste Land"* (Princeton: Princeton University Press, 1973), 23–49, hereafter cited as "UA"; Grover Smith, "The Making of *The Waste Land*," *Mosaic* 6, no. 1 (1972): 127–141, hereafter cited as "MOTWL."

3. Lyndall Gordon, *Eliot's Early Years* (New York: Farrar, Straus, 1977), appendix II, "Dating *The Waste Land* Fragments," 143–146, hereafter cited as "DTWLF."

4. Peter Barry, "The *Waste Land* Manuscript: Picking Up the Pieces—In Order," *Forum for Modern Language Studies* 15 (1979): 237–248. See also David Moody, "Appendix B: The Drafts of 'The Waste Land,'" in *Thomas Stearns Eliot: Poet* (Cambridge: Cambridge University Press, 1979), 310–318; Moody assumed that the poem was written straightforwardly in the sequence that we know from the published version, and he set aside the question of the various typewriters that had sparked debate about the priority of parts I and II or part III, while offering a judicious synthetic account for dating some of the ancillary poems and fragments.

5. Ronald Bush, *T. S. Eliot: A Study in Character and Style* (Oxford: Oxford University Press, 1984), chapter 5, "'Unknown Terror and Mystery': *The Waste Land*," 53–78.

6. Christine Froula, "Corpse, Monument, *Hypocrite Lecteur:* Text and Transference in the Reception of *The Waste Land*," *Text: An Interdisciplinary Journal of Textual Studies* 6 (1996): 297–314, here 313.

7. "I am not anxious to produce another [book of criticism] for a year or two; and meanwhile have a long poem in mind and partly on paper which I am wishful to finish." T. S. Eliot to John Quinn, 9 May 1921, in Valerie Eliot, ed., *The Letters of T. S. Eliot*, vol. 1, *1898–1922* (New York: Harcourt Brace, 1988), 451; hereafter cited as *LOTSE*.

8. Smith furnished no reference for this claim allegedly made by Pound, and I can find no evidence that Pound said anything of the sort.

9. This was but one of several overlapping chronologies Smith offered for part III's composition. He suggested at one point that the "long poem . . . partly on paper" to which Eliot referred in his letter of 9 May to John Quinn, "probably . . . included . . . Part III or the outlines of Part IV" ("MOTWL," 133). But later he observed: "Part III, or some prototype of it, existed by the time Eliot and Vivienne went to Margate about the middle of October" ("MOTWL," 133).

10. See the headnote of Table 1 for the numbering system used here. The sixteen letters for which no original is extant are:

DATE	RECIPIENT	*LOTSE* PP.	NO.
23 August 1914	Mother	51–54	T.13
December 1917	Editor of the *Egoist*	211–212	T.119
March 1918	Editor of the *Egoist*	225	T.130
4 Sept. 1918	Robert Ross	243	T.148
1 June 1919	Lytton Strachey	298–299	T.200
3 Oct. 1919	John Rodker	338	T.231
[24 Oct. 1919]	Editor of the *Athenaeum*	341–342	T.235
[7 Nov. 1919]	Editor of the *Athenaeum*	344	T.238
[7 Feb. 1920]	Editor of the *Athenaeum*	369–370	T.264
[22 Apr. 1920]	Editor of the *TLS*	380–381	T.275
[25 June 1920]	Editor of the *Athenaeum*	387	T.282
[6 Aug. 1920]	Editor of the *Athenaeum*	396	T.292
[28 Oct. 1920]	Editor of the *TLS*	415–417	T.312
[3 Nov. 1920]	Editor of the *TLS*	483	T.377
[24 Nov. 1920]	Editor of the *TLS*	489	T.384
[30 Nov. 1922]	Editor of the *Liverpool Daily Post*	602–603	T.495

The six letters for which the originals have been lost since they were located by Mrs. Eliot are:

DATE	RECIPIENT	*LOTSE* PP.	NO.	INSTITUTION
5 Aug. [1915]	Conrad Aiken	11	T.45	Huntington
15 Aug. [1915]	J. H. Woods	112–113	T.47	Harvard Archive
[25? Aug. 1919]	Lytton Strachey	327	T.220	British Library
[24 Aug. 1920]	Mother	403–404	T.299	Houghton Libr.
15 Aug. 1922	Sydney Schiff	561	T.454	British Library
17 Aug. 1922	Paul Valéry	562	T.456	Bib. Nat. Paris

The thirteen letters for which the originals are in private collections that could not be consulted:

DATE	RECIPIENT	*LOTSE* PP.	NO.	OWNER
4 Aug. 1917	Robert Nichols	190	T.101	Mrs. Charlton
10 Nov. 1918	Hugh Walpole	253–254	T.156	Valerie Eliot
[20 Oct. 1919]	Sydney Schiff	340–341	T.234	Valerie Eliot
5 Nov. 1920	Walter de la Mare	420–421	T.314	De la Mare Estate
8 Nov. 1920	Walter de la Mare	421	T.315	De la Mare Estate
2 Jan. 1921	Maxwell Bodenheim	431–432	T.323	E. Goldsmith Estate
14 Dec. 1921	André Gide	494	T.388	Mme. C. Gide
24 Jan. 1921	André Gide	502	T.392	Mme. C. Gide
[21 Feb. 1922]	J. M. Murry	506	T.396	Valerie Eliot
2 Aug. 1922	Sydney Schiff	555	T.446	Valerie Eliot
9 Aug. 1922	Sydney Schiff	557	T.449	Valerie Eliot
7 Nov. 1922	Ezra Pound	592	T.483	Valerie Eliot
1 Dec. 1922	Gilbert Seldes	604	T.497	Valerie Eliot

The two letters for which I could not obtain permission, both at the Houghton Library, to see the originals are:

DATE	RECIPIENT	*LOTSE* PP.	NO.
8 Dec. 1922	Henry Eliot	608–610	T.500
31 Dec. 1922	Henry Eliot	616–618	T.509

11. The myth that the name Madame Sosostris was derived from "Sesostris, the Sorceress of Ecbatana" in Huxley's *Crome Yellow* was first promulgated by Grover Smith, "The Fortuneteller in Eliot's *Waste Land*," *American Literature* 25 (1954): 490–492. In support of his claim Smith cited a letter he had received from Eliot, dated 10 March 1952, in which Eliot had said it was "almost certain" that he had borrowed the name from *Crome Yellow*. "Almost

certain" are the only words of the letter which were directly quoted by Smith. He then paraphrased the rest of the letter: Eliot "has also said that, being unconscious of the borrowing, he was unaware of any connection between the name of the clairvoyant and that assumed by Mr. Scogan," the character in *Crome Yellow* who pretends to be a fortune-teller. Eliot had better reason than he knew for being "unaware of any connection" between the two characters. As we shall see below, Eliot had probably completed the scene with Madame Sosostris by early February, if we accept the evidence of a letter by Wyndham Lewis; and at the very latest he completed the typescript of parts I and II sometime in mid-May, 1921. Aldous Huxley, then living in Italy, did not even start to write his novel until the beginning of June that same year, "pledging himself to finish it within two months," according to his biographer. It took just a bit longer, and he finished it in the second week of August, the same biographer says (see Sybille Bedford, *Aldous Huxley: A Biography,* vol. 1, *1894–1939* [London: Chatto and Windus, 1973], 117, 119). Eliot and Huxley did not correspond during this period, as the two men were not close; Eliot, writing late in January 1921, had damned Huxley's recent long poem "Leda" as "a concession to the creamy top of the General Reading Public" (see T. S. Eliot, "London Letter, March 1921," in Lawrence Rainey, ed., *The Annotated "Waste Land" with Eliot's Contemporary Prose* [New Haven: Yale University Press, 2005], 139.) Smith went on to diffuse the claim in his subsequent monographs on Eliot: *T. S. Eliot's Poetry and Plays: A Study in Sources and Influence* (Chicago: University of Chicago Press, 1956), 76, a work that went through numerous impressions and a second edition in 1974; and *The Waste Land* (London: George Allen and Unwin, 1983), 47, 67–68. Through these it has become a standard note in all commentaries on the poem. See, for example: B. C. Southam, *A Guide to the Selected Poems of T. S. Eliot* (New York: Harcourt, 1968), 74–75, note to line 43; and Michael North, ed., *The Waste Land: A Norton Critical Edition* (New York: Norton, 2001), 6 n. 4, which also reprints the entire passage from *Crome Yellow,* 40–42. It is fairly likely that Huxley, in adopting the name Sesostris, was drawing on a name common to three rulers of ancient Egypt during the Middle Kingdom, who were named Senusret, or in a variant rendering, Sesostris: Senusret or Sesostris I, II, and III ruled for various spells between 1971 and 1841 B.C. Whether Eliot also had these names in mind is a matter of speculation.

12. Wyndham Lewis, "Early London Environment," in Tambimuttu and Richard March, eds., *T. S. Eliot: A Symposium* (London: Frank and Cass, 1965; 1st ed., 1948), 24–32, here 30.

13. "Mr. Apollinax" is assigned to 1916 by Christopher Ricks in his edition of T. S. Eliot, *Inventions of the March Hare* (New York: Harcourt Brace, 1996), xli, evidently on the basis of its first publication in *Poetry* 8, no. 6 (September 1916): 294. For the text of both the autograph draft and the fair-copy versions of the poem see ibid., 344, 345. Gordon urges that both "The Death of St. Narcissus" and "Mr. Apollinax" were "written by January 1915 for, on 2 February, Eliot alluded to them in a letter to Pound ('I understand that

Priapism, Narcissism etc. are not approved of . . .')" ("DTWLF," 143). But Gordon misunderstands Eliot's comment. He is referring to the infamous King Bolo poems that Wyndham Lewis chose not to publish in *Blast* 2, not to "The Death of St. Narcissus" and "Mr. Apollinax."

14. Gordon, "DTWLF," 43, claims that the paper "matches that of an unpublished 1916 review of H.D.'s translation of choruses from *Iphigenia in Aulis*." I have been unable to locate this unpublished review of H.D., *Choruses from Iphigeneia in Aulis* (London: Egoist, 1916), no. 3 in the Poets' Translation series.

15. On 9 April Lewis held a private viewing of his exhibition "Tyros and Portraits" at the Leicester Galleries, where he distributed the first copies of the journal to visitors; see Paul O'Keefe, *Some Sort of Genius: A Life of Wyndham Lewis* (London: Jonathan Cape, 2000), 229–230.

16. The British Bond [A] paper was used for only a single extant letter, from Eliot to Wyndham Lewis, dated November[?] 1915, T.55, in *LOTSE*, 122. Between the British Bond [B] and the British Bond [C] there is also a small distinction in color: the British Bond [B] used for "Song" is yellow white (Centroid 92; see the headnote to Table 1 for notes on these terms for standardized color descriptions), while British Bond [C], used in other *Waste Land* manuscripts described below, is white. Lyndall Gordon confuses the two papers because, although she notes their distinct colors, she fails to note that [B] has chainlines while [C] does not: "Eliot used . . . British Bond paper for the *Waste Land* copy. Parts I and II of *The Waste Land* use the same typewriter and paper [as 'Song'], though the paper of 'Song' is slightly yellower, perhaps a different batch" ("DTWLF," 144).

17. The sixteen letters written on British Bond [B] are:

DATE	RECIPIENT	*LOTSE* PP.	NO.
13 Sept. 1920	Henry Eliot	406	T.303
20 Sept. 1920	Mother	408	T.304
17 Oct. 1920	Scofield Thayer	413	T.310
23 Oct. 1920	Leonard Woolf	415	T.311
31 Oct. 1920	Mother	417	T.313
2 Dec. 1920	Mother	423	T.317
8 Dec. 1920	Edgar Jepson		U.75
10 Dec. 1920	R. C. Trevelyan	426	T.319
[22 Dec. 1920]	Ezra Pound	426	T.320
26 Dec. 1920	Leonard Woolf	427	T.321
1 Jan. 1921	Scofield Thayer	428	T.322
16 Jan. 1921	Mother	432	T.324
18 Jan. 1921	Leonard Woolf		U.77
22 Jan. 1921	Mother	432	T.325
30 Jan. 1921	Scofield Thayer	434	T.326
30 Jan. 1921	Scofield Thayer	435	T.327

18. That Eliot did not begin working on *The Waste Land* sometime during 1920 is abundantly evident from his own comments in various letters written throughout that year. True, already on 5 November 1919 he had made a statement widely interpreted as his earliest reference to *The Waste Land* when, writing to the New York lawyer and cultural patron John Quinn, he enumerated his current projects: "I am at work now on an article ordered by the *Times*, and when that is off I hope to get started on a poem that I have in mind" (*LOTSE*, 344). But throughout 1920 Eliot was prevented from working on the "poem that I have in mind" by a combination of events. First, writing *The Sacred Wood* proved far more difficult than he had anticipated: Eliot had originally hoped to complete it by the end of May, but the final manuscript was not posted to the publisher until 9 August 1920, more than two months late. Second, there was the flat at Crawford Mansions, which he and Vivien had "come to loathe on account of the noise and sordidness." In June he began searching for another one, horrified to learn that many were priced at "two to four times what we pay now" (*LOTSE*, 390). Only at the end of October did Eliot finally agree on rental terms for a new flat at 9, Clarence Gate Gardens, and only at the end of November did he move in. But there was a third event which further consumed his time, an enormous stomach abscess which nearly killed Vivien's father, requiring an emergency operation and weeks of painful recovery attended by Vivien. Finally, throughout 1920 Eliot complained of poor health and exhaustion—sometimes his own, sometimes Vivien's, often that of both. Eliot's regrets over not working on his projected poem recur throughout the year. To a novelist who was finding it difficult to concentrate he wrote in January 1920: "I have been trying to start work myself, and it is very difficult when *both* people in a household are run down" (*LOTSE*, 355). To his brother he wrote in September: "I have not done any writing for months, and now we are both sleeping very badly. . . . I feel maddened now because I want to get settled quietly and write some poetry" (*LOTSE*, 407). A week later he wrote to his mother: "I do not suppose that I shall be properly settled at work again till November; I have several things I want to do; and I want a period of tranquility to do a poem that I have in mind" (*LOTSE*, 408). "Am I writing much?" he asked himself in another letter, echoing his correspondent's question. "Only signing my name to leases and agreements" (*LOTSE*, 409). In October he advised his mother regretfully: "I have of course been unable to write, or even read and think, for some weeks" (*LOTSE*, 412). "You see," he explained to one correspondent, "we began looking for a flat in June, and since then I have simply not had the time to do a single piece of work. . . . But I want to get to work on a poem I have in mind" (*LOTSE*, 419). By December even the success of *The Sacred Wood* was beginning to irritate him: "I am rather tired of the book now, as I am so anxious to get on to new work, and I should more enjoy being praised if I were engaged on something which I thought better or more important. I think I shall be able to do so soon" (*LOTSE*, 424).

19. That Eliot sent off the manuscript of his "London Letter, May 1921" by

around 1 May can be inferred from his comment, made on 21 May, to Scofield Thayer, editor of the *Dial*, who was then in Berlin: "I am glad to hear that my letter was received in time." Given how long it would take for Eliot to send his essay to the *Dial*'s office in New York (nine days), for the office then to notify Thayer in Berlin (another nine days), and for Thayer to acknowledge receipt to Eliot, the essay must have been posted by early May.

20. Ezra Pound to Agnes Bedford, 20 April 1921, Indiana University, Lilly Library, Pound Mss. II.

21. Ezra Pound to Isabel Pound, 24 April [1921], Yale University, Beinecke Library, YCAL ms. 43.

22. That the manuscript reached Eliot after 9 May can be inferred from Eliot's comment to John Quinn in his letter of 9 May: "I have had no news whatever from Pound, beyond two postcards with no address, since he left this country" (*LOTSE*, 451).

23. Wyndham Lewis to Sydney Schiff, 7 February 1921, British Library, ms. add. 52919. The existence of this letter was first noted by Peter Ackroyd, *T. S. Eliot: A Life* (New York: Simon and Schuster, 1984), 110, 345 n. 6.

24. Unpublished letter (U.82) from T. S. Eliot to Mary Hutchinson [15 June 1921; postmark 16 June 1921], University of Texas, Harry Ransom Humanities Research Center.

25. T. S. Eliot, "The Metaphysical Poets," *Times Literary Supplement*, no. 1031 (20 October 1921): 669–670. Rpt. in Rainey, *Annotated "Waste Land,"* 192–201.

26. Unpublished letter from Ezra Pound to Dorothy Pound, 14 [October 1921], Indiana University, Lilly Library, Pound Mss. III.

27. Valerie Eliot assigns Eliot's departure from Paris to "22? November" (*LOTSE*, xxxvi). But a difficulty for this date is posed by Eliot's letter to the editor of the *Times Literary Supplement*, which was datelined Lausanne and published on 24 November. Surely it had to have been set in type by at least 23 November, and surely it must have been posted at least one day earlier, on 22 November. It seems to ask too much to suppose that Eliot could have taken the train from Paris to Lausanne, arrived, and then written and posted a letter the same afternoon. It seems more likely that he left Paris on 21 November, perhaps even 20 November. Pound, in a letter to Scofield Thayer, indicated that Eliot was simply "on his way through Paris," not staying for a more extended period.

28. Unpublished letters from Ezra Pound to his father, Homer Pound, 3 December [1921] and 25[–26] December 1921, Beinecke Library, YCAL ms. 43.

29. Unpublished letter from Ezra Pound to Scofield Thayer, 5 December 1921, Beinecke Library, *Dial* Papers.

30. Hieratica Bond [A] was used for Eliot's letters of [14 October 1914] to William Greene (T.19, *LOTSE*, 65) and 21 November [1914] to Conrad Aiken (T.23, *LOTSE*, 69).

31. Hieratica Bond [B] was used for a letter from Eliot to Wyndham Lewis, 5 August 1918 (T.143, *LOTSE*, 240).

32. Hieratica Bond [C] was used for two letters, one dated 6 August 1919 to Harold Monro (T.218, *LOTSE*, 325), the other dated 3 September 1919 to Eliot's mother (T.222, *LOTSE*, 328).

33. This dating differs sharply from that of Lyndall Gordon, "DTWLF," 144, who urges: "It is impossible, so far, to date the Hieratica cluster exactly, but 1918 seems a reasonable guess." The guess is just that, a guess, and it is by no means a reasonable one. Her arguments are followed by Ronald Bush, *T. S. Eliot: A Study in Character and Style* (Oxford: Oxford University Press, 1984), 53–78, in particular 56–57 and 248, nn. 14–15, who then uses this early dating of the passage of "London, the swarming life" to make an argument about Eliot having programmatic intentions which later "fell away" (57).

34. The letter to Pound is misdated by Valerie Eliot, who assigns it to [24? January 1922]. The mistake results from her error in dating an earlier letter by Pound, one which he had dated "24 Saturnus" according to an arcane calendar ("The Little Review Calendar") that he published in the *Little Review* 7, no. 2 (Spring 1922): 2. The month "Saturnus" was to correspond with January. Mrs. Eliot, in her edition of *LOTSE*, mistakenly assigned the letter to December, following D. D. Paige, the editor of Ezra Pound, *Selected Letters, 1907–1941* (New York: New Directions, 1971), 169. Paige's error was first noticed back in 1972 by Hugh Kenner, "UA," 44 n. 7, but it evidently had not come to Mrs. Eliot's attention before she published her edition of the letters in 1988.

35. On these discussions over publishing the poem see Chapter 2.

36. Ibid.

37. On the various publication dates see Chapter 2, n. 3.

38. Much of the discussion has focused on Eliot and Wagner. See Sarah Wintle, "Wagner and *The Waste Land*—Again," *English: The Journal of the English Association* 38, no. 162 (Autumn 1989): 227–250; Philip Waldron, "The Music of Poetry: Wagner in *The Waste Land*," *Journal of Modern Literature* 18, no. 4 (Fall 1993): 421–434; and Margaret Dana, "Orchestrating *The Waste Land*: Wagner, Leitmotiv, and the Play of Passion," in John Xiros Cooper, ed., *T. S. Eliot's Orchestra: Critical Essays on Poetry and Music* (New York: Garland, 2000), 267–294.

39. My transcription departs from Valerie Eliot's at line 5. She seems to think that the word "there" replaces "where"; but exactly the opposite is true, as a glance at the facsimile reproduction of the manuscript (*TWL:AF*, 36) suffices to indicate. My reading is also confirmed by the published text of the poem, which in all versions has always given "where" as a final reading.

40. Indeed, the form which these lines will assume in the published poem only accentuates both their relatedness and their difference:
    But at my back in a cold blast I hear (line 185)
    But at my back from time to time I hear (line 196)
    O City City, I can sometimes hear (line 259)

41. Readers will recognize that I am drawing here on Michael Levenson's excellent discussion of the opening passage in his *A Genealogy of Modernism* (Cambridge: Cambridge University Press, 1984), 165–173.

42. Calvin Bedient, *He Do the Police in Different Voices: "The Waste Land" and Its Protagonist* (Chicago: University of Chicago Press, 1986), 56.

43. Michael Levenson, "Does *The Waste Land* Have a Politics?" *Modernism/ Modernity* 6, no. 3 (September 1999): 1–13, here 1.

44. The ten essays which Eliot published while writing *The Waste Land* are conveniently collected in Lawrence Rainey, ed., *The Annotated "Waste Land" with Eliot's Contemporary Prose* (New Haven: Yale University Press, 2005). The first note to each essay provides the rationale used to assign it a date of composition, and those dates of composition (as opposed to publication) are followed in the discussion below.

45. T. S. Eliot, "Andrew Marvell," *Times Literary Supplement* 1002 (31 March 1921): 201–202. Rpt. in Rainey, *Annotated "Waste Land,"* 149, 150.

46. T. S. Eliot, "John Dryden," *Times Literary Supplement* 1012 (9 June 1921): 361–362. Rpt. in Rainey, *Annotated "Waste Land,"* 174, 175.

47. T. S. Eliot, London Letter, July 1921, *Dial* 71, no. 2 (August 1921): 213–217. Rpt. in Rainey, *Annotated "Waste Land,"* 186.

48. T. S. Eliot, London Letter, May 1921, *Dial* 70, no. 6 (June 1921): 448–453. Rpt. in Rainey, *Annotated "Waste Land,"* 168.

49. Ibid. Rpt. in Rainey, *Annotated "Waste Land,"* 169.

50. T. S. Eliot, "The Metaphysical Poets," *Times Literary Supplement* 1031 (20 October 1921): 669–670. Rpt. in Rainey, *Annotated "Waste Land,"* 194.

51. Eliot, "John Dryden." Rpt. in Rainey, *Annotated "Waste Land,"* 180.

52. Eliot, London Letter, May 1921. Rpt. in Rainey, *Annotated "Waste Land,"* 169.

53. Carol Christ, "Gender, Voice, and Figuration in Eliot's Early Poetry," in Ronald Bush, ed., *T. S. Eliot: The Modernist in History* (Cambridge: Cambridge University Press, 1991), 33; Martin Scofield, *T. S. Eliot: The Poems* (Cambridge: Cambridge University Press, 1988), 118.

54. See Clara del Rio, *Confessions of a Type-Writer* (Chicago: Del Rio Publishing, 1893), and Elinor Dawson, *Confessions of a Typewriter; or, Merciful Unto Me, a Sinner* (Chicago: Charles Thompson, 1903). The Library of Congress catalogues the latter under the title *Merciful Unto Me, a Sinner* and dates it to 1905; but the copy of the novel I own, a 1912 reprint, has the title as I've given it here and dates the copyright to 1903. See also Elizabeth Baker, *Miss Robinson: A Play in Three Acts* (London: Sidgwick and Jackson, 1920), 58.

55. Examples include T. W. H. [Thomas William Hodgson] Crosland (1865–1924), "To the American Invader," in his *Outlook Odes* (London: At the Unicorn, 1902), 30–32; Enoch Miner [pseud.: Topsy Typist], *Our Phonographic Poets: Written by Stenographers and Typists upon Subjects Pertaining to Their Arts. Compiled by "Topsy Typist"* (New York: Popular Publishing, 1904); Samuel Ellsworth Kiser, *Love Sonnets of an Office Boy* (Chicago: Forbes, 1907), twenty-eight sonnets addressed to the office typewriter girl; Andrew Lang,

"Matrimony," in *The Poetical Works of Andrew Lang*, ed. Leonora Blanche Lang (London: Longmans, 1923), 3: 179–180. A serious and hence rare poem about a typist is "Interlude: Eurydice," by Arthur Henry Adams, in his *London Streets* (London: T. N. Foulis, 1906), 34–36.

56. See Christopher Keep, "The Cultural Work of the Type-Writer Girl," *Victorian Studies* 40 (1997): 401–426; Morag Shiach, "Modernity, Labour, and the Typewriter," in Hugh Stevens and Caroline Howlett, eds., *Modernist Sexualities* (Manchester: Manchester University Press, 2000), 114–129; and Pamela Thurschwell, "Supple Minds and Automatic Hands: Secretarial Agency in Early-Twentieth-Century Literature," *Forum for Modern Language Studies* 37 (2001): 155–168.

57. The discussion which follows draws on J. R. Winton, *Lloyds Bank, 1918–1969* (Oxford: Oxford University Press, 1982), 1–43.

58. JoAnne Yates, *Control Through Communication: The Rise of System in American Management* (Baltimore: Johns Hopkins University Press, 1989), 37.

59. On the changes detailed here and below see Elyce J. Rotella, "The Transformation of the American Office: Changes in Employment and Technology," *Journal of Economic History* 41 (1981): 51–57; Thomas Whalen, "Office Technology and Socio-Economic Change, 1870–1955," *IEEE* [Institute of Electrical and Electronic Engineers] *Technology and Society Magazine* 2, no. 2 (June 1983): 12–18; and Yates, "Communication Technology and the Growth of Internal Communication," in *Control Through Communication*, 21–64.

60. Peter D. McDonald, *British Literary Culture and Publishing Practice, 1880–1914* (Cambridge: Cambridge University Press, 1997), 96.

61. "Frances," "Five O'Clock Tea Talk: A Woman's Restaurant," *T.P.'s Weekly*, 11 December 1903, 918. All subsequent citations are from this page. My thanks to Tom Holland for drawing my attention to this essay.

62. The Prudential Assurance headquarters, Holborn Bars, was constructed between 1899 and 1906, designed by Alfred Waterhouse (1830–1905). The neo-Gothic edifice was one of fifteen office buildings which Waterhouse designed for Prudential. See Alastair Service, *London 1900* (New York: Rizzoli, 1979), 97–98.

63. Ivy Low, *The Questing Beast* (London: Martin Secker, 1914), hereafter cited within the text as *TQB*. In 1916 Ivy Low married Maxim Litvinov and changed her name; she moved with him to the new Soviet Union after 1917, where ultimately he became foreign minister under Stalin. After his death she returned to England. *The Questing Beast* was her second novel. Her first, *Growing Pains* (London: William Heinemann), was published in 1913; while her next, *His Master's Voice* (London: William Heinemann), appeared in 1930. Low/Litvinov also translated many works from Russian literature. See John Carswell, *Exile: The Life of Ivy Litvinov* (London: Faber, 1983).

64. Anonymous, "Suffragette Secretaries: A Report on Office Life 60 Years Ago," *Survey of Secretarial and Clerical Salaries: Alfred Marks Bureau, Statistical Services Division* (October 1979): 19–29.

65. Sophie Cole, *Money Isn't Everything* (London: Mills and Boon, 1923), 24–25.

66. Tom Gallon, *The Girl Behind the Keys* (London: Hutchinson, 1903), 5.

67. David Graham Phillips, *The Grain of Dust* (New York: D. Appleton, 1911), 300.

68. Ibid., 326.

69. T. S. Eliot, "London Letter, March 1921," *Dial* 70, no. 4 (April 1921): 448–453, here 450. Rpt. in Rainey, *Annotated "Waste Land,"* 135–140, here 137.

70. For Low's rapport with Mansfield and Murry, see Carswell, *Exile*, 74, 96–97, 165. Eliot's publications in the *Athenaeum* are catalogued by Donald Gallup, *T. S. Eliot: A Bibliography*, rev. ed. (New York: Harcourt Brace, 1963), 203–207.

71. The following discussion on novels about typists, secretaries, and stenographers in fiction is based on a book-length study of the typist in modern culture from 1890 to the present, a study that I currently am at work on.

72. See, for example, Grace Miller White, *Edna, the Pretty Typewriter* (New York: J. S. Ogilvie, 1907), and Eliza Margaret J. Humphreys (pseud. Rita), *Betty Brent, Typist* (London: T. Werner Laurie, 1908).

73. See, for example, Sophie Cole, *A Plain Woman's Portrait* (London: Mills and Boon, 1912); Ruby M. Ayre, *The Winds of the World* (London: Hodder and Stoughton, 1918); Elinor Glynn, *Man and Maid* (London: Duckworth, 1922); Sophie Cole, *Money Isn't Everything* (London: Mills and Boon, 1923); and the novel cited below, n. 77.

74. Warren Titus, *Winston Churchill* (New York: Twayne, 1963), 7.

75. The four novels which portray a heroine having consensual sex before marriage are Low, *The Questing Beast*; Winston Churchill, *The Dwelling-Place of Light* (New York: Macmillan, 1917); Arnold Bennett, *Lilian* (London: Cassell, 1922); and Rebecca West, *The Judge* (London: Hutchinson, 1922; rpt. London: Virago, 1980). The other two realistic novels about a typist or stenographer are by Phillips, *The Grain of Dust*, and Sinclair Lewis, *The Job: An American Novel* (New York: Harper, 1917; rpt. Lincoln: University of Nebraska Press, 1994).

76. Carswell, *Exile*, 72. The offending passage was the seduction of Rachel by Giles Goodey, quoted further below.

77. The identification of the typist and Tiresias is noted by Christ, "Gender, Voice, and Figuration," 33; that of machine, typist, and Tiresias by Michael North, *The Political Aesthetic of Yeats, Eliot, and Pound* (Cambridge: Cambridge University Press, 1991), 99.

78. Charlton Lewis and Charles Short, *A Latin Dictionary* (Oxford: Oxford University Press, 1980), s.v. *vanus*.

79. Propertius compares his relation to Cynthia to military service at 1.6.40 and 4.1.135–138. Ovid extends the conceit with comic hyperbole in *Amores* 1.9. For the view that this conceit has no history but is a timeless propensity of the human mind, see George Laskoff and Mark Johnson, *Metaphors We Live By* (Chicago: University of Chicago Press, 1980), 49.

80. Elenore Meherin, *"Chickie": A Hidden, Tragic Chapter from the Life of a Girl of This Strange "Today"* (New York: Grosset and Dunlap, 1925), 272–273.

81. See Jonathan Barnes, ed., *The Complete Works of Aristotle* (Princeton: Princeton University Press, 1984), vol. 1, *Parts of Animals*, 1071–1072; for Heidegger see the terms "presence-at-hand" and "ready-to-hand," which recur throughout his *Being and Time*, trans. John Macquarrie and Edward Robinson (New York: Harper and Row, 1961). For a view of the hand in English and American literature, see Katherine Rowe, *Dead Hands: Fictions of Agency, Renaissance to Modern* (Stanford: Stanford University Press, 1999).

82. See Martin Kirigin, *La mano divina nell'iconografia cristiana* (Vatican City: Istituto pontefice di archeologia cristiana, 1976); for a discussion of the hand in Byzantine churches and its development from Jewish tradition, see André Grabar, *L'Art de la din de l'antiquité et du moyen age*, vol. 2 (Paris: Collège de France, 1968), 791–794.

83. T. S. Eliot, "'The Duchess of Malfi' at the Lyric; and Poetic Drama," *Art and Letters* 3, no. 1 (Winter [1919/]1920): 36–39, here 37.

2. THE PRICE OF MODERNISM

1. The quotations are from Joyce's *Ulysses*, Eliot's "Gerontion," and Pound's *Guide to Kulchur*.

2. Richard Ellmann and Charles Feidelson, Jr., eds., *The Modern Tradition: Backgrounds of Modern Literature* (New York: Oxford University Press, 1965), vi.

3. For the English publication, see T. S. Eliot to Henry Ware Eliot, 11 October 1922: "The Criterion is due to appear next Monday [16 October]," in *LOTSE*, 580. See also Eliot to Richard Cobden-Sanderson, 16 October 1922, in *LOTSE*, 582. The exact date of the American publication in the *Dial* is less clear. "We are to publish the text of the poem, without the notes, in the November Dial, which will be published about October 20th" (carbon copy of Gilbert Seldes to Horace Liveright, 7 September 1922, Yale, Beinecke Library, *Dial* Papers, box 41, folder 1153; hereafter *Dial* Papers). With a delay of perhaps one or two days, the *Dial* apparently met its schedule: Burton Rascoe reported that he received his copy of the November issue on Thursday, 26 October 1922 (see Burton Rascoe, "A Bookman's Day Book," *New York Tribune*, 5 November 1922, section V, 8). More mystery surrounds the exact date of the Liveright release. In a letter to Seldes of 12 September, Liveright confirmed that his firm was "not to publish The Waste Land prior to its appearance in The Dial," and speculated, "I don't think that we'll publish it before January" (*Dial* Papers, ms. 34, box 41, folder 1153). However, it is clear that the book had already been typeset in August, for Eliot had received and corrected the proofs by 15 September (see *LOTSE*, 570), and by late October the volume must have needed only binding. Apparently Liveright hastened to release it on 15 December in order to capitalize on the publicity generated by the announcement of the Dial Award in its December issue (presumably released around 20 November). For the date, see Donald Gallup, *T. S. Eliot:*

A Bibliography, rev. ed. (New York: Harcourt, 1969), A6, 29–32. For an earlier study on *The Waste Land*'s publication, see Daniel Woodward, "Notes on the Publishing History and Text of The Waste Land," *Papers of the Bibliographical Society of America* 58 (1964): 252–269.

4. James E. B. Breslin, *From Modern to Contemporary American Poetry, 1945–1965* (Chicago: University of Chicago Press, 1984), 11 and 11 n. 53. Breslin cannot assign the epithet "drunken Bolshevik" to a source because it has none. The ultimate source of the phrase is a book review by Arthur Waugh (1866–1943), father of the two novelists Alec and Evelyn. Writing in 1916, he assessed the *Catholic Anthology, 1914–1915* (London: Elkin Mathews, 1915), a collection of poems edited by Ezra Pound which included Eliot's "The Love Song of J. Alfred Prufrock." Waugh condemned the entire volume for being "the very stronghold of literary rebellion, if not of anarchy," and he singled out "Prufrock" for special attention, saying that it called for "a hint of warning": "It was a classic custom in the family hall, when the feast was at its height, to display a drunken slave among the sons of the household, to the end that they, being ashamed at the ignominious folly of his gesticulations, might determine never to be tempted into such a pitiable condition themselves." Ezra Pound, in an angry defense of Eliot's work, seized upon the phrase "drunken slave," transformed it ever so slightly into "drunken helot," and charged Waugh with applying it to Eliot. From there, in the lore of the young, it went on to become "drunken Bolshevik" and lodged itself in the memory of Stephen Spender, and from Spender it was taken up by Breslin and turned into a comment representing public opinion of the 1920s, or even a judgment on *The Waste Land*. For the review by Waugh and the counterblast by Pound, see *T. S. Eliot: The Critical Heritage*, ed. Michael Grant (London: Routledge, 1942), 67–73. For Spender's contribution, see his essay "The New Orthodoxies," in Robert Richman, ed., *The Arts at Mid-Century* (New York: Horizon, 1954), 11, which in turn is the source that is cited by Breslin.

5. On Bishop see Elizabeth Carroll Spindler, *John Peale Bishop* (Morgantown: West Virginia University Library, 1980), chapters 5–7. It should be noted that Spindler often errs on points of detail, especially in transcribing letters. See below, note 8, for examples.

6. Gilbert Seldes to Scofield Thayer, cable of 6 March 1922 (*Dial* Papers, box 40, folder 1138); Thayer to Seldes, cable of 9 March 1922; Seldes to Thayer, letter of 11 March 1922 (both in the *Dial* Papers, box 40, folder 1139).

7. Ezra Pound to Jeanne Foster, 6 May 1922 (Harvard University, Houghton Library, bMS Am 1635). On Foster and Quinn, see B. L. Reid, *The Man from New York: John Quinn and His Friends* (New York: Oxford University Press, 1968), 313, 367 (her background and their meeting in 1918), 464–465, 579 (her poetry), and 549 (her work for *Vanity Fair*). On Quinn's own work for *Vanity Fair* and his relations with its editor, Frank Crowninshield, see ibid., 276–277, 302–304, 373. For a Foster contribution to *Vanity Fair* that was

inspired by Pound, see "New Sculptures by Constantin Brancusi," *Vanity Fair* 18 (May 1922): 68. On her relations with Bishop, see Pound to Jeanne Foster, [20 April] 1922 (Harvard University, Houghton Library, bMS Am 1635).

8. John Peale Bishop to Edmund Wilson, 5 August 1922 (Yale, Beinecke Library, Edmund Wilson Papers, Series 2). The letter is reported by Spindler, *John Peale Bishop*, 68–69, though with numerous errors. Whereas Bishop states that he met Pound extended on a "bright green couch swathed in a hieratic bathrobe," Spindler reports him on "a *high* green couch swathed in a *heraldric* bathrobe"—curious garb indeed. And whereas Bishop describes the bathrobe as "made of a maiden aunt's shit-brown blanket," Spindler fabricates "a maiden aunt's *shirt*-brown blanket" (68; all emphases added). Spindler also omits the three sentences from "Here's the thing . . ." to ". . . written in English since 1900." It is important to note that Bishop was apparently acting in collaboration with Edmund Wilson in his effort to purchase *The Waste Land,* a point elaborated below.

9. Pound himself was conscious of the dilemma presented by his role as impresario and its effects on his literary reputation. Consider his remarks to Margaret Anderson in 1921: "Point I never can seem to get you to take is that I have done more log rolling and attending to other people's affairs, Joyce, Lewis, Gaudier, etc. (don't regret it). But I am in my own small way, a writer myself, and as before stated I shd. like (and won't in any case get) the chance of being considered as the author of my own poems rather than as a literary politician and a very active stage manager of rising talent." See Pound to Margaret Anderson, [22? April 1921], *Pound/The Little Review: The Letters of Ezra Pound to Margaret Anderson,* ed. Thomas L. Scott and Melvin J. Riedman (New York: New Directions, 1988), 266.

10. Pound to Felix Schelling, 8–9 July 1922, in Ezra Pound, *Selected Letters, 1907–1941,* ed. D. D. Paige (New York: New Directions, 1971), 180.

11. It should be stressed that Pound did not at this time have a copy of the manuscript and so could not lend it to Bishop. One week before their meeting, on 27 July, Pound had written to Eliot requesting a copy of the manuscript precisely because he had none available to show James Sibley Watson, Jr., who was then visiting Pound and wished to read it. This can be inferred from Eliot's reply of 18 July, when he stated that he had only one copy to hand but would make another and send it as soon as he could (see *LOTSE,* 552). Equally important, the typescript did not arrive until 14 August, or seven days after Bishop's departure, as reported by Watson to Thayer when he sent it on to him in Vienna (James Sibley Watson to Thayer, 16 August 1922, *Dial* Papers, box 44, folder 1260).

12. The dates of Eliot's arrival and departure are inferred from Vivien Eliot to Mary Hutchinson, 12 January 1922, in *LOTSE,* 501. She reports that "Tom has been here ten days," implying that he arrived on 2 January; and she states that "he will be back [in London] on Monday," 17 January 1922, suggesting that he would leave the day before, or 16 January. The new dates also make

clear that all of Pound's editorial interventions occurred between 2 and 16 January 1922. Further, as scholars have previously suspected, these consisted principally of two editorial sessions. This hypothesis is confirmed by Eliot's letter of 20 January 1922 to Scofield Thayer, in which he reports that his poem "will have been three times through the sieve by Pound as well as myself" (*LOTSE*, 503). In other words, in addition to the two times that Pound had already gone over the poem while the two men were in Paris, Eliot was planning to send it to him for yet a third time. Eliot probably sent the poem to Pound on 19 or 20 January, at roughly the same time he was writing to Thayer, and in response Pound wrote his letter dated "24 Saturnus," or 24 January 1922 (mistakenly assigned to 24 December 1921 by Valerie Eliot, and printed in *LOTSE*, 497–498).

13. On *Instigations*, see Gallup, *Eliot*, A18. For Liveright's acceptance of *Poems, 1918–1921*, see Liveright to Pound, 13 September 1920, Indiana University, Lilly Library, Pound Mss. II, Liveright. For his helpful role in Pound's personal finances in 1921, see Lawrence Rainey, *Ezra Pound and the Monument of Culture* (Chicago: University of Chicago Press, 1991), 48.

14. Copy of Liveright to John Quinn, 24 March 1922, Indiana University, Lilly Library, Pound Mss. I, Quinn: "I am attaching to this letter a card which James Joyce gave me in Paris one evening when I had dinner with him. . . . Ezra Pound and T. S. Eliot had dinner with us that night and as I am publishing Ezra Pound, and I'm about to publish Eliot, providing that Knopf has no legal claim on his next book, I think Joyce belongs in the Boni and Liveright fold.

"I saw Pound each day during the six days I was in Paris, and I made a little arrangement with him that will take care of his rent over there for the next two years anyhow."

Liveright's contract with Pound is dated 4 January 1922, and this is also the date he apparently left Paris. He refers to his departure in a postcard from London to Pound, dated 11 January 1922, where he reports that he met May Sinclair "last Thursday," 5 January 1922; presumably, therefore, he left Paris on 4 January. If so, and if he stayed "six days in Paris" (as he reports), then he must have arrived there on 29 or 30 December 1921. Since Eliot himself did not arrive in Paris until 2 January, the dinner could have occurred only on the evenings of 2 or 3 January. The latter date is more likely, as Eliot would have been tired after arriving from Lausanne on 2 January, and as some time must be allowed for plans to have been formulated and accepted by all the parties. There are three other references to the dinner. Eliot reports on his offer from Liveright in a letter to Alfred A. Knopf, dated 3 April 1922, in which he explains that "Mr. Liveright, whom I met in Paris," has made an offer for the poem (see *LOTSE*, 519). Pound also refers to the dinner in a letter to Jeanne Foster, dated 5 April 1922: "Liveright saw the right people in Paris. . . . He saw Joyce and Eliot with me" (see Pound to Jeanne Foster, 5 April 1922, Harvard University, Houghton Library, bMS Am 1635). Finally,

Eliot reports the meeting again in a letter to John Quinn, dated 25 June: "Pound introduced me to Liveright in Paris, and Liveright made me the offer" (see *LOTSE*, 530).

15. Pound to Jeanne Foster, 5 April 1922.

16. Pound to Quinn, 20 June 1920, New York Public Library, Quinn Papers, box 34, folder 4.

17. Liveright to Pound, 11 January 1922, Yale, Beinecke Library, Bird Papers, folder 23; hereafter Bird Papers. It is Liveright's concern with the length of the poem that explains Eliot's repeated proposals designed to make the book longer by adding as prefatory material to *The Waste Land*: (1) three minor pieces, a suggestion that Pound rejected on 24 January, (2) a reprint of "Gerontion," an idea advanced to Pound in a letter circa 26 January (assigned to "24? January" by Valerie Eliot), and (3) one or two poems by Pound, also advanced in the same letter of circa 26 January to Pound. In addition, however, Liveright was nervous about its publication in periodical form, and whether it would be printed in a single issue: "And does it *all* appear in *one* issue of the Dial—please let me know." This concern prompted Eliot to worry about the same question, as emerges in his letter offering the poem to the *Dial* on 20 January 1922: "It could easily go into 4 issues if you like, but not more" (T. S. Eliot to Scofield Thayer, 20 January 1922, *Dial* Papers, box 31, folder 810). Liveright may have communicated his concerns directly to Eliot after he arrived in London on 17 January, for Liveright did not depart for the United States until 28 January and could easily have met or contacted the poet until then. Surely this explains Eliot's anxiety in his letters to Thayer (20 January) and Pound (circa 26 January) on precisely those matters raised earlier in Liveright's note of 11 January to Pound.

18. See Liveright to Pound, 12 October 1922, Bird Papers, folder 23: "It doesn't seem that we've found the right thing yet, does it? . . . And if Yeats insists on sticking to Macmillan, and I firmly believe that Yeats has more to do with it than Watt [his agent] because I did have a long talk with Watt and he seemed inclined to let me have a look-in,—well, all the worse for Yeats."

19. Pound to Thayer, 18 February 1922, *Dial* Papers, box 38, folder 1070; Thayer to Pound, 5 March 1922, and Pound to Thayer, 9–10 March 1922, *Dial* Papers, box 38, folder 1071.

20. Thayer's marginalia on Eliot's letter of 20 January 1922 (*Dial* Papers, box 31, folder 810) record his diligent calculations of the poem's price at normal rates: if typeset at thirty-five lines per page, the poem would come to slightly less than twelve pages, yielding a price of $120; if typeset at forty lines per page, it would come to eleven and a quarter pages, yielding a price slightly more than $110. Summarizing his results, Thayer firmly concludes: "12 pp. $120." His offer of $150, then, was already 25 percent higher than normal rates.

21. It must be stressed that there is no straightforward procedure that would enable us to establish an exact value in current dollars for a specific income from 1922. One can make an estimate based on the consumer price index,

which by 1986 (to take a random year) had risen to 5.79 times its level in 1922. However, this may produce misleading figures, insofar as it fails to indicate the relative position of a given income within the larger economy. If, for example, we assume that the average per capita income was $735 in 1922 and multiply this by 5.79, it yields a 1986 average per capita income of $4,256. In reality, however, the national income per capita in 1986 was more than three times as high: $14,166. The reason for this discrepancy is that the average person enjoys more wealth today than he did in 1922, a fact that must also be taken into account when attempting to estimate an equivalent income figure. A better approach, then, is to take the given sum as a percentage of national income per capita. In that case, the offer of $150 was 20 percent of the national income per capita of $750 (hereafter the figure of $735 is rounded to $750), and the equivalent figure in 1986 dollars would be $2,833. Again, these figures are offered as rough estimates, not precise equivalents. It is impossible to be more exact because it was not until the 1940s that the minimum income requirement for annual tax returns was lowered enough to facilitate accurate nationwide estimates of income distribution for families and individuals. Before then, higher minimums meant that information was available for only a small fraction of the population, those with the highest incomes. For various estimates of national income per capita, see Wesley C. Mitchell, Willford I. King, et al., *Income in the United States: Its Amount and Distribution, 1909–1919* (New York: Harcourt, Brace, 1921), with relevant figures on 13, 76, and 144–147; they concluded that income per capita in 1918 and 1919 totaled $586 and $629, respectively. See also *Historical Statistics of the United States: Colonial Times to 1970, Part 1* (Washington: Department of Commerce, 1976), 166–167 and 284ff.; this study shows that the average annual earnings of employees in the educational services in 1922 were $1,109. See also Robert F. Martin, *National Income in the United States, 1799–1958* (New York: National Industrial Conference Board, 1941), 7; and Simon Kuznets, *National Income and Its Composition, 1919–1938*, vol. 1 (New York: National Bureau of Economic Research, 1941). For help in considering these economic questions, I am grateful to Lance Davis.

22. Eliot to Thayer, 16 March 1922, *Dial* Papers, box 31, folder 810.

23. Eliot to Pound, 12 March 1922, *LOTSE*, 507.

24. Thayer visited Pound for the first time on 12 July 1921. Pound's initial contract to serve as writer and talent scout for the *Dial* had expired twelve days earlier, and Thayer had advised him that it would not be renewed. When the two met for a second time on 13 July, however, the contract was renewed, though only in part: Pound would continue to write for the *Dial* but not serve as talent scout, and he would receive roughly half his former salary. These meetings were only part of a series that continued throughout the month: 12 July, 13 July, circa 20 July, 26 July, and 28 July. For the meetings, see Pound to Dorothy Shakespear Pound, 12 July, 14 July, 21 July, 26 July, 30 July 1921, Indiana University, Lilly Library, Pound Mss. III, 1921.

25. Pound to Thayer, 23 April 1922, *Dial* Papers, box 38, folder 1072.

26. Pound to Thayer, 6 May 1922, *Dial* Papers, box 38, folder 1073.

27. The visit is mentioned in Eliot to Sydney Schiff, attributed to "early June 1922" by Valerie Eliot in *LOTSE*, 528: "I also went to Verona and saw Pound." On Pound's travels in 1922 see Rainey, "The Earliest Manuscripts of the Malatesta Cantos by Ezra Pound," Ph.D. diss., University of Chicago, 1986, 70–91, especially 85–88. His meeting with Eliot is rehearsed in various drafts for the Malatesta Cantos, in particular: draft B, lines 3–4, transcribed ibid., 406–407; draft C1, lines 82–85, transcribed ibid., 482–488; and draft C3, lines 61–100, transcribed ibid., 566–571, with annotations for specific passages. For Pound's later reminiscences, see Cantos 29 and 78.

28. Eliot to Pound, 12 March 1922, *LOTSE*, 508. Eliot mentions the *Little Review* only twice in his correspondence for 1922, both times in letters to Pound. Clearly he considered the journal to be largely Pound's.

29. Pound to Dorothy Shakespear Pound, 21 July 1922, Indiana University, Lilly Library, Pound Mss. III, 1922.

30. Thayer to Seldes, 20 July 1922, *Dial* Papers, box 40, folder 1148. Thayer reports that Watson "is present as I dictate," leaving no doubt that Watson departed within hours of his meeting with Pound on 19 July (date of meeting from Pound to Dorothy Shakespear Pound, 21 July 1922).

31. Thayer to Eliot, 5 October 1922, *Dial* Papers, box 31, folder 810: "I have been very glad to learn from New York that the suggestion I made to Mr. Watson while he was with me in Berlin last July has borne fruit and that we are despite your asperity to have the pleasure of recognizing publicly your contribution to contemporary letters."

32. Pound to Dorothy Shakespear Pound, 29 July 1922, Indiana University, Lilly Library, Pound Mss. III, 1922.

33. Watson to Thayer, 29 July 1922, *Dial* Papers, box 44, folder 1260.

34. Eliot to Pound, 28 July 1922, *LOTSE*, 552.

35. Watson to Thayer, 16 August 1922, *Dial* Papers, box 44, folder 1260.

36. Eliot to Watson, 15 August 1922, *LOTSE*, 560.

37. Watson to Thayer, 19 August 1922, *Dial* Papers, box 44, folder 1260.

38. Eliot to Quinn, 21 August 1922, *LOTSE*, 564.

39. Eliot to Pound, 30 August 1922, *LOTSE*, 567.

40. Eliot to Watson, 21 August 1922, *LOTSE*, 564–565; Seldes to Thayer, 31 August 1922, *Dial* Papers, box 40, folder 1151.

41. Liveright to Pound, 5 February 1922, Indiana University, Lilly Library, Pound Mss. I, Liveright.

42. Tom Dardis, *Firebrand: The Life of Horace Liveright* (New York: Random House, 1995), 97.

43. "A Group of Poems by T. S. Eliot: A Selection from the Dramatic Lyrics of a Much Discussed American Poet," *Vanity Fair* 20, no. 4 (June 1923): 67. The other articles by Eliot appeared in *Vanity Fair* 20, no. 5 (July 1923): 51, 98; 21, no. 3 (November 1923): 44, 118; and 21, no. 6 (February 1924): 29, 98.

44. On the *Egoist*, see Jane Lidderdale and Mary Nicholson, *Dear Miss Weaver* (New York: Viking, 1970).

45. On the *Little Review*, see Frank Luther Mott, *A History of American Magazines*, vol. 5, *Sketches of Twenty-one Magazines, 1905–1930* (Cambridge: Harvard University Press, 1968), 166–178. Mott considers it "unlikely that the circulation ever rose to much over a thousand" (171). His figure is offered as a correction to the earlier estimate of 2,000 given by Frederick J. Hoffman et al., *The Little Magazine: A History and Bibliography* (Princeton: Princeton University Press, 1946), 57. My figures are from Pound to Quinn, 8 February 1927, New York Public Library, Quinn Papers. For the *Egoist*, see Lidderdale and Nicholson, *Dear Miss Weaver*, 460; Jane Lidderdale reports that its largest circulation was 400 copies per issue, with about 268 by subscription, during the first six months of its life (1913). "Then it went into a long decline, with a sharp drop in November 1916 when the long-term subscriptions ran out; and the circulation never rose again above 200."

46. In the second half of 1925 the *Egoist* earned £37 in sales and subscriptions, and one surmises that its advertising revenues were around £5 (see Lidderdale and Nicholson, *Dear Miss Weaver*, 99). In *Sketches of Twenty-one Magazines*, Mott estimates that advertising revenues for the *Little Review* "seldom or never exceeded $500 a year" (171); sales and subscriptions probably earned around $4,000 in 1917, according to my estimate.

 The "revolution" in the magazine industry is usually dated to 1893, when several magazines dramatically dropped their prices and achieved unprecedented circulation rates; the price of a magazine was now less than the cost of its production, and the difference was made up with expanded revenues from advertisers. The most perceptive discussion of this transformation appears in Richard Ohmann, *Selling Culture: Magazines, Markets, and Class at the Turn of the Century* (London: Verso, 1996), 24–38.

47. All figures are from the annual financial reports of the *Dial*, in *Dial* Papers, box 9, folders 327–332.

48. For the *Little Review* figure, see Mott, *Sketches of Twenty-one Magazines*, 171, and Reid, *Man from New York*, 343. The four donors were John Quinn, Otto Kahn, Mrs. James Byrne, and Max Pam. Quinn's patronage included a standing subsidy of $750 per year, in addition to his $400 gift as part of the syndicate. For the *Egoist*, see Lidderdale and Nicholson, *Dear Miss Weaver*, 459. Weaver's contributions were, respectively, £251, £342, £234, and £185.

49. Lewis appeared in the *Little Review* of November 1918 and the *Dial* of August 1921. Zadkine appeared in the *Little Review* of December 1918 and the *Dial* of October 1921.

50. Thayer to Seldes, 28 November 1922, *Dial* Papers, box 41, folder 1157.

51. See [Scofield Thayer,] "Comment," *Dial* 73, no. 1 (July 1922): 119. Springarn's major essays are collected in Joel Springarn, *Creative Criticism: Essays on the Unity of Genius and Taste* (New York: Henry Holt, 1917). The book is dedicated "to my friend Benedetto Croce, the most original of all modern thinkers on Art," and it reports that the central essay, "The New Criticism," was originally delivered as a lecture at Columbia University in 1910 (iii). For Springarn's influence on the *Dial*, see William Wasserstrom, *The Time of the Dial*

(Syracuse: Syracuse University Press, 1963), 17–19. See also Nicholas Joost, *Scofield Thayer and the Dial* (Carbondale: Southern Illinois University Press, 1964); and Nicholas Joost, *The "Dial," 1912–1920* (Barre, Mass.: Barre, 1967).

52. Eliot to Thayer, 1 January 1921, *LOTSE*, 429.

53. Thayer to Seldes, 12 October 1922, *Dial* Papers, box 41, folder 1153. The practice was a regular one at the *Dial*, and newspaper clippings from 1920–1929 fill three boxes; *Dial* Papers, boxes 16–18.

54. On *Vanity Fair*, see Martha Cohn Cooper, "Frank Crowninshield and *Vanity Fair*," Ph.D. diss., University of North Carolina, 1976; Kitty Hoffman, "A History of *Vanity Fair*: A Modernist Journal in America," Ph.D. diss., University of Toronto, 1980; and Cynthia L. Ward, "*Vanity Fair* Magazine and the Modern Style, 1914–1936 (New York City)," Ph.D. diss., State University of New York at Stony Brook, 1983. Also useful is Caroline Seebohm, *The Man Who Was Vogue: The Life and Times of Condé Nast* (New York: Viking, 1982). For a survey of the magazine market and industry see Theodore Peterson, *Magazines in the Twentieth Century* (Urbana: University of Illinois Press, 1964). For Nast's strategy of market segmentation see Cohn Cooper, "Frank Crowninshield and *Vanity Fair*," 38.

55. Thayer to Mrs. Edward D. Thayer, 16 December 1922, *Dial* Papers, box 43, 1922; Thayer to Seldes, 26 December 1922, *Dial* Papers, box 441, folder 1159; Thayer to Seldes, 18 January, 28 May, 8 June 1923, *Dial* Papers, box 41, folders 1160, 1166, 1167. "I was recently sent a copy of *Vanity Fair* and was interested to see how many of my friends are now writing for that paper. In the number for December I find the names of Kenneth MacGowan, Henry McBride, Kenneth Burke, Gilbert Seldes and of my acquaintance Miss Millay" (Thayer to Mrs. Edward D. Thayer, 16 December 1922). Thayer also complains that "Mr. Burke's review [in the *Dial*] interested me, but I do not find it so good as his recent article developing more or less the same theme in Vanity Fair" (Thayer to Seldes, 26 December 1922).

56. As a point of comparison, the two leading weeklies, *Collier's* and the *Saturday Evening Post*, had circulations of 1 million and 2.1 million, respectively. For the advertising revenues of *Vanity Fair*, I rely on Peterson, *Magazines in the Twentieth Century*, 271. For the circulation figures of all the journals discussed here, *N. W. Ayer and Son's American Newspaper Annual and Directory* (Philadelphia: N. W. Ayer and Son's, 1922), 1224–1226, reports figures from the Audit Bureau of Circulation. On advertising as "an integral part of the magazine" (that is, *Vanity Fair*), see Cohn Cooper, "Frank Crowninshield and *Vanity Fair*," 42.

57. Reid, *Man from New York*, 594.

58. Less is known about Thayer's collecting; but see Joost, *Scofield Thayer*, 23–36.

59. See Nicholas Fox Weber, *Patron Saints: Five Rebels Who Opened America to a New Art* (New York: Knopf, 1992), 56; and *The Frank Crowninshield Collection of Modern French Art*, Auction Catalogue, Parke-Bernet Galleries (20–21 October 1943).

60. Ward, "*Vanity Fair* Magazine and the Modern Style," 91–92, 100–101; see Alfred H. Barr, Jr., "An American Museum of Modern Art," *Vanity Fair* 33 (November 1929): 79, 136.

61. John Quinn, "Jacob Epstein, Sculptor," *Vanity Fair* 9 (1917): 76, 114; John Quinn, "James Joyce, A New Irish Novelist," *Vanity Fair* 8 (1917): 49, 128; see Reid, *Man from New York,* 580–590; on Gregg and *Vanity Fair,* see Ward, "*Vanity Fair* Magazine and the Modern Style," 91.

62. See Peter Bürger, *Theory of the Avant-Garde,* trans. Michael Shaw (Minneapolis: University of Minnesota Press, 1984); Andreas Huyssen, *After the Great Divide* (Bloomington: Indiana University Press, 1986); and Marjorie Perloff, *The Poetics of Indeterminacy* (Princeton: Princeton University Press, 1981; rpt., Evanston: Northwestern University Press, 1983). See also Charles Russell, *Poets, Prophets, and Revolutionaries: The Literary Avant-Garde from Rimbaud Through Postmodernism* (Oxford: Oxford University Press, 1985).

63. See Walker Gilmore, *Horace Liveright: Publisher of the Twenties* (New York: David Lewis, 1970), 38. A normal budget would have been twelve to fifteen cents per copy; Liveright spent twenty-five cents per copy. Gilmore draws his information from interviews with Manuel Komroff, a former Liveright employee.

64. On the multiple collected editions of Tennyson, see June Steffensen Hagen, *Tennyson and His Publishers* (University Park: Pennsylvania State University Press, 1979), 149–150. See also Hagen's entire study on the emergence of this practice and Tennyson's use of it throughout his later career.

65. See Liam Miller, *The Dun Emer Press, Later the Cuala Press* (Dublin: Dolmen, 1973).

66. See John Dreyfus, *Bruce Rogers and American Typography* (Cambridge: Cambridge University Press, 1959).

67. Conrad Aiken to Maurice Firuski, 15 February 1922, Chapin Library, Williams College, T. S. Eliot Collection. I wish to thank Robert L. Volz, Rare Book Custodian, for his kindness in drawing this letter to my attention.

68. T. S. Eliot to Maurice Firuski, 26 February 1922, Chapin Library, Williams College, T. S. Eliot Collection. Mention of this letter is made by Valerie Eliot in *LOTSE,* 515 n. 1. I am grateful to Mrs. Eliot for permission to quote this letter in its entirety. The letter from T. S. Eliot to Edmund Wilson quoted below is also printed by permission of Mrs. Eliot, and both are copyrighted by her.

69. T. S. Eliot to Ezra Pound, 12 March 1922, *LOTSE,* 507.

70. T. S. Eliot to Edmund Wilson, 14 August 1922, Yale, Beinecke Library, Edmund Wilson Papers.

71. For the wages of Crowninshield's executive secretary, Jeanne Ballot, who earned $22 per week, or $1,144 per year, see Cohn Cooper, "Frank Crowninshield and *Vanity Fair,*" 48. The $2,000 paid to Eliot in the form of the Dial Award was a remarkable figure: the highest sum *Vanity Fair* ever paid was $100, to F. Scott Fitzgerald in 1925 for a short story.

3. IMMENSE. MAGNIFICENT. TERRIBLE.

1. John Peale Bishop to Edmund Wilson, 3 November [1922] and [c. 10 November 1922], Yale, Beinecke Library, Edmund Wilson Papers.

2. In this discussion I am indebted to Steven Connor, *Dumbstruck: A Cultural History of Ventriloquism* (Oxford: Oxford University Press, 2000), especially chapters 1 and 2, 3–74.

3. Burton Rascoe, "A Bookman's Day Book," *New York Tribune*, 5 November 1922, section V, 8.

4. Edmund Wilson, "The Poetry of Drouth," *Dial* 73, no. 6 (December 1922): 611–616. Rpt. in Michael Grant, ed., *T. S. Eliot: The Critical Heritage* (London: Routledge, 1982), 138–144.

5. All ten essays are found in Lawrence Rainey, ed., *The Annotated "Waste Land" with Eliot's Contemporary Prose* (New Haven: Yale University Press, 2005), 138–201.

6. Ibid., 168, 169, 167, 189.

7. Gilbert Seldes, "T. S. Eliot," *Nation* 115 (6 December 1922): 614–616. Rpt. in Grant, *Eliot*, 144–150.

8. Conrad Aiken, "Prefatory Note (1958)," in Charles Brian Cox and Arnold P. Hinchliffe, eds., *T. S. Eliot: "The Waste Land," a Casebook* (London: Macmillan, 1978), 91.

9. Conrad Aiken, "An Anatomy of Melancholy," *New Republic* 33 (7 February 1923): 294–295. Rpt. in Grant, *Eliot*, 156–161.

10. The nine reviews, in chronological order, are an anonymous one in the *TLS* and eight others by Desmond McCarthy, Harold Monro, Edgell Rickword, Clive Bell, J. C. Squire, Charles Powell, F. L. Lucas, and Humbert Wolfe. In addition to these, published in 1922 and 1923, there were three further reviews in 1924 and 1925 devoted not specifically to *The Waste Land* but to Eliot's oeuvre to date, and written by Irish and Scottish reviewers. All twelve are listed in Rainey, *Annotated "Waste Land,"* 256–259, along with forty-seven American notices and reviews. The reviews frequently cite one another: they make reference to four more, as yet unidentified, reviews by Edward Anthony, Keith Preston, and two anonymous reviewers in the *Christian Science Monitor* and a journal called *Measure*.

11. T. S. Eliot, *For Lancelot Andrewes* (London: Faber and Gwyer, 1928), ix.

12. On the misdating of "Tradition and the Individual Talent" in the first edition of Eliot's *Selected Essays*, see Donald Gallup, *T. S. Eliot: A Bibliography*, rev. ed. (New York: Harcourt, 1969), 47, A21.a.

13. See Rainey, *Annotated "Waste Land,"* 138–201.

14. The Baudelaire essay stands conspicuously as the first in a section treating modern authors, a position it still occupies today. The sentence by Eliot quoted here is found in his *Selected Essays* (New York: Harcourt, 1950), 380.

15. Cleanth Brooks, "*The Waste Land*: A Critique of the Myth," *Southern Review* 3 (1937–1938): 106–136. Rpt. in Cleanth Brooks, *Modern Poetry and the Tradition* (Chapel Hill: University of North Carolina Press, 1939), 136–172.

Although there are some minor changes made in the reprinted version, I cite it because it is the most widely available version of the essay. All page references hereafter are given in parentheses within the text.

16. T. S. Eliot, "Religion and Literature" (1935), in *Selected Prose of T. S. Eliot,* ed. Frank Kermode (New York: Harcourt, 1975), 104–105.

17. F. R. Leavis, *New Bearings in English Poetry* (London: Chatto and Windus, 1932), 103.

18. Aristotle, *Metaphysics,* trans. Hugh Tredennich (London: Putnam's Sons, 1933), 1: 13.

19. *The Poetics of Aristotle,* trans. Stephen Halliwell (Chapel Hill: University of North Carolina Press, 1987), 42.

20. *Poetics,* 60.

21. Stephen Halliwell, *Aristotle's "Poetics"* (London: Duckworth, 1986), 75 n. 41.

22. *The Iliad,* trans. Richmond Lattimore (Chicago: University of Chicago Press, 1951), XXII, 199–201.

23. Connor, *Dumbstruck,* 25.

24. Ibid., 27; Frank Kermode, *The Genesis of Secrecy* (Cambridge: Harvard University Press, 1979), 64.

25. T. S. Eliot, "The Frontiers of Criticism," in *On Poetry and Poets* (London: Faber, 1957), 109–110.

26. T. S. Eliot, "The Art of Poetry, I: T. S. Eliot," *Paris Review* 21 (Spring/Summer, 1959): 47–50, rpt. in *Writers at Work: The Paris Review Interviews,* second series, ed. George Plimpton (Harmondsworth: Penguin, 1977), 91–110, here 96, 105.

27. Ithaca: Cornell University Press.

28. Christine Froula, "Corpse, Monument, *Hypocrite Lecteur:* Text and Transference in the Reception of *The Waste Land,*" *Text: An Interdisciplinary Annual of Textual Studies* 9 (1996): 304–314.

DOCUMENTING THE DOCUMENTS:
SYNOPTIC BIBLIOGRAPHICAL DESCRIPTIONS
OF ELIOT'S WRITINGS, 1898–1922

TABLE ONE LETTERS, 1898–1922

TABLE 1 LISTS ALL the letters by T. S. Eliot which have been consulted and gives a synoptic bibliographical description of them. In the first column (and repeated in the last), each letter is listed in chronological order and assigned a number. Although this table primarily records *the kinds of paper* which Eliot used in his letters, doing so to collate them with those used in his student papers (Table 2), poems and essays (Table 3), and *The Waste Land* manuscripts (Table 4), for most scholars the unit of reference will remain not the kind of paper but the dated letter. Therefore, in the seven cases where a letter is written on leaves of more than one kind of paper, the number assigned to it remains the same and an alphabetical suffix is added, such as 97A and 97B, to register the presence of different papers. In the second column appears the date for each letter. When the date of a letter, or a portion of the date, has been conjectured (whether by Mrs. Eliot or by me), it appears in square brackets. When the date is derived from a postmark, it is preceded by the initials "PM."

The corpus of letters registered in this table corresponds largely with the letters printed by Valerie Eliot in *The Letters of T. S. Eliot*, vol. 1, *1898–1922* (hereafter *LOTSE*), an edition that contains transcriptions of 509 letters by Eliot. For ease of reference, those 509 letters have each been assigned a number according to the sequence of their appearance in *The Letters of T. S. Eliot*, preceded by the letter "T" to indicate Eliot's authorship (the volume also includes letters by Vivien Eliot and various third parties): hence "T.1," "T.2," and so forth, found in the third column of Table 1, headed *LOTSE*. In the fourth column, headed "Pg. No.," the reader is referred to the page in Valerie Eliot's edition where the letter's published transcription begins.

It should be noted that not all the originals of the 509 published letters by Eliot were examined. There were 37 published letters whose originals could not be consulted, and those are detailed in note 10 to Chapter 1. That leaves 472 of the published letters whose originals were consulted. In addition, a further 166 unpublished letters by Eliot were examined, dating from 1914 to the end of 1922, making a total of 638 letters whose originals have been consulted. These unpublished letters are consecutively numbered and placed in chronological order, preceded by the letter "U" in the fifth column of Table 1: hence "U.1," "U.2," and so on. To assist scholars who wish to identify, consult, and refer to these letters, Appendix 1 to Table 1 gives a chronological list of all the unpublished letters, their dates, recipients, locations, and incipits. Forty-four of the unpublished letters are without dates. Appendix 2 to Table 1 lists these undated letters in chronological order and gives the rationale used in assigning them dates.

Following the indications of a letter's date, its place and its page number in the sequence established by *LOTSE* if the letter has been published, or its number in a chronological ordering if the letter has not been published, the table gives the name of the letter's recipient in the sixth column, followed in the seventh by the name of the library or private collection which holds the original document, and in the eighth by the number of leaves which the letter contains.

The next three columns, nine through eleven, detail the most basic features of the paper: height, width, and thickness. Height and width are given in millimeters, thickness in hundredths of a millimeter as measured by a micrometer. (The micrometer used was a pocket model no. 1010, manufactured by the L. S. Starrett Company of Athol, Massachusetts.) A word about tolerances for these values is in order. Machine-trimmed papers vary in their size by one and in some cases two millimeters. In some, for example, the width on the top edge of a leaf will prove 1–2 millimeters more or less than the width on the bottom edge. Likewise, from one leaf to another the same kind of paper may differ by 1–2 millimeters. As I have tried to record the actual measurements of each leaf, rather than making leaves conform to an ideal type, readers will note minor variations among different leaves of what is obviously the same type of paper. Likewise, a single leaf can vary in thickness by as much as one-hundredth of a millimeter; the same leaf can be 0.07 millimeter at the top edge, and 0.08 millimeter elsewhere. In reporting the thickness of a given leaf, I've reported the figure most commonly found in three or more of five readings. But since, as before, I have not adjusted measurements to conform to an ideal or standard type, readers will discern minor variations in the thickness of different leaves that are clearly the same type of paper. Very thin papers meant to serve as carbon copies, for example, can alternate between 0.05 and 0.06 millimeters, while somewhat thicker papers intended to serve as top leaves may alternate between 0.08 and 0.09 millimeters.

The next seven columns, or twelve through eighteen, describe the markings of the paper—chainlines and watermarks. (These terms are explained in the preface.) Column twelve, headed "Texture," indicates whether a paper is "laid" or "wove." If it is wove, there is no further discussion of chainlines; but if laid, the next three columns record the direction of the chain lines, their distance from one another, and the number of them which are visible on a leaf.

Most, though not all, laid papers also have a watermark, usually a decorative design which accompanies the name of the paper manufacturer or a brand name. Such names are sometimes fairly long, and only an abbreviated form of them is given here in the column headed "Watermark." One device used in several watermarks is a picture of a crown, represented in the table by an asterisk. Thus "* Bond" indicates a watermark which undoubtedly meant "Crown Bond." When the same watermark is used for different kinds of paper, either in *The Waste Land* manuscripts or in Eliot's student papers or his poetry and prose, I have differentiated these appearances by adding a capital letter in square brackets (e.g., "British Bond [A]") to facilitate their identification. The abbreviated indication of the watermark or brand name is followed by an indication of the watermark's position on the paper and its dimensions.

In the nineteenth column appears a description of the paper's color. The color terms which are used here (and the number assigned to each color other than white) are taken from the Centroid Color Chart, which was devised by the Inter-Society Color Council and the National Bureau of Standards. It gives 267 color names and matches them with color chips which enable readers to identify the intended shade or hue. Inevitably papers age differently under different conditions, and comparing the paper color of one letter located in, say, Boston, with that of another seen months later under different lighting conditions in Tulsa, Oklahoma, is plainly a delicate enterprise. But in practice, the color descriptions merely confirm or corroborate other evidence concerning the identity of a particular paper. Readers who wish to see the colors described here should consult the *ISCC-NBS Color-Name Charts Illustrated with Centroid Colors (Supplement to National Bureau of Standards Circular 553)* (Washington, D.C.: National Bureau of Standards, n.d.). See also G. Thomas Tanselle, "A System of Color Identification for Bibliographical Description," *Studies in Bibliography* 20 (1967): 203–234.

The twentieth column, headed "Printing," gives a synoptic register of letterheads and other matters printed on the paper (for example, black borders). The next column registers the characteristics of a specific kind of printed paper which Eliot recurrently uses, lined or quadruled papers. Here the pattern of horizontal printed lines presents distinctive features that can be quantified and arranged in a formula that reflects their order as seen on a leaf:

1. The "top" margin, which is blank or does not have printed lines, given in millimeters;
2. The block of space occupied by the horizontal lines, given first in millimeters (2.1) and then by the number of lines (2.2) that occupy that block of space, the latter set apart between parentheses;
3. The "bottom" margin, which is blank or has no printed lines, given again in millimeters.

Finally, columns twenty-two through twenty-four register whether a letter is written on a postcard ("PC") and whether it was written by hand ("MS" for "manuscript") or with a typewriter ("TS" for "typescript"). Column twenty-five, under the heading "Script," indicates the material used for writing: typically "black ink" or "pencil" for handwritten letters, and "black ribbon" for typewritten ones. In a few instances where the letters took the form of a telegram, this

NO.	DATE	LOTSE	PG. NO.	UNPBD.	RECIPIENT	LOCATION	LVS.	HEIGHT	WIDTH	THICK.	TEXTURE	CHAINLINES	DIST.	NO.
1	23 June 1898	T.1	p. 3		Father	Houghton	1	212	177	0.11	Wove			
2	4 August [1904]	T.2	p. 4		Smith, C. E.	Houghton	1	231	175	0.13	Wove			
3	PM 23 Dec. 1910	T.3	p. 15		Smith, T. E.	Houghton	1	139	88	0.40	Wove			
4	[Late Feb.? 1911]	T.4	p. 16		Smith, T. E.	Houghton	3	416	250	0.12	Wove			
5	PM 24 Mar. 1911	T.5	p. 17		Hinkley, E.	Houghton	1	139	90	0.29	Wove			
6	26 Apr. [1911]	T.6	p. 17		Hinkley, E.	Houghton	3	264	205	0.07	Wove			
7	PM 29 June 1913	T.7	p. 37		Hinkley, E.	Houghton	1	139	89	0.27	Wove			
8	PM 7 July 1914	T.8	p. 37		Hinkley, E.	Houghton	1	266	203	0.10	Wove			
9	19 July 1914	T.9	p. 40		Aiken, C.	Huntington	2	289	190	0.07	Wove			
10	23 July 1914	T.10	p. 43		Aiken, C.	Huntington	1	288	190	0.07	Wove			
11	26 July 1914	T.11	p. 48		Hinkley, E.	Houghton	2	287	190	0.07	Wove			
12	PM 22 Aug. 1914	T.12	p. 51		Hinkley, E.	Houghton	1	137	89	0.26	Wove			
13	8 Sept. 1914	T.14	p. 54		Eliot, H.	Houghton	2	250	202	0.06	Wove			
14	8 Sept. [1914]	T.15	p. 56		Hinkley, E.	Houghton	3	251	202	0.07	Wove			
15	30 Sept. [1914]	T.16	p. 58		Aiken, C.	Huntington	2.5	250	202	0.07	Wove			
16	2 Oct. 1914			U.1	Briggs, L. B. R.	Harvard	0.5	126	202	0.06	Wove			
17	5 Oct. 1914	T.17	p. 60		Woods, J. H.	Williams	1	250	202	0.07	Wove			
18	14 Oct. 1914	T.18	p. 60		Hinkley, E.	Houghton	3	258	202	0.07	Laid	Horizontal	26	10
19	[14 Oct. 1914]	T.19	p. 65		Greene, W. C.	Greene	2	226	152	0.11	Wove			
20	23 Oct. 1914			U.2	Wiener, N.	M.I.T.	1	113	88	0.46	Wove			
21	[9? Nov. 1914]	T.20	p. 66		Wiener, N.	M.I.T.	1	113	88	0.40	Laid	Horizontal	26.5	9
22	9 Nov. [1914]	T.21	p. 67		Woods, J. H.	Williams	2	253	208	0.10	Wove			
23	16 Nov. [1914]	T.22	p. 68		Aiken, C.	Huntington	1	255	208	0.09	Laid	Horizontal	26.5	10
24	21 Nov. [1914]	T.23	p. 69		Aiken, C.	Huntington	1	227	152	0.10	Wove			
25	27 Nov. 1914	T.24	p. 70		Hinkley, E.	Houghton	3	258	201	0.07	Laid	Horizontal	26	10
26	[20? Dec. 1914]			U.3	Wiener, N.	M.I.T.	1	249	201	0.07	Wove			
27	31 Dec. 1914	T.25	p. 73		Aiken, C.	Huntington	2	254	203	0.10	Wove			
28	3 Jan. 1915	T.26	p. 76		Hinkley, E.	Houghton	2	253	202	0.10	Wove			
29	6 Jan. 1915	T.27	p. 79		Wiener, N.	M.I.T.	2	253	202	0.09	Wove			
30	PM 7 Jan. 1915			U.4	Thayer, S.	Beinecke	1	140	90	0.27	Wove			
31	PM 27 Jan. 1915	T.28	p. 82		Hinkley, E.	Houghton	1	258	202	0.07	Laid	Horizontal	26	10
32	28 Jan. 1915	T.29	p. 83		Woods, J. H.	Williams	1	254	202	0.10	Wove			
33	28 Jan. 1915	T.30	p. 84		Briggs, L. B. R.	Harvard	1	254	203	0.09	Wove			
34	2 Feb. [1915]	T.31	p. 86		Pound, E.	Beinecke	1	259	202	0.07	Laid	Horizontal	26	10
35	25 Feb. [1915]	T.32	p. 87		Aiken, C.	Huntington	1	253	203	0.09	Wove			
36	2 Mar. 1915	T.33	p. 89		Woods, J. H.	Williams	1	253	203	0.09	Wove			
37	21 Mar. [1915]	T.34	p. 90		Hinkley, E.	Houghton	2.5	252	203	0.10	Wove			
38	4 Apr. [1915]	T.35	p. 93		Gardner, I. S.	Gardner	2	252	203		Wove			
39	15 Apr. [1915]	T.36	p. 95		Pound, E.	Beinecke	2	251	203	0.09	Laid	Vertical	26	8
40	24 Apr. [1915]	T.37	p. 96		Hinkley, E.	Houghton	1.5	254	203	0.10	Wove			
41	6 May [1915]	T.38	p. 98		Woods, J. H.	Williams	1	215	144	0.20	Laid	Horizontal	27	8
42	PM 2 July 1915	T.39	p. 104		Eliot, H.	Houghton	2	228	178	0.19	Laid	Horizontal	26	9
43	10 July 1915	T.40	p. 106		Monroe, H.	Chicago	1	228	150	0.15	Laid	Vertical	27	6
44	[10? July 1915]	T.41	p. 107		Gardner, I. S.	Gardner	2	225	177	0.21	Laid	Horizontal	26	9
45	10 July 1915	T.42	p. 108		Woods, J. H.	Williams	1	228	150	0.15	Laid	Vertical	27	6
46	10 July 1915	T.43	p. 109		Briggs, L. B. R.	Harvard	1	228	151	0.15	Laid	Vertical	27	5
47	23 July 1915	T.44	p. 110		Father	Maryland	1	286	190	0.18	Laid	Horizontal	25.5	11
48	[9 Aug. 1915]	T.46	p. 112		Thayer, S.	Beinecke	1	310	184	0.14	Wove			
49	[16 Aug. 1915]			U.5	Woods, J. H.	Williams	1	274	175	0.15	Wove			
50	4 Sept. 1915	T.48	p. 113		Thayer, S.	Beinecke	1	228	151	0.15	Laid	Vertical	26	5
51	10 Sept. [1915]	T.49	p. 113		Father	Houghton	1	284	190	0.18	Laid	Horizontal	25.5	11
52	11 Sept. [1915]	T.50	p. 115		Russell, B.	McMaster	1	284	191	0.19	Laid	Horizontal	25.5	11
53	[11 Sept.? 1915]	T.51	p. 116		Woods, J. H.	Williams	2	228	151	0.15	Laid	Vertical	27	6
54	27 Sept. 1915	T.52	p. 117		Father	Houghton	3	228	199	0.08	Wove			
55	11 Oct. 1915	T.53	p. 119		Russell, B.	McMaster	1	286	190	0.19	Laid	Horizontal	25.5	11
56	17 Oct. 1915			U.6	Monroe, H.	Chicago	1	285	190	0.18	Laid	Horizontal	25.5	11
57	18 Nov. 1915	T.54	p. 120		Mother	Houghton	2	250	199	0.10	Laid	Vertical	26.5	8
58	[Nov.? 1915]	T.55	p. 122		Lewis, W.	Cornell	1	266	201	0.06	Wove			
59	28 Dec. 1915	T.56	p. 123		Woods, J. H.	Williams	1	225	156	0.16	Laid	Horizontal	27	9
60	[2 Jan. 1916]			U.7	Russell, B.	McMaster	1	253	208	0.12	Wove			

column is left blank. Column twenty-six, headed "Typewr.," specifies the size of the typewriter's characters in millimeters, a handy device which readily identifies the distinctive typewriters which Eliot used in these years. Finally, column twenty-seven refers the reader to a set of notes which immediately follow Table 1 and register variants in the paper or papers used in a particular letter, or in its dating or location.

WATERMARK	POSITION	DIMENSIONS	COLOR	PRINTING	LINED PAPER	PC	MS	TS	SCRIPT	TYPEWR.	NOTE	NO.
Crescent	Vertical	Incomplete	White		31.138(12).8	X			Pencil			1
None			Yellow white 92				X		Black ink			2
None			Yellow gray 93	Post Card		X	X		Black ink			3
None			Light gray 264				X		Black ink		1.1	4
None			White			X	X		Black ink			5
None			White				X		Black ink			6
None			White			X	X		Black ink			7
Marcus Ward's	Vertical	12 x 122	White					X	Black ribbon 2.12		5.1	8
None			White				X		Black ink			9
None			White				X		Black ink			10
None			White				X		Black ink			11
None			White			X	X		Black ink			12
None			Green white 153				X		Black ink			13
None			Green white 153				X		Black ink			14
None			Green white 153				X		Black ink			15
None			Green white 153				X		Black ink			16
None			Green white 153				X		Black ink			17
Croxley Manifest	Vertical	121 x 156	White					X	Black ribbon 2.12			18
Hieratica Bond [A]	Vertical	42 x 50	Blue white 189	Merton College			X		Black ink			19
None			White	Merton College			X		Black ink			20
Original Milton	Vertical	74 x 136	Yellow white 92	Merton College		X	X		Black ink			21
None			White	Merton College			X		Black ink			22
Original Milton	Vertical	74 x 136	Yellow white 92	Merton College			X		Black ink			23
Hieratica Bond [A]	Vertical	43 x 50	White	Merton College			X		Black ink			24
Croxley Manifest	Vertical	121 x 157	Yellow white 92	Merton College				X	Black ribbon 2.12			25
None			Green white 153				X		Black ink			26
None			White				X		Black ink			27
None			White				X		Black ink			28
None			White				X		Black ink			29
None			White			X	X		Black ink			30
Croxley Manifest	Vertical	121 x 157	Yellow white 92					X	Black ribbon 2.12			31
None			White				X		Black ink			32
None			White				X		Black ink			33
Croxley Manifest	Vertical	122 x 156	Yellow white 92				X		Black ink			34
None			White				X		Black ink			35
None			White				X		Black ink			36
None			White				X		Black ink			37
None			White				X		Black ink		2.1	38
Excelsior Fine	Horizontal	71 x 125	Yellow white 92					X	Black ribbon 2.12			39
None			White				X		Black ink			40
Society Hand Made	Vertical	58 x 160	White				X		Black ink		1.2	41
None			White				X		Black ink		4.1	42
None			White	Thyme Cottage			X		Black ink			43
St. aker L.... Ltd.	Vertical	Incomplete	White				X		Black ink			44
None			White	Thyme Cottage			X		Balck ink			45
None			White	Thyme Cottage			X		Black ink			46
Waldorf Club [A]	Vertical	35 x 210	Blue white 189				X		Black ink			47
Wardwove Boston	Vertical	29 x 73	White				X		Black ink			48
Wardwove Boston	Horizontal	Incomplete	White				X		Black ink			49
None			Lt blue gray 190				X		Black ink			50
Waldorf Club [A]	Vertical	36 x 210	Blue white 189				X		Black ink			51
Waldorf Club [A]	Vertical	36 x 210	Blue white 189				X		Black ink			52
None			Lt blue gray 190				X		Black ink		3.1	53
Aberdeen Bond	Horizontal	12 x 129	White				X		Black ink			54
Waldorf Club [A]	Vertical	Incomplete	White				X		Black ink			55
Waldorf Club [A]	Vertical	Incomplete	White				X		Black ink			56
None			White		24.208(24).12	X			Black ink			57
British Bond [A]	Horizontal	65 x 125	White					X	Black ribbon 2.12			58
None			Yellow white 92				X		Black ink		4.1	59
Devon Valley	Horizontal	40 x 55	White	Dolphin Hotel			X		Black ink			60

NO.	DATE	LOTSE	PG. NO.	UNPBD.	RECIPIENT	LOCATION	LVS.	HEIGHT	WIDTH	THICK.	TEXTURE	CHAINLINES	DIST.	NO.
61	10 Jan. 1916	T.57	p. 125		Aiken, C.	Huntington	2	251	199	0.11	Wove			
62	[11 Jan. 1916]	T.58	p. 127		Russell, B.	McMaster	1	251	199	0.11	Wove			
63	14 Jan. 1916	T.59	p. 127		Father	Houghton	1	223	176	0.14	Laid	Horizontal	26	9
64	[14 Jan. 1916]	T.60	p. 128		Russell, B.	McMaster	1	224	177	0.15	Laid	Horizontal	26	9
65	[16 Jan. 1916]	T.61	p. 129		Russell, B.	McMaster	1	224	176	0.15	Laid	Horizontal	26	9
66	[17 Jan.1916]	T.62	p. 130		Russell, B.	McMaster	1	223	177	0.15	Laid	Horizontal	26	9
67	27 Jan. 1916			U.8	Waterlow, S.	Waterlow	1	224	156	0.16	Laid	Horizontal	27	8
68	20 Feb. 1916	T.63	p. 132		Woods, J. H.	Williams	1	285	190	0.18	Laid	Horizontal	26	11
69	[6? Mar. 1916]	T.64	p. 133		Russell, B.	McMaster	1	226	156	0.17	Laid	Horizontal	27	10
70	6 Mar. 1916	T.65	p. 134		Woods, J. H.	Williams	1	286	191	0.16	Laid	Horizontal	26	11
71	27 Mar. 1916	T.66	p. 135		Monroe, H.	Chicago	1	285	191	0.16	Laid	Horizontal	26	11
72	3 May 1916	T.67	p. 136		Woods, J. H.	Williams	1	285	191	0.16	Laid	Horizontal	26	11
73	7 May 1916	T.68	p. 137		Thayer, S.	Beinecke	1	288	190	0.16	Wove			
74	14 May [1916]	T.69	p. 138		Russell, B.	McMaster	1	254	201	0.11	Wove			
75	7 June 1916	T.70	p. 140		Monroe, H.	Chicago	1	253	201	0.11	Wove			
76	7 June 1916	T.71	p. 141		Russell, B.	McMaster	1	255	203	0.06	Wove			
77	21 Aug. 1916	T.72	p. 143		Aiken, C.	Huntington	4	258	202	0.07	Laid	Vertical	26	8
78	5 Sept. 1916	T.73	p. 146		Hinkley, E.	Houghton	3	259	202	0.07	Laid	Horizontal	27	9
79	6 Sept. 1916	T.74	p. 148		Mother	Houghton	3	259	203	0.07	Laid	Horizontal	27	9
80	6 Sept. 1916	T.75	p. 151		Eliot, H.	Houghton	1	259	203	0.07	Laid	Horizontal	27	9
81	6 Sept. 1916	T.76	p. 151		Hutchinson, M.	Texas	1	249	158	0.08	Wove			
82	7 Sept. 1916	T.77	p. 152		Woods, J. H.	Williams	2	259	203	0.07	Laid	Horizontal	26	9
83	7 Sept. 1916	T.78	p. 153		Monroe, H.	Chicago	1	259	202		Laid	Horizontal	26	9
84	28 Sept. 1916			U.9	Monroe, H.	Chicago	1	249	158	0.08	Wove			
85	27 Oct. 1916			U.10	Zimmern, A.	Bodleian	1	252	202	0.08	Wove			
86	5 Nov. 1916	T.79	p. 157		Eliot, H.	Houghton	2	252	202	0.08	Wove			
87	1 Jan. 1917			U.11	Hutchinson, M.	Texas	1	228	178	0.15	Laid	Horizontal	25.5	9
88	16 Jan. 1917			U.12	Huxley, J.	Fondren	1	254	203	0.11	Wove			
89	5 Feb. 1917	T.80	p. 159		Father	Houghton	1	227	178	0.16	Laid	Horizontal	25.5	8
90	1 Mar. 1917	T.81	p. 160		Father	Houghton	2	259	203	0.07	Laid	Horizontal	27	9
91	13 Mar. 1917	T.82	p. 162		Russell, B.	McMaster	1	228	177	0.16	Laid	Horizontal	25.5	9
92	15 Mar.? 1917	T.83	p. 163		Russell, B.	McMaster	1	228	177	0.16	Laid	Horizontal	25.5	9
93	21 Mar. 1917	T.84	p. 163		Mother	Houghton	2	228	177	0.16	Laid	Horizontal	25.5	9
94	21 Mar. 1917	T.85	p. 165		Smith, C. E.	Houghton	2	228	177	0.16	Laid	Horizontal	25.6	9
95	23 Mar. 1917	T.86	p. 167		Wallas, G.	LSE	1	227	177	0.12	Wove			
96	23 Mar. 1917	T.87	p. 167		Hinkley, E.	Houghton	3	252	203	0.07	Laid	Vertical	27	8
97A	23 Mar. 1917	T.88	p. 169		Woods, J. H.	Williams	1	252	202	0.07	Laid	Vertical	27	7
97B	23 Mar. 1917	T.88	p. 169		Woods, J. H.	Williams	2	227	177	0.12	Wove			
98	23 Mar. 1917	T.89	p. 171		Eliot, H.	Houghton	1	252	203	0.07	Laid	Vertical	27	7
99	28 Mar. 1917			U.13	Hutchinson, M.	Texas	1	227	177	0.12	Wove			
100	29 Mar. 1917	T.90	p. 172		Squire, J. C.	Texas	1	227	177	0.12	Wove			
101	11 Apr. 1917	T.91	p. 174		Mother	Houghton	2	227	177	0.12	Wove			
102	18 Apr. 1917	T.92	p. 175		Father	Houghton	2	227	177	0.12	Wove			
103	13 May 1917	T.93	p. 179		Mother	Houghton	3	252	203	0.07	Laid	Vertical	27	8
104	20 May 1917	T.94	p. 180		Mother	Houghton	3	253	186	0.07	Wove			
105	28 May 1917	T.95	p. 182		Mother	Houghton	2	254	186	0.07	Wove			
106	13 June 1917	T.96	p. 183		Father	Houghton	3	253	186	0.07	Wove			
107	27 June 1917	T.97	p. 184		Mother	Houghton	1	253	186	0.07	Wove			
108	1 July 1917	T.98	p. 187		Mother	Houghton	2	253	186	0.07	Wove			
109	2 July 1917	T.99	p. 188		Hutchinson, M.	Texas	1	225	176	0.13	Wove			
110	23 July 1917	T.100	p. 189		Hinkley, E.	Houghton	2	253	202	0.07	Laid	Vertical	27	8
111	8 Aug. 1917	T.102	p. 191		Mother	Houghton	1	253	202	0.07	Laid	Vertical	27	8
112	8 Aug. 1917	T.103	p. 192		Hinkley, E.	Houghton	1	253	202	0.07	Laid	Vertical	27	7
113	2 Sept. 1917	T.104	p. 193		Mother	Houghton	2	202	126	0.12	Wove			
114	12 Sep. 1917	T.105	p. 194		Mother	Houghton	2	202	126	0.12	Wove			
115	19 Sept. 1917	T.106	p. 195		Mother	Houghton	2	202	126	0.12	Wove			
116	19 Sept. 1917	T.107	p. 196		Huxley, J.	Fondren	1	202	126	0.11	Wove			
117	19 Sept. 1917	T.108	p. 197		Hutchinson, M.	Texas	2	202	126	0.11	Wove			
118	23 Sept. 1917			U.14	Huxley, J.	Fondren	1	202	126	0.11	Wove			
119	23 Sept. 1917	T.109	p. 197		Pound, E.	Beinecke	1	202	126	0.12	Wove			
120	3 Oct. 1917	T.110	p. 198		Mother	Houghton	2	202	126	0.11	Wove			
121	14 Oct. 1917	T.111	p. 199		Mother	Houghton	2	202	126	0.12	Wove			
122	24 Oct. 1917	T.112	p. 203		Mother	Houghton	1	259	206	0.10	Wove			
123	31 Oct. 1917	T.113	p. 203		Father	Houghton	2	253	202	0.07	Laid	Vertical	27	8
124	31 Oct. 1917	T.114	p. 205		Hinkley, E.	Houghton	2	253	202	0.07	Laid	Vertical	27	7
125	31 Oct. 1917	T.115	p. 206		Pound, E.	Beinecke	1	253	202	0.07	Laid	Vertical	27	7
126	15 Nov. 1917	T.116	p. 207		Mother	Houghton	1	259	206	0.10	Wove			
127	15 Nov. 1917	T.117	p. 208		Hutchinson, M.	Texas	1	259	206	0.10	Wove			
128	22 Nov. 1917	T.118	p. 208		Father	Houghton	1	259	206	0.10	Wove			
129	[15? Dec. 1917]			U.15	Mother	Virginia	0.5	178	114	0.11	Wove			
130	22 Dec. 1917	T.120	p. 212		Mother	Houghton	2	224	175	0.16	Wove			
131	23 Dec. 1917	T.121	p. 213		Father	Houghton	1	224	175	0.16	Wove			
132	30 Dec. 1917	T.122	p. 214		Mother	Houghton	1	224	175	0.17	Wove			
133	30 Dec. 1917	T.123	p. 215		Eliot, H.	Houghton	1	224	175	0.17	Wove			
134	31 Dec. 1917	T.124	p. 216		Hinkley, E.	Houghton	1	224	175	0.17	Wove			

WATERMARK	POSITION	DIMENSIONS	COLOR	PRINTING	LINED PAPER	PC	MS	TS	SCRIPT	TYPEWR.	NOTE	NO.
			Pale orange yellow 73		43.194(24).12	X			Black ink			61
			Pale orange yellow 73		43.194(24).12	X			Pencil			62
None			White	Torbay Hotel		X			Black ink			63
None			White	Torbay Hotel		X			Black ink			64
None			White	Torbay Hotel		X			Black ink			65
None			White	Torbay Hotel		X			Black ink			66
None			Yellow white 92			X			Black ink		4.1	67
Waldorf Club [A]	Vertical	35 x 210	White			X			Black ink			68
None			White			X			Black ink			69
Waldorf Club [A]	Vertical	Incomplete	White			X			Black ink			70
Waldorf Club [A]	Vertical	Incomplete	White			X			Black ink			71
Waldorf Club [A]	Vertical	Incomplete	White			X			Black ink			72
Newton Mill	Vertical	53 x 81	Yellow white 92	18 Crawford Mansions		X			Black ink			73
None			White			X			Black ink			74
None			White			X			Black ink			75
None			White		27.215(26).13	X			Black ink			76
None			Yellow white 92					X	Black ribbon	2.12		77
None			White					X	Black ribbon	2.12		78
None			White					X	Black ribbon	2.12		79
None			White					X	Black ribbon	2.12		80
None			Lt. Green gray 154			X			Black ink			81
None			Yellow white 92					X	Black ribbon	2.12		82
None			Yellow white 92					X	Black ribbon	2.12	2.2	83
None			Lt. Green gray 154			X			Black ink			84
None			White			X			Black ink			85
None			White			X			Black ink			86
Waldorf Club [B]	Vertical	Incomplete	Lt. Green gray 154			X			Black ink			87
None			Yellow white 92			X			Black ink			88
Waldorf Club [B]	Vertical	Incomplete	Lt. Green gray 154			X			Black ink			89
None			Yellow white 92					X	Black ribbon	2.12		90
Waldorf Club [B]	Vertical	35 x 212	Lt. Green gray 154			X			Black ink			91
Waldorf Club [B]	Vertical	Incomplete	Lt. Green gray 154			X			Black ink			92
Waldorf Club [B]	Vertical	Incomplete	Lt. Green gray 154			X			Black ink		3.3	93
Waldorf Club [B]	Vertical	Incomplete	Lt. Green gray 154			X			Black ink			94
Society Bond	Vertical	20 x 84	White			X			Black ink			95
Silver Linen [A]	Horizontal	18 x 156	Yellow white 92					X	Black ribbon	2.12	3.5	96
Silver Linen [A]	Horizontal	18 x 156	Yellow white 92			X			Black ink			97A
Society Bond	Vertical	20 x 83	White			X			Black ink			97B
Silver Linen [A]	Horizontal	Incomplete	Yellow white 92					X	Black ribbon	2.12		98
Society Bond	Vertical	20 x 84	White			X			Black ink			99
Society Bond	Vertical	20 x 84	White			X			Black ink			100
Society Bond	Vertical	20 x 84	White			X			Black ink			101
Society Bond	Vertical	20 x 83	White			X			Black ink			102
Silver Linen [A]	Horizontal	Incomplete	Yellow white 92			X			Black ink		3.4	103
None			White		27.214(26).12	X			Black ink			104
None			White		27.214(26).12	X			Black ink			105
None			White		27.214(26).12	X			Black ink			106
None			White		27.214(26).12	X			Black ink			107
None			White		27.214(26).12	X			Black ink			108
None			White			X			Black ink			109
Silver Linen [A]	Horizontal	17 x 156	Yellow white 92					X	Black ribbon	2.12	3.2	110
Silver Linen [A]	Horizontal	17 x 156	Yellow white 92					X	Black ribbon	2.12		111
Silver Linen [A]	Horizontal	Incomplete	Yellow white 92					X	Black ribbon	2.12		112
Society Bond	Horizontal	Incomplete	White			X			Black ink			113
Society Bond	Horizontal	Incomplete	White			X			Black ink			114
Society Bond	Horizontal	19 x 75	White			X			Black ink			115
Society Bond	Horizontal	Incomplete	White			X			Black ink			116
Society Bond	Horizontal	Incomplete	White			X			Black ink			117
Society Bond	Horizontal	Incomplete	White			X			Black ink			118
Society Bond	Horizontal	Incomplete	White			X			Black ink			119
Society Bond	Horizontal	Incomplete	White			X			Black ink			120
Society Bond	Horizontal	Incomplete	White			X			Black ink			121
None			White	The Egoist		X			Black ink			122
Silver Linen [A]	Horizontal	17 x 156	Yellow white 92					X	Black ribbon	2.12		123
Silver Linen [A]	Horizontal	18 x 156	Yellow white 92					X	Black ribbon	2.12		124
Silver Linen [A]	Horizontal	Incomplete	Yellow white 92					X	Black ribbon	2.12		125
None			White	The Egoist		X			Black ink			126
None			White	The Egoist		X			Black ink			127
None			White	The Egoist		X			Black ink			128
None			White			X			Black ink		1.3	129
None			White			X			Black ink			130
None			White			X			Black ink			131
None			White			X			Black ink			132
None			White			X			Black ink			133
None			White			X			Black ink			134

NO.	DATE	LOTSE	PG. NO.	UNPBD.	RECIPIENT	LOCATION	LVS.	HEIGHT	WIDTH	THICK.	TEXTURE	CHAINLINES	DIST.	NO.
135	17 Jan. 1918	T.125	p. 218		Mother	Houghton	1	253	202	0.12	Wove			
136	6 Feb. 1918	T.126	p. 219		Mother	Houghton	2	253	202	0.12	Wove			
137	14 Feb. 1918	T.127	p. 220		Mother	Houghton	2	255	184	0.06	Wove			
138	4 Mar. 1918	T.128	p. 221		Mother	Houghton	2	254	204	0.09	Laid	Vertical	27	7
139	4 Mar. 1918	T.129	p. 222		Quinn, J.	NYPL	3	254	204	0.09	Laid	Vertical	27	7
140	24 Mar. 1918	T.131	p. 225		Mother	Houghton	2	255	184	0.06	Wove			
141	1 Apr. 1918	T.132	p. 226		Hinkley, E.	Houghton	4	254	204	0.09	Laid	Vertical	27	7
142	13 Apr. 1918	T.133	p. 229		Russell, B.	McMaster	1	254	202	0.12	Wove			
143	28 Apr. 1918	T.134	p. 229		Mother	Houghton	2	254	202	0.12	Wove			
144	1 May 1918			U.16	Hutchinson, M.	Texas	1	164	123	0.21	Wove			
145	10 May 1918	T.135	p. 231		Mother	Houghton	1	254	202	0.12	Wove			
146	22 May 1918	T.136	p. 232		Mother	Houghton	2	254	202	0.12	Wove			
147	2 June 1918	T.137	p. 232		Mother	Houghton	2	162	125	0.10	Wove			
148	9 June 1918	T.138	p. 233		Mother	Houghton	3	162	125	0.10	Wove			
149	23 June 1918	T.139	p. 234		Mother	Houghton	2	259	202	0.05	Wove			
150	30 June 1918	T.140	p. 236		Thayer, S.	Beinecke	2	259	202	0.05	Wove			
151	1 July 1918			U.17	Hutchinson, M.	Texas	1	161	123	0.23	Wove			
152	6 July 1918			U.18	Monroe, H.	Chicago	1	253	203		Wove			
153	7 July 1918	T.141			Mother	Houghton	1	253	203	0.08	Wove			
154	28 July 1918	T.142	p. 238		Mother	Houghton	2	253	203	0.08	Wove			
155	4 Aug. 1918			U.19	Hutchinson, M.	Texas	1	253	203	0.07	Wove			
156	5 Aug. 1918	T.143	p. 240		Lewis, W.	Cornell	1	224	151	0.11	Wove			
157	11 Aug. 1918	T.144	p. 240		Lewis, W.	Cornell	1	259	185	0.18	Wove			
158	15 Aug. 1918			U.20	Hutchinson, M.	Texas	1	259	185	0.17	Wove			
159	[19 Aug. 1918]			U.21	Lewis, W.	Cornell	1	176	122	0.12	Wove			
160	23 Aug. 1918	T.145	p. 240		Dulac, E.	Virginia	1	163	123	0.08	Wove			
161	25 Aug. 1918	T.146	p. 241		Eliot, H.	Houghton	2	259	205	0.09	Wove			
162	25 Aug. 1918			U.22	Hutchinson, J.	Texas	2	163	123	0.08	Wove			
163	25 Aug. 1918			U.23	Hutchinson, M.	Texas	2	163	123	0.08	Wove			
164	4 Sept. 1918	T.147			Rodker, J.	Tulsa	1	202	126	0.12	Wove			
165	8 Sept. 1918	T.149	p. 243		Father	Houghton	2	202	126	0.12	Wove			
166	8 Sept. 1918	T.150	p. 244		Quinn, J.	NYPL	3	202	126	0.12	Wove			
167	27 Oct. 1918			U.24	Eliot, H.	Houghton	1	175	112	0.11	Wove			
168	4 Nov. 1918	T.151	p. 246		Father	Houghton	3	254	205	0.09	Laid	Vertical	27	7
169	4 Nov. 1918	T.152	p. 249		Eliot, H.	Houghton	2	259	166	0.10	Laid	Vertical	29	6
170	7 Nov. 1918	T.153	p. 250		Gardner, I.	Gardner	2	251	207	0.09	Laid	Vertical	26	7
171	7 Nov. 1918	T.154	p. 252		Rodker, J.	Virginia	1	175	112	0.11	Wove			
172	7 Nov. 1918	T.155	p. 252		Goldring, D.	Virginia	1	259	166	0.09	Laid	Vertical	29	6
173	7 Nov. 1918			U.25	Monroe, H.	Chicago	1	259	166	0.09	Laid	Vertical	29	6
174	9 Nov. 1918			U.26	Hutchinson, M.	Texas	2	259	166	0.09	Laid	Vertical	29	6
175	10 Nov. 1918			U.27	Hutchinson, J.	Texas	1	259	166	0.09	Laid	Vertical	29	5
176	12 Nov. 1918			U.28	Woolf, V.	Berg	1	175	112	0.12	Wove			
177	13 Nov. 1918	T.157	p. 254		Quinn, J.	NYPL	2	254	204	0.09	Laid	Vertical	27	7
178	13 Nov. 1918	T.158	p. 255		Mother	Houghton	1	254	204	0.10	Laid	Vertical	27	7
179	20 Nov. 1918	T.159	p. 256		Woods, J. H.	Williams	1	254	204	0.09	Laid	Vertical	27	8
180	2 Dec. 1918			U.29	Rodker, J.	Virginia	1	114	88	0.39	Wove			
181	8 Dec. 1918	T.160	p. 259		Mother	Houghton	2	175	112	0.10	Wove			
182	9 Dec. 1918	T.161	p. 260		Rodker, J.	Gallup	1	251	205	0.09	Wove			
183	14 Dec. 1918	T.162	p. 260		Bennett, A.	Gallup	1	175	112	0.12	Wove			
184	14 Dec. 1918			U.30	Wallas, G.	LSE	1	175	112	0.12	Wove			
185	22 Dec. 1918	T.163	p. 262		Mother	Houghton	3	175	112	0.11	Wove			
186	29 Dec. 1918	T.164	p. 263		Mother	Houghton	4	175	112	0.11	Wove			
187	6 Jan. 1919	T.165	p. 266		Quinn, J.	NYPL	3	175	112	0.11	Wove			
188	12 Jan. 1919	T.166	p. 267		Mother	Houghton	1	228	177	0.12	Wove			
189	12 Jan. 1919	T.167	p. 267		Eliot, H.	Houghton	1	227	177	0.12	Wove			
190	19 Jan. 1919	T.168	p. 268		Mother	Houghton	1.5	228	177	0.13	Wove			
191	22 Jan. 1919			U.31	Hutchinson, M.	Texas	1	227	177	0.12	Wove			
192	26 Jan. 1919	T.169	p. 269		Quinn, J.	NYPL	1	226	177	0.13	Wove			
193	26 Jan. 1919	T.170	p. 269		Mother	Houghton	1	226	176	0.13	Wove			
194	29 Jan. 1919			U.32	Woolf, V.	Berg	0.5	113	176	0.13	Wove			
195	3 Feb. 1919	T.171	p. 270		Russell, B.	Berg	1	224	176	0.13	Wove			
196	14 Feb. 1919	T.172	p. 271		Russell, B.	McMaster	2	176	112	0.11	Wove			
197	27 Feb. 1919	T.173	p. 272		Eliot, H.	Houghton	2	254	204	0.10	Laid	Vertical	27	8
198	27 Feb. [1919]	T.174	p. 273		Mother	Houghton	2	254	204	0.10	Laid	Vertical	27	8
199	4 Mar. 1919	T.175	p. 275		Hutchinson, M.	Texas	1	175	111	0.14	Wove			
200	4 Mar. 1919	T.176	p. 275		Jepson, E.	Gallup	1	175	111	0.14	Wove			
201	12 Mar. 1919	T.177	p. 276		Mother	Houghton	3	175	111	0.14	Wove			
202	12 Mar. 1919	T.178	p. 277		Jepson, E.	Gallup	1	175	110	0.14	Wove			
203	26 Mar. 1919	T.179	p. 278		Woolf, V.	Berg	1	175	111	0.14	Wove			
204	26 Mar. 1919	T.180	p. 278		Read, H.	Victoria	1	175	111	0.14	Wove			
205	26 Mar. 1919	T.181	p. 279		Russell, B.	McMaster	1	175	111	0.13	Wove			
206	29 Mar. 1919	T.182	p. 279		Mother	Houghton	6	174	111	0.13	Wove			
207	1 Apr. 1919			U.33	Hutchinson, J.	Texas	1	174	111	0.14	Wove			
208	[April? 1919?]	T.183	p. 281		Patmore, B.	Gallup	2	259	206	0.08	Wove			
209A	6 Apr. 1919	T.184	p. 282		Eliot, H.	Houghton	1	253	208	0.11	Wove			

WATERMARK	POSITION	DIMENSIONS	COLOR	PRINTING	LINED PAPER	PC	MS	TS	SCRIPT	TYPEWR.	NOTE	NO.
None			White				X		Black ink			135
None			White				X		Black ink			136
None			White				X		Pencil			137
Silver Linen	Horizontal	17 x 155	Yellow white 92					X	Black ribbon	2.12		138
Silver Linen	Horizontal	17 x 155	Yellow white 92					X	Black ribbon	2.12		139
None			White				X		Black ink			140
Silver Linen	Horizontal	27 x 155	Yellow white 92					X	Black ribbon	2.12		141
None			White				X		Black ink			142
None			White				X		Black ink			143
None			Yellow white 92	Letter * Card		X	X		Balck ink			144
None			White				X		Black ink			145
None			White				X		Black ink			146
Emissary bond	Vertical	Incomplete	White				X		Black ink			147
Emissary bond	Vertical	Incomplete	White				X		Black ink			148
None			White					X	Black ribbon	2.12		149
None			White					X	Black ribbon	2.12		150
None			Yellow white 92	Letter * Card		X	X		Black ink			151
None			White				X		Black ink		2.2	152
None			White				X		Black ink			153
None			White				X		Black ink			154
None			White				X		Black ink			155
Hieratica Bond [B]	Vertical	Incomplete	White				X		Black ink			156
None			Gray green yellow 105				X		Black ink			157
None			Gray green yellow 105				X		Black ink			158
None			White				X		Black ink			159
Emissary bond	Vertical	Incomplete	White				X		Black ink			160
None			White	The Egoist			X		Black ink			161
Emissary bond	Vertical	Incomplete	White				X		Black ink			162
Emissary bond	Vertical	Incomplete	White				X		Black ink			163
Society Bond	Horizontal	20 x 83	White				X		Black ink			164
Society Bond	Horizontal	Incomplete	White				X		Black ink			165
Society Bond	Horizontal	Incomplete	White				X		Black ink			166
None			White				X		Black ink		6.1	167
Silver Linen [B]	Horizontal	18 x 155	Yellow white 92					X	Black ribbon	2.12		168
None			Yellow white 92		44.198(24).17		X		Pencil			169
Silver Linen [B]	Horizontal	18 x 155	Yellow white 92					X	Black ribbon	2.12		170
None			White				X		Black ink			171
None			Yellow white 92		44.198(24).17		X		Black ink			172
None			Yellow white 92		44.198(24).17		X		Black ink			173
None			Yellow white 92		44.198(24).17		X		Black ink		3.1	174
None			Yellow white 92		44.198(24).17		X		Black ink			175
None			White				X		Black ink			176
Silver Linen [B]	Horizontal	18 x 155	Yellow white 92					X	Black ribbon	2.12		177
Silver Linen [B]	Horizontal	18 x 155	Yellow white 92					X	Black ribbon	2.12		178
Silver Linen [B]	Horizontal	18 x 155	Yellow white 92					X	Black ribbon	2.12		179
None			Yellow white 92	From T. S. Eliot		X	X		Black ink			180
Society Bond	Horizontal	Incomplete	White				X		Black ink			181
None			White	The Egoist			X		Black ink		6.2	182
None			White				X		Black ink			183
None			White				X		Black ink			184
Society Bond	Horizontal	Incomplete	White				X		Black ink			185
Society Bond	Horizontal	20 x 84	White				X		Black ink			186
Society Bond	Horizontal	20 x 84	White				X		Black ink			187
Society Bond	Vertical	20 x 83	White	[Black border - 2mm]			X		Black ink			188
Society Bond	Vertical	20 x 83	White	[Black border - 2mm]			X		Black ink			189
Society Bond	Vertical	20 x 83	White	[Black border - 2mm]			X		Black ink			190
Society Bond	Vertical	20 x 83	White	[Black border - 2mm]			X		Black ink			191
Society Bond	Vertical	20 x 82	White	[Black border - 2mm]			X		Black ink			192
Society Bond	Vertical	20 x 83	White	[Black border - 2mm]			X		Black ink			193
Society Bond	Vertical	Incomplete	White	[Black border - 2mm]			X		Black ink		1.4	194
Society Bond	Vertical	20 x 83	White	[Black border - 2mm]			X		Black ink			195
None			White				X		Black ink			196
Silver Linen [B]	Horizontal	18 x 155	Yellow white 92					X	Black ribbon	2.12		197
Silver Linen [B]	Horizontal	18 x 155	Yellow white 92					X	Black ribbon	2.12		198
Society Bond	Horizontal	23 x 83	White				X		Black ink			199
Society Bond	Horizontal	23 x 83	White				X		Black ink			200
Society Bond	Horizontal	23 x 83	White				X		Black ink			201
Society Bond	Horizontal	23 x 83	White				X		Black ink			202
Society Bond	Horizontal	23 x 83	White				X		Black ink			203
Society Bond	Horizontal	23 x 83	White				X		Black ink			204
Society Bond	Horizontal	23 x 83	White				X		Black ink			205
Society Bond	Horizontal	23 x 83	White				X		Black ink			206
Society Bond	Horizontal	23 x 83	White				X		Black ink			207
None			White	The Egoist			X		Black ink			208
W. T. & Co.	Vertical	66 x 106	White	The Manchester			X		Black ink			209A

NO.	DATE	LOTSE	PG. NO.	UNPBD.	RECIPIENT	LOCATION	LVS.	HEIGHT	WIDTH	THICK.	TEXTURE	CHAINLINES	DIST.	NO.
209B	6 Apr. 1919	T.184	p. 282		Eliot, H.	Houghton	1	260	202	0.11	Wove			
209C	6 Apr. 1919	T.184	p. 282		Eliot, H.	Houghton	1	163	211	0.11	Laid	Vertical	28	8
210	12 Apr. 1919	T.185	p. 284		Woolf, V.	Berg	1	223	177	0.13	Wove			
211	21 Apr. 1919	T.186	p. 284		Woods, J. H.	Williams	2	228	170	0.12	Laid	Vertical	25.5	7
212	23 Apr. 1919	T.187	p. 286		Mother	Houghton	3	228	170	0.12	Laid	Vertical	25.5	6
213	[1 May 1919]			U.34	Hutchinson, M.	Texas	1	175	113	0.14	Wove			
214	4 May 1919	T.188	p. 289		Mother	Houghton	3	175	113	0.14	Wove			
215	4 May 1919	T.189	p. 290		Patmore, B.	Gallup	2	175	113	0.14	Wove			
216	[7 May 1919]	T.190	p. 291		Patmore, B.	Gallup	1	175	113	0.14	Wove			
217	[12 May 1919]	T.191	p. 292		Patmore, B.	Gallup	1	263	202	0.07	Wove			
218	[14 May 1919]	T.192	p. 293		Patmore, B.	Gallup	2	175	113	0.13	Wove			
219	16 May 1919			U.35	Hutchinson, M.	Texas	1	228	171	0.12	Wove			
220	[16 May 1919]	T.193	p. 293		Patmore, B.	Gallup	1	175	113	0.14	Wove			
221	17 May 1919	T.194	p. 294		Rodker, J.	Virginia	1	263	203	0.07	Wove			
222	19 May 1919	T.195	p. 295		Strachey, L.	British Libr.	1	175	113	0.14	Wove			
223	[21 May 1919]			U.36	Rodker, J.	Virginia	1	175	113	0.14	Wove			
224	[21 May 1919]			U.37	Strachey, L.	British Libr.	1	175	113	0.14	Wove			
225	25 May 1919	T.196	p. 295		Mother	Houghton	2	175	113	0.14	Wove			
226	25 May 1919	T.197	p. 296		Quinn, J.	NYPL	2	175	113	0.14	Wove			
227	[26 May 1919]		p. 291	U.38	Hutchinson, M.	Texas	1	175	113	0.14	Wove			
228	[27? May? 1919?]	T.198	p. 297		Patmore, B.	Gallup	1	259	165	0.10	Laid	Vertical	29	6
229	1 June 1919	T.199	p. 298		Hutchinson, M.	Texas	2	175	113	0.14	Wove			
230	1 June 1919	T.201	p. 299		Rodker, J.	Virginia	2	175	113	0.13	Wove			
231	5 June 1919	T.202	p. 300		Weaver, H.	British Libr.	1	257	205	0.15	Wove			
232	[10 June 1919]			U.39	Hutchinson, M.	Texas	1	164	123	0.19	Wove			
233	[15? June 1919]	T.203	p. 302		Hutchinson, M.	Texas	1	259	206	0.09	Wove			
234	15 June 1919	T.204	p. 303		Patmore, B.	Gallup	1	259	206	0.09	Wove			
235	17 June 1919	T.205	p. 304		Hinkley, E.	Houghton	3	259	206	0.09	Wove			
236	[23 June 1919]	T.206	p. 306		Morrell, O.	Texas	2	259	206	0.08	Wove			
237	29 June 1919	T.207	p. 308		Mother	Houghton	2	259	206	0.09	Wove			
238	[1 July 1919]			U.40	Hutchinson, M.	Texas	1	175	113	0.14	Wove			
239	2 July 1919	T.208	p. 309		Eliot, H.	Houghton	5	176	113	0.11	Wove			
240	[9? July? 1919]	T.209	p. 311		Hutchinson, M.	Texas	1	263	203	0.07	Wove			
241	9 July 1919	T.210	p. 312		Rodker, J.	Virginia	1	263	203	0.07	Wove			
242	9 July 1919	T.211	p. 312		Quinn, J.	NYPL	2	263	202	0.07	Wove			
243	10 July 1919	T.212	p. 315		Mother	Houghton	2	263	203	0.07	Wove			
244	[11? July 1919]	T.213	p. 316		Hutchinson, M.	Texas	2	263	203	0.07	Wove			
245	11 July 1919			U.41	Jepson, E.	Gallup	1	176	113	0.11	Wove			
246	16 July 1919	T.214	p. 319		Schiff, S.	British Libr.	2	176	113	0.11	Wove			
247	21 July 1919	T.215	p. 322		Schiff, V.	British Libr.	2	176	113	0.11	Wove			
248	25 July 1919	T.216	p. 324		Schiff, S.	British Libr.	1	176	113	0.11	Wove			
249	29 July 1919	T.217	p. 325		Murry, J. M.	Northwest.	1	176	113	0.11	Wove			
250	6 Aug. 1919	T.218	p. 325		Monro, H.	Texas	1	178	114	0.10	Wove			
251	6 Aug. 1919	T.219	p. 326		Hutchinson, M.	Texas	2	178	113	0.11	Wove			
252	6 Aug. 1919	T.220	p. 327		Strachey, L.	British Libr.	2	178	113	0.11	Wove			
253	PM 7 Aug. 1919			U.42	Hutchinson, M.	Texas	1							
254	3 Sept. 1919	T.222	p. 328		Mother	Houghton	4	178	114	0.10	Wove			
255	[4 Sept. 1919]			U.43	Hutchinson, M.	Texas	1	228	177	0.10	Wove			
256	9 Sept. 1919	T.223	p. 329		Mother	Houghton	1	228	178	0.10	Wove			
257	10 Sept. 1919			U.44	Squire, J. C.	UCLA	1	229	178	0.11	Wove			
258	[12? Sept. 1919]	T.224	p. 330		Pound, E.	Beinecke	1	264	203	0.06	Wove			
259	14 Sept. 1919	T.225	p. 330		Eliot, H.	Houghton	2	229	178	0.10	Wove			
260	[14 Sept. 1919]	T.226	p. 331		Schiff, S.	British Libr.	1	229	178	0.11	Wove			
261	22 Sept. 1919	T.227	p. 332		Jepson, E.	Gallup	1	229	178	0.10	Wove			
262	24 Sept. 1919	T.228	p. 333		Schiff, S.	British Libr.	1	229	178	0.10	Wove			
263	28 Sept. 1919	T.229	p. 335		Quinn, J.	NYPL	1	263	203	0.08	Wove			
264	2 Oct. 1919	T.230	p. 336		Mother	Houghton	2	229	178	0.11	Wove			
265	14 Oct. 1919	T.232	p. 339		Mother	Houghton	1	229	178	0.11	Wove			
266	17 Oct. 1919	T.233	p. 340		Schiff, S.	British Libr.	1	229	178	0.11	Wove			
267	31 Oct. 1919	T.236	p. 343		Jepson, E.	Gallup	1	227	177	0.11	Wove			
268	[3 Nov. 1919]			U.45	Jepson, E.	Gallup	1	227	177	0.11	Wove			
269	5 Nov. 1919	T.237	p. 343		Quinn, J.	NYPL	2	265	202	0.06	Laid	Vertical	25	8
270	[Nov.? 1919]	T.239	p. 345		Murry, J. M.	Northwest.	1	265	202	0.05	Laid	Vertical	25	8
271	10 Nov. 1919			U.46	Hutchinson, M.	Texas	1	140	85	0.37	Wove			
272	10 Nov. 1919	T.240	p. 345		Mother	Houghton	2	227	177	0.11	Wove			
273	18 Nov. 1919	T.241	p. 347		Mother	Houghton	1	227	177	0.11	Wove			
274	23 Nov. 1919	T.242	p. 347		Mother	Houghton	1	227	177	0.11	Wove			
275	24 Nov. 1919			U.47	Morrell, O.	Texas	1	227	177	0.11	Wove			
276	[Late Nov.? 1919]	T.243	p. 348		Rodker, J.	Virginia	1	227	177	0.12	Wove			
277	1 Dec. 1919	T.244	p. 348		Hutchinson, M.	Texas	1	228	175	0.12	Wove			
278	2 Dec. 1919	T.245	p. 349		Mother	Houghton	1	228	178	0.11	Wove			
279	2 Dec. 1919	T.246	p. 350		Pound, E.	Lilly	1	140	85	0.34	Wove			
280	13 Dec. 1919			U.48	Jepson, E.	Gallup	1	228	178	0.11	Wove			
281	[16 Dec. 1919]	T.247	p. 350		Monro, H.	Gallup	1	228	178	0.11	Wove			
282	[17 Dec. 1919]			U.49	Jepson, E.	Gallup	1	228	178	0.11	Wove			

WATERMARK	POSITION	DIMENSIONS	COLOR	PRINTING	LINED PAPER	PC	MS	TS	SCRIPT	TYPEWR.	NOTE	NO.
Excelsior Super	Horizontal	65 x 139	White	The New Statesman		X			Black ink			209B
Cyclostyle	Horizontal	Incomplete	White			X			Black ink		4.2	209C
Society Bond	Vertical	23 x 83	White	[Black border - 2mm]		X			Black ink			210
Waldorf Club	Horizontal	Incomplete	White			X			Black ink			211
Waldorf Club	Horizontal	Incomplete	White			X			Black ink		3.2	212
Society Bond	Horizontal	23 x 83	White			X			Black ink			213
Society Bond	Horizontal	23 x 83	White			X			Black ink			214
Society Bond	Horizontal	23 x 83	White			X			Black ink			215
Society Bond	Horizontal	23 x 83	White			X			Black ink			216
None			White					X	Red ribbon	2.12	5.2	217
Society Bond	Horizontal	23 x 83	White			X			Pencil			218
Waldorf Club	Horizontal	Incomplete	White			X			Black ink			219
Society Bond	Horizontal	23 x 83	White			X			Pencil			220
None			White					X	Black ribbon 2.12			221
Society Bond	Horizontal	23 x 83	White			X			Black ink			222
Society Bond	Horizontal	23 x 83	White			X			Black ink			223
Society Bond	Horizontal	23 x 83	White			X			Black ink			224
Society Bond	Horizontal	23 x 83	White			X			Black ink			225
Society Bond	Horizontal	23 x 83	White			X			Black ink			226
Society Bond	Horizontal	23 x 83	White			X			Black ink			227
None			Light gray 264		44.198(24).17	X			Black ink			228
Society Bond	Horizontal	23 x 83	White			X			Balck ink			229
Society Bond	Horizontal	23 x 83	White			X			Black ink			230
None			White	The Egoist		X			Black ink			231
None			Yellow white 92	Letter * Card		X	X		Pencil			232
None			White	The Egoist		X			Black ink			233
None			White	The Egoist		X			Black ink			234
None			White	The Egoist		X			Black ink			235
None			White	The Egoist		X			Black ink			236
None			White	The Egoist		X			Black ink			237
Society Bond	Horizontal	23 x 83	White			X			Black ink			238
None			White			X			Black ink			239
None			White			X			Black ink			240
None			White			X			Black ink			241
None			White					X	Black ribbon 2.12			242
None			White			X			Black ink			243
None			White			X			Black ink			244
None			White			X			Black ink			245
None			White			X			Black ink			246
None			White			X			Black ink			247
None			White			X			Black ink			248
None			White			X			Black ink			249
Hieratica Bond [C]	Horizontal	45 x 48	White			X			Black ink			250
None			White			X			Black ink			251
None			White			X			Black ink			252
				[Telegram]								253
Hieratica Bond [C]	Horizontal	45 x 48	White			X			Black ink			254
Basildon Bond	Vertical	14 x 133	Gray yellow 90			X			Black ink			255
Basildon Bond	Vertical	14 x 133	Gray yellow 90			X			Black ink			256
Basildon Bond	Vertical	Incomplete	Gray yellow 90									257
None			White			X			Pencil			258
Basildon Bond	Vertical	14 x 133	Gray yellow 90			X			Black ink			259
Basildon Bond	Vertical	14 x 133	Gray yellow 90			X			Black ink			260
Basildon Bond	Vertical	14 x 133	Gray yellow 90			X			Black ink			261
Basildon Bond	Vertical	14 x 133	Gray yellow 90			X			Black ink			262
None			White					X	Black ribbon 2.12			263
Basildon Bond	Vertical	14 x 133	Gray yellow 90			X			Black ink			264
Basildon Bond	Vertical	14 x 133	Gray yellow 90			X			Black ink			265
Basildon Bond	Vertical	14 x 133	Gray yellow 90			X			Black ink			266
Basildon Bond	Horizontal	Incomplete	Gray yellow 90			X			Black ink			267
Basildon Bond	Horizontal	Incomplete	Gray yellow 90			X			Black ink			268
None			White					X	Black ribbon 2.12		3.2	269
None			White					X	Black ribbon 2.12			270
None			White	Post Card		X	X		Black ink			271
Basildon Bond	Horizontal	Incomplete	Gray yellow 90			X			Black ink			272
Basildon Bond	Horizontal	Incomplete	Gray yellow 90			X			Black ink			273
Basildon Bond	Horizontal	Incomplete	Gray yellow 90			X			Black ink			274
Basildon Bond	Horizontal	Incomplete	Gray yellow 90			X			Black ink			275
Basildon Bond	Horizontal	Incomplete	Gray yellow 90			X			Black ink			276
* Bond	Vertical	27 x 73	White	18 Crawford M.		X			Black ink			277
Basildon Bond	Horizontal	Incomplete	Gray yellow 90			X			Black ink		4.2	278
None			Yellow white 92			X	X		Black ink			279
Basildon Bond	Horizontal	130 x 14	Gray yellow 90			X			Black ink			280
Basildon Bond	Horizontal	130 x 14	Gray yellow 90			X			Black ink			281
Basildon Bond	Horizontal	130 x 14	Gray yellow 90			X			Black ink			282

NO.	DATE	LOTSE	PG. NO.	UNPBD.	RECIPIENT	LOCATION	LVS.	HEIGHT	WIDTH	THICK.	TEXTURE	CHAINLINES	DIST.	NO.
283	PM 18 Dec. 1919	T.248	p. 350		Mother	Houghton	2	228	178	0.11	Wove			
284	6 Jan. 1920	T.249	p. 352		Eliot, H.	Houghton	1	228	178	0.11	Wove			
285	6 Jan. 1920	T.250	p. 352		Mother	Houghton	3	228	178	0.11	Wove			
286	7 Jan. 1920			U.50	Knopf, A.	Texas	1	228	178	0.11	Wove			
287	7 Jan. 1920			U.51	Hutchinson, M.	Texas	1	228	175	0.12	Wove			
288	11 Jan. 1920	T.251	p. 354		Mother	Houghton	1	228	175	0.12	Wove			
289	12 Jan. 1920	T.252	p. 355		Schiff, S.	British Libr.	3	225	175	0.13	Wove			
290	[14 Jan. 1920]	T.253	p. 357		Hutchinson, M.	Texas	1	225	175	0.12	Wove			
291	[14? Jan. 1920]			U.52	Morrell, O.	Texas	1	228	175	0.12	Wove			
292	[18? Jan. 1920]			U.53	Hutchinson, M.	Texas	1	225	175	0.12	Wove			
293	20 Jan. 1920			U.54	Rodker, J.	Gallup	1	265	201	0.05	Laid	Vertical	25	8
294	25 Jan. 1920	T.254	p. 357		Quinn, J.	NYPL	3	225	175	0.13	Wove			
295	26 Jan. 1920	T.255	p. 359		Mother	Houghton	2	225	175	0.12	Wove			
296	1 Feb. 1920	T.256	p. 360		Rodker, J.	Virginia	1	225	175	0.13	Wove			
297	6 Feb. 1920	T.257	p. 361		Rodker, J.	Virginia	1	201	166	0.12	Wove			
298	14 Feb. 1920	T.258	p. 361		Thayer, S.	Beinecke	3	265	202	0.05	Laid	Vertical	25.5	8
299	15 Feb. 1920	T.259	p. 363		Eliot, H.	Houghton	3	265	202	0.05	Laid	Vertical	25.5	8
300	[15 Feb. 1920]			U.55	Morrell, O.	Texas	1	225	175	0.12	Wove			
301	15 Feb. 1920	T.260	p. 365		Mother	Houghton	2	225	175	0.12	Wove			
302	17 Feb. 1920	T.261	p. 367		Strachey, L.	British Libr.	1	225	175	0.12	Wove			
303	21 Feb. 1920	T.262	p. 367		Hutchinson, M.	Texas	1	225	175	0.12	Wove			
304	21 Feb. 1920			U.56	Monro, H.	Gallup	1	265	202	0.05	Laid	Vertical	25.5	8
305	22 Feb. 1920	T.263	p. 368		Mother	Houghton	2	265	202	0.06	Laid	Vertical	25.5	8
306	[5? Mar. 1920]	T.265	p. 370		Monro, H.	Gallup	1	228	177	0.13	Wove			
307	16 Mar. 1920	T.266	p. 371		Mother	Houghton	2	265	202	0.06	Laid	Vertical	25.5	8
308	[19? Mar. 1920]	T.267	p. 373		Lewis, W.	Cornell	1	229	178	0.11	Wove			
309	[21 Mar. 1920]	T.268	p. 373		Morrell, O.	Texas	4	255	204	0.06	Wove			
310	24 Mar. 1920	T.269	p. 375		Schiff, S.	British Libr.	2	229	177	0.10	Wove			
311	[25 Mar. 1920]			U.57	Hutchinson, M.	Texas	1	229	177	0.10	Wove			
312	26 Mar. 1920	T.270	p. 376		Thayer, S.	Beinecke	1	265	202	0.05	Laid	Vertical	25.5	8
313	26 Mar. 1920	T.271			Quinn, J.	Beinecke	2	228	277	0.10	Wove			
314	PM 4 Apr. 1920			U.58	Hutchinson, M.	Texas	1	137	90	0.24	Wove			
315	10 Apr. 1920	T.272	p. 379		Morrell, O.	Texas	1	229	177	0.10	Wove			
316	[12 Apr. 1920]			U.59	Hutchinson, M.	Texas	1	229	177	0.10	Wove			
317	[15 Apr. 1920]			U.60	Hutchinson, M.	Texas	1	178	161	0.25	Wove			
318	19 Apr. 1920	T.273	p. 379		Shorter, C.	Gallup	1	227	177	0.10	Wove			
319	[19? Apr.? 1920]	T.274	p. 380		Murry, J. M.	Northwest.	1	228	177	0.11	Wove			
320	[25? Apr. 1920]	T.276	p. 381		Murry, J. M.	Northwest.	1	228	177	0.10	Wove			
321	10 May 1920	T.277	p. 382		Quinn, J.	NYPL	1	265	202	0.06	Laid	Vertical	25.5	8
322	[13 May 1920]			U.61	Monro, H.	Gallup	1	227	177	0.10	Wove			
323	16 May 1920	T.278	p. 383		Rodker, J.	Tulsa	1	227	177	0.10	Wove			
324	30 May 1920	T.279	p. 383		Pound, E.	Beinecke	1	228	178	0.10	Wove			
325	[June? 1920]	T.280	p. 385		Pound, E.	Beinecke	1	265	202	0.05	Laid	Vertical	25.5	8
326	PM 6 June 1920			U.62	Hutchinson, M.	Texas	1	140	85	0.34	Wove			
327	9 June 1920			U.63	Aiken, C.	Huntington	1	113	89	0.27	Wove			
328	[10 June 1920]			U.64	Aiken, C.	Huntington	1	228	177	0.10	Wove			
329	20 June 1920	T.281	p. 386		Read, H.	Victoria	1	228	177	0.10	Wove			
330	1 July 1920	T.283	p. 388		Monro, H.	Gallup	1	227	176	0.10	Wove			
331	3 July 1920	T.284	p. 388		Pound, E.	Beinecke	2	265	202	0.06	Laid	Vertical	25.5	8
332	3 July 1920	T.285	p. 389		Mother	Houghton	4	265	202	0.06	Laid	Vertical	25.5	8
333	PM 13 July 1920	T.286	p. 392		Pound, E.	Beinecke	1	116	89	0.26	Wove			
334	14 July 1920	T.287	p. 392		Strachey, L.	British Libr.	1	227	175	0.11	Wove			
335	PM 20 July 1920			U.65	Aiken, C.	Huntington	1	114	89	0.27	Wove			
336	27 July 1920	T.288	p. 393		Mother	Houghton	1	228	175	0.11	Wove			
337	[28 July 1920]	T.289	p. 394		Lewis, W.	Cornell	2	228	177	0.11	Wove			
338	[4 Aug. 1920]	T.290	p. 394		Schiff, S.	British Libr.	1	228	177	0.11	Wove			
339	[4 Aug. 1920]	T.291	p. 395		Aiken, C.	Huntington	1	114	89	0.29	Wove			
340	9 Aug. 1920	T.293	p. 397		Brooks, V. W.	Gallup	1	227	175	0.11	Wove			
341	9 Aug. 1920	T.294	p. 399		Mother	Houghton	2	227	175	0.11	Wove			
342	[9? Aug. 1920]	T.295	p. 400		Pound, E.	Beinecke	1	227	175	0.11	Wove			
343	10 Aug. 1920	T.296	p. 401		Thayer, S.	Beinecke	1	227	175	0.11	Wove			
344	11 Aug. 1920	T.297	p. 402		Joyce, J.	Buffalo	1	223	171	0.08	Wove			
345	[14 Aug. 1920]			U.66	Jepson, E.	Gallup	1	222	171	0.08	Wove			
346	22 Aug. 1920	T.298	p. 402		Schiff, S.	British Libr.	1	268	211		Wove			
347	PM 26 Aug. 1920	T.300	p. 404		Pound, E.	Beinecke	1	140	92	0.23	Wove			
348	[27 Aug. 1920]			U.67	Lewis, W.	Cornell	1	175	134	0.09	Wove			
349A	31 Aug. 1920	T.301	p. 404		Schiff, S.	British Libr.	1	222	171		Wove			
349B	31 Aug. 1920	T.301	p. 404		Schiff, S.	British Libr.	1	268	211	0.22	Wove			
350	[5 Sept. 1920]			U.68	Schiff, S.	British Libr.	1	222	171	0.09	Wove			
351	[10? Sept. 1920]	T.302	p. 405		Schiff, S.	British Libr.	1	222	171	0.11	Wove			
352	13 Sept. 1920	T.303	p. 406		Eliot, H.	Houghton	2	263	201	0.07	Laid	Vertical	26	7
353	20 Sept. 1920	T.304	p. 408		Mother	Houghton	1	263	201	0.07	Laid	Vertical	26	7
354	[22 Sept. 1920]	T.305	p. 409		Hutchinson, M.	Texas	1	227	174	0.12	Wove			
355	23 Sept. 1920	T.306	p. 409		Fletcher, J. G.	Arkansas	1	227	174	0.12	Wove			
356	23 Sept. 1920			U.69	Torrence, R.	Princeton	1	227	174	0.12	Wove			

WATERMARK	POSITION	DIMENSIONS	COLOR	PRINTING	LINED PAPER	PC	MS	TS	SCRIPT	TYPEWR.	NOTE	NO.
Basildon Bond	Horizontal	Incomplete	Gray yellow 90				X		Black ink		4.2	283
Basildon Bond	Horizontal	130 x 14	Gray yellow 90				X		Black ink			284
Basildon Bond	Horizontal	Incomplete	Gray yellow 90				X		Black ink			285
Basildon Bond	Horizontal	130 x 14	Gray yellow 90				X		Black ink			286
* Bond	Vertical	27 x 73	White				X		Black ink			287
* Bond	Vertical	27 x 73	White				X		Black ink			288
None			Yellow white 92	18 Crawford M.			X		Black ink			289
None			Yellow white 92				X		Black ink			290
* Bond	Vertical	27 x 73	White				X		Black ink			291
None			Yellow white 92				X		Pencil			292
None			White					X	Black ribbon	2.12		293
None			Yellow white 92				X		Black ink			294
None			Yellow white 92				X		Black ink			295
None			Yellow white 92				X		Black ink			296
None			Yellow white 92				X		Black ink			297
None			White					X	Black ribbon	2.12		298
None			White					X	Black ribbon	2.12		299
None			Yellow white 92				X		Black ink			300
None			Yellow white 92				X		Black ink			301
None			Yellow white 92				X		Black ink			302
None			Yellow white 92				X		Black ink			303
None			White					X	Black ribbon	2.12		304
None			White					X	Black ribbon	2.12		305
* Bond	Vertical	27 x 73	White	18 Crawford M.			X		Black ink			306
None			White					X	Black ribbon	2.12		307
Basildon Bond	Vertical	14 x 129	White				X		Black ink			308
None			Yellow white 92		24.216(26).15		X		Pencil			309
Basildon Bond	Vertical	14 x 129	White				X		Black ink			310
Basildon Bond	Vertical	14 x 129	White				X		Black ink			311
None			White					X	Black ribbon	2.12		312
Basildon Bond	Vertical	14 x 130	White				X		Black ink			313
None			Pale green yellow 104			X	X		Pencil			314
Basildon Bond	Vertical	14 x 129	White				X		Black ink			315
Basildon Bond	Vertical	14 x 129	White				X		Black ink			316
None			Yellow white 92	Assoc. Harvard Clubs			X		Black ink			317
Basildon Bond	Vertical	14 x 130	White				X		Black ink			318
Basildon Bond	Vertical	14 x 129	White				X		Black ink			319
Basildon Bond	Vertical	14 x 129	White				X		Black ink			320
None			White					X	Black ribbon	2.12		321
Basildon Bond	Vertical	14 x 130	White				X		Black ink			322
Basildon Bond	Vertical	14 x 130	White				X		Black ink			323
Basildon Bond	Vertical	14 x 130	White					X	Black ribbon	2.12		324
None			White					X	Black ribbon	2.12		325
None			White	Post Card		X		X	Black ribbon	2.12		326
None			Light yellow 86			X	X		Black ink			327
Basildon Bond	Vertical	14 x 129	White				X		Black ink			328
Basildon Bond	Vertical	14 x 130	White				X		Black ink			329
Basildon Bond	Vertical	14 x 130	White				X		Black ink			330
None			White					X	Black ribbon	2.12		331
None			White					X	Black ribbon	2.12		332
None			Yellow white 92	Post * Card		X	X		Black ink			333
Basildon Bond	Vertical	14 x 131	White				X		Black ink			334
None			Light yellow 86				X		Black ink			335
Basildon Bond	Vertical	14 x 131	White					X	Black ribbon	2.12		336
Basildon Bond	Vertical	14 x 131	White				X		Black ink			337
Basildon Bond	Vertical	14 x 131	White				X		Black ink			338
None			Light yellow 86			X	X		Black ink			339
Basildon Bond	Vertical	14 x 130	White				X		Black ink			340
Basildon Bond	Vertical	14 x 131	White				X		Black ink			341
Basildon Bond	Vertical	14 x 131	White				X		Black ink			342
Basildon Bond	Vertical	14 x 129	White				X		Black ink			343
London Bond	Horizontal	Incomplete	White				X		Black ink			344
London Bond	Horizontal	Incomplete	White				X		Black ink			345
None			White		20.174(23).17		X		Black ink		2.2	346
None			Yellow white 92				X		Black ink			347
None			White				X		Pencil			348
London Bond	Horizontal	13 x 122	White				X		Black ink		2.2	349A
None			White		20.174(23).17		X		Black ink			349B
London Bond	Horizontal	13 x 122	White				X		Black ink			350
None			White					X	Black ribbon	2.12		351
British Bond [B]	Horizontal	65 x 125	White					X	Black ribbon	2.12		352
British Bond [B]	Horizontal	65 x 125	White					X	Black ribbon	2.12		353
None			White				X		Black ink			354
None			White				X		Black ink			355
None			White				X		Black ink			356

NO.	DATE	*LOTSE*	PG. NO.	UNPBD.	RECIPIENT	LOCATION	LVS.	HEIGHT	WIDTH	THICK.	TEXTURE	CHAINLINES	DIST.	NO.
357	28 Sept. 1920	T.307	p. 410		Hutchinson, M.	Texas	2	227	174	0.12	Wove			
358	6 Oct. 1920	T.308	p. 412		Mother	Houghton	2	227	173	0.13	Wove			
359	15 Oct. 1920			U.70	Jepson, E.	Gallup	1	227	174	0.13	Wove			
360	15 Oct. 1920	T.309	p. 413		Lewis, W.	Cornell	1	227	114	0.13	Wove			
361	17 Oct. 1920	T.310	p. 413		Thayer, S.	Beinecke	2	263	201	0.07	Laid	Vertical	26	7
362	18 Oct. 1920			U.71	Lewis, W.	Cornell	1	227	174	0.13	Wove			
363	23 Oct. 1920	T.311	p. 415		Woolf, L.	Berg	1	263	200	0.07	Laid	Vertical	26	8
364	PM 30 Oct. 1920			U.72	Hutchinson, M.	Texas	1	114	89	0.26	Wove			
365	31 Oct. 1920	T.313	p. 417		Mother	Houghton	5	263	200	0.07	Laid	Vertical	26	8
366	2 Nov. 1920			U.73	Methuen, A.	Lilly	1	175	134	0.12	Wove			
367	[5 Nov. 1920]			U.74	Monro, H.	Gallup	1	259	186	0.16	Wove			
368	16 Nov. 1920			U.75	Green, Russell	Texas	1	114	88	0.25	Wove			
369	30 Nov. 1920	T.316	p. 422		Schiff, S.	British Libr.	2	229	177	0.10	Wove			
370	2 Dec. 1920	T.317	p. 423		Mother	Houghton	3	263	200	0.07	Laid	Vertical	26	7
371	6 Dec. 1920	T.318	p. 425		Schiff, S.	British Libr.	1	228	177	0.10	Wove			
372	8 Dec. 1920			U.76	Jepson, E.	Gallup	1	263	201	0.07	Laid	Vertical	26	8
373	10 Dec. 1920	T.319	p. 426		Trevelyan, R. C.	Trinity	1	263	201	0.07	Laid	Vertical	26	8
374	[22 Dec. 1920]	T.320	p. 426		Pound, E.	Lilly	1	263	201	0.07	Laid	Vertical	26	8
375	26 Dec. 1920	T.321	p. 427		Woolf, L.	Berg	1	263	201	0.07	Laid	Vertical	26	7
376	1 Jan. 1921	T.322	p. 428		Thayer, S.	Beinecke	3	263	201	0.07	Laid	Vertical	26	7
377	[2 Jan. 1921]			U.77	Woolf, L.	Berg	1	228	177	0.10	Wove			
378	16 Jan. 1921	T.324	p. 432		Mother	Houghton	1	263	200	0.07	Laid	Vertical	26	8
379	18 Jan. 1921			U.78	Woolf, L.	Berg	1	263	200	0.07	Laid	Vertical	26	8
380	22 Jan. 1921	T.325	p. 432		Mother	Houghton	2	263	200	0.07	Laid	Vertical	26	7
381	30 Jan. 1921	T.326	p. 434		Thayer, S.	Beinecke	1	263	201	0.07	Laid	Vertical	26	8
382	30 Jan. 1921	T.327	p. 435		Thayer, S.	Beinecke	2	263	201	0.07	Laid	Vertical	26	8
383	3 Feb. 1921	T.328	p. 435		Hutchinson, M.	Texas	1	227	178	0.10	Wove			
384	13 Feb. 1921	T.329	p. 436		Mother	Houghton	2	265	204	0.09	Wove			
385	2 Mar. [1921]	T.330	p. 437		Patmore, B.	Gallup	1	177	110	0.14	Laid	Vertical	25	4
386	6 Mar. 1921	T.331	p. 438		Mother	Houghton	2	227	177	0.10	Wove			
387	8 Mar. 1921	T.332	p. 439		Mother	Houghton	3	277	178	0.11	Wove			
388	8 Mar. 1921	T.354	p. 463		Rodker, J.	Tulsa	1	228	178	0.10	Wove			
389	17 Mar. [1921]	T.334	p. 441		Hutchinson, M.	Gallup	1	225	177	0.15	Wove			
390	3 Apr. 1921	T.335	p. 442		Moore, M.	Rosenbach	1	226	177	0.10	Wove			
391	3 Apr. 1921	T.336	p. 442		Mother	Houghton	2	227	177	0.10	Wove			
392	3 Apr. 1921	T.337	p. 443		Schiff, S.	British Libr.	2	227	177	0.10	Wove			
393	7 Apr. 1921			U.79	Aldington, R.	Texas	2	265	204	0.09	Wove			
394	14 Apr. 1921	T.338	p. 444		Mother	Houghton	2	227	177	0.10	Wove			
395	[16? Apr. 1921]	T.339	p. 445		Lewis, W.	Cornell	1	152	104	0.10	Wove			
396	[22 Apr. 1921]			U.80	Jepson, E.	Gallup	1	227	177	0.10	Wove			
397	22 Apr. 1921	T.340	p. 446		Murry, J. M.	Northwest.	2	227	177	0.10	Wove			
398	27 Apr. 1921	T.341	p. 448		Mother	Houghton	2	227	177	0.10	Wove			
399	9 May 1921	T.343	p. 450		Quinn, J.	NYPL	2	264	203	0.09	Wove			
400	9 May [1921]	T.344	p. 453		Mother	Houghton	1	228	176	0.10	Wove			
401	18 May 1921			U.81	Jepson, E.	Gallup	1	228	176	0.10	Wove			
402	21 May 1921	T.345	p. 453		Thayer, S.	Beinecke	1	264	203	0.08	Wove			
403	21 May 1921	T.346	p. 455		Joyce, J.	Buffalo	1	264	203	0.08	Wove			
404	22 May 1921	T.342	p. 449		McAlmon	Beinecke	1	264	203	0.08	Wove			
405	22 May 1921	T.347	p. 456		Pound, D.	Lilly	1	264	203	0.08	Wove			
406	2 June 1921	T.348	p. 457		Read, H.	Victoria	1	229	176	0.10	Wove			
407	[15 June 1921]			U.82	Hutchinson, M.	Texas	1	264	203	0.08	Wove			
408	15 June 1921	T.349	p. 457		Woolf, L.	Berg	1	227	176	0.10	Wove			
409	21 June 1921	T.350	p. 458		Morrell, O.	Texas	1	227	176	0.10	Wove			
410	23 June 1921	T.351	p. 458		Aldington, R.	Texas	2	227	176	0.10	Wove			
411	6 July 1921	T.352	p. 459		Aldington, R.	Texas	2	265	202	0.06	Wove			
412	14 July 1921	T.353	p. 461		Morrell, O.	Texas	2	228	176	0.10	Wove			
413	15 August 1921	T.355	p. 463		Hutchinson, M.	Texas	1	228	177	0.10	Wove			
414	16 August 1921	T.356	p. 463		Aldington, R.	Texas	2	228	177	0.10	Wove			
415	PM 18 Aug. 1921			U.83	Pound, D.	Lilly	1							
416	21 Aug. 1921			U.84	Pound, D.	Lilly	1	228	177	0.11	Wove			
417	[23 Aug. 1921]	T.357	p. 464		Mother	Houghton	1	228	177	0.11	Wove			
418	25 Aug. 1921	T.358	p. 466		Schiff, S.	British Libr.	1	228	177	0.11	Wove			
419	1 Sept. 1921	T.359	p. 467		Hutchinson, M.	Texas	2	228	177	0.11	Wove			
420	[7 Sept. 1921]	T.360	p. 468		Aldington, R.	Texas	1	248	200	0.07	Wove			
421	8 Sept. 1921	T.361	p. 468		Aldington, R.	Texas	1	254	203	0.06	Laid	Vertical	25.5	8
422	16 Sept. 1921	T.362	p. 469		Aldington, R.	Texas	2	228	177	0.11	Wove			
423	23 Sept. 1921			U.85	Jepson, E.	Gallup	1	228	177	0.11	Wove			
424	[28? Sept. 1921]	T.363	p. 470		Aldington, R.	Texas	1	228	177	0.11	Wove			
425	[30? Sept. 1921]	T.364	p. 470		Lewis, W.	Cornell	1	228	177	0.11	Wove			
426	2 Oct. 1921			U.86	C.-Sanderson, R.	Gallup	2	254	202	0.07	Laid	Vertical	25.5	8
427	3 Oct. 1921	T.365	p. 471		Eliot, H.	Houghton	2	228	177	0.11	Wove			
428	3 Oct. 1921	T.366	p. 472		Hutchinson, J.	Texas	1	228	177	0.11	Wove			
429	[3? Oct. 1921]	T.367	p. 473		Aldington, R.	Texas	1	228	177	0.11	Wove			
430	[4? Oct. 1921]	T.368	p. 475		Hutchinson, J.	Texas	1	228	177	0.11	Wove			
431	PM 5 Oct. 1921			U.87	Hutchinson, M.	Texas	1	113	89	0.26	Wove			

WATERMARK	POSITION	DIMENSIONS	COLOR	PRINTING	LINED PAPER	PC	MS	TS	SCRIPT	TYPEWR.	NOTE	NO.
None			White				X		Black ink			357
None			White				X		Black ink			358
None			White				X		Black ink			359
None			White				X		Black ink			360
British Bond [B]	Horizontal	65 x 125	White					X	Black ribbon	2.12		361
None			White				X		Black ink			362
British Bond [B]	Horizontal	65 x 125	White					X	Black ribbon	2.12		363
None			Light yellow 86	Post * Card		X	X		Black ink			364
British Bond [B]	Horizontal	65 x 125	White					X	Black ribbon	2.12		365
San . . . Lin . . .	Horizontal	Incomplete	Yellow white 92				X		Black ink			366
None			Light gray 264				X		Black ink			367
None			Light yellow brown 76			X	X		Black ink			368
* Bond	Vertical	Incomplete	White				X		Black ink			369
British Bond [B]	Horizontal	65 x 125	White					X	Black ribbon	2.12		370
* Bond	Vertical	Incomplete	White				X		Black ink			371
British Bond [B]	Horizontal	65 x 125	White					X	Black ribbon	2.12		372
British Bond [B]	Horizontal	65 x 125	White					X	Black ribbon	2.12		373
British Bond [B]	Horizontal	65 x 125	White					X	Black ribbon	2.12		374
British Bond [B]	Horizontal	65 x 125	White					X	Black ribbon	2.12		375
British Bond [B]	Horizontal	65 x 125	White					X	Black ribbon	2.12		376
* Bond	Vertical	26 x 73	White					X	Black ribbon	2.12	6.3	377
British Bond [B]	Horizontal	65 x 125	White				X		Black ink			378
British Bond [B]	Horizontal	65 x 125	White					X	Black ribbon	2.12		379
British Bond [B]	Horizontal	65 x 125	White					X	Black ribbon	2.12		380
British Bond [B]	Horizontal	65 x 125	White					X	Black ribbon	2.12		381
British Bond [B]	Horizontal	65 x 125	White					X	Black ribbon	2.12		382
Basildon Bond	Vertical	Incomplete	White				X		Black ink			383
British Bond [C]	Horizontal	65 x 125	White					X	Black ribbon	2.12		384
None			White	9 Clarence Gate			X		Black ink			385
Basildon Bond	Vertical	Incomplete	White				X		Black ink			386
Basildon Bond	Vertical	Incomplete	White				X		Black ink			387
Basildon Bond	Vertical	Incomplete	White				X		Black ink		6.4	388
None			White	9 Clarence Gate	11.155 (24).12		X		Black ink			389
Basildon Bond	Vertical	Incomplete	White				X		Black ink			390
Basildon Bond	Vertical	14 x 129	White				X		Black ink			391
Basildon Bond	Vertical	14 x 129	White				X		Black ink			392
British Bond [C]	Horizontal	65 x 125	White					X	Black ribbon	2.12		393
Basildon Bond	Vertical	14 x 129	White				X		Black ink			394
Watt and Seekam	Vertical	24 x 132	Brilliant orange yellow 67				X		Pencil			395
Basildon Bond	Vertical	14 x 129	White				X		Black ink			396
Basildon Bond	Vertical	14 x 129	White				X		Black ink			397
Basildon Bond	Vertical	14 x 129	White				X		Black ink			398
British Bond [C]	Horizontal	Incomplete	White					X	Black ribbon	2.12		399
Utility Bond	Vertical	71 x 112	White				X		Black ink			400
Utility Bond	Vertical	71 x 112	White				X		Black ink			401
British Bond [C]	Horizontal	65 x 125	White					X	Black ribbon	2.12		402
British Bond [C]	Horizontal	65 x 125	White					X	Black ribbon	2.12		403
British Bond [C]	Horizontal	65 x 125	White					X	Black ribbon	2.12	6.5	404
British Bond [C]	Horizontal	65 x 125	White					X	Black ribbon	2.12		405
Utility Bond	Vertical	71 x 112	White					X	Black ribbon	2.12		406
British Bond [C]	Horizontal	Incomplete	White					X	Black ribbon	2.12		407
Basildon Bond	Vertical	Incomplete	White				X		Black ink			408
Basildon Bond	Vertical	Incomplete	White				X		Black ink			409
Basildon Bond	Vertical	Incomplete	White				X		Black ink			410
Verona Linen	Horizontal	14 x 128	White					X	Black ribbon	2.12		411
Basildon Bond	Vertical	Incomplete	White				X		Black ink			412
Basildon Bond	Vertical	Incomplete	White				X		Black ink			413
Basildon Bond	Vertical	Incomplete	White				X		Black ink			414
				[Telegram]								415
Basildon Bond	Vertical	Incomplete	White				X		Black ink			416
Basildon Bond	Vertical	Incomplete	White				X		Black ink			417
Basildon Bond	Vertical	Incomplete	White				X		Black ink			418
Basildon Bond	Vertical	Incomplete	White				X		Black ink			419
None			White		29.216(25).3		X		Pencil			420
Verona Linen	Horizontal	14 x 128	White					X	Black ribbon	2.10	1.6	421
Basildon Bond	Vertical	Incomplete	White				X		Black ink			422
Basildon Bond	Vertical	14 x 129	White				X		Black ink			423
Basildon Bond	Vertical	14 x 129	White				X		Black ink			424
Basildon Bond	Vertical	14 x 129	White				X		Black ink			425
Verona Linen	Horizontal	14 x 128	White					X	Black ribbon	2.10		426
Basildon Bond	Vertical	14 x 129	White					X	Black ribbon	2.10		427
Basildon Bond	Vertical	14 x 129	White				X		Black ink			428
Basildon Bond	Vertical	14 x 129	White				X		Black ink			429
Basildon Bond	Vertical	14 x 129	White				X		Black ink			430
None			Light yellow brown 76	Post * Card		X	X		Black ink			431

NO.	DATE	LOTSE	PG. NO.	UNPBD.	RECIPIENT	LOCATION	LVS.	HEIGHT	WIDTH	THICK.	TEXTURE	CHAINLINES	DIST.	NO.
432	[8 Oct. 1921]	T.369	p. 475		Aldington, R.	Texas	1	113	89	0.26	Wove			
433	12 Oct. 1921	T.370	p. 475		Monro, H.	Gallup	1	227	177	0.11	Wove			
434	[13 Oct. 1921]	T.371	p. 476		Aldington, R.	Texas	3	228	177	0.11	Wove			
435	13 Oct. 1921	T.372	p. 477		Hutchinson, J.	Texas	1	228	177	0.11	Wove			
436	PM 15 Oct. 1921	T.373	p. 479		Aldington, R.	Texas	1	113	89	0.27	Wove			
437	26 Oct. 1921	T.374	p. 480		Huxley, J.	Fondren	2	204	129	0.12	Wove			
438	PM 29 Oct. 1921	T.375	p. 481		Aldington, R.	Texas	1	139	87	0.37	Wove			
439	31 Oct. 1921	T.376	p. 482		Huxley, J.	Fondren	1	228	177	0.11	Wove			
440	PM 1 Nov. 1921			U.88	Eliot, H.	Houghton	1	136	94	0.40	Wove			
441	PM 3 Nov. 1921	T.378	p. 484		Aldington, R.	Texas	1	139	87	0.37	Wove			
442	[4? Nov. 1921]	T.379	p. 484		Schiff, S.	British Libr.	1	204	129	0.12	Wove			
443	5? Nov. 1921	T.380	p. 485		Aldington, R.	Texas	1	204	129	0.12	Wove			
444	6 Nov. 1921	T.381	p. 486		Aldington, R.	Texas	2	204	129	0.12	Wove			
445	[16? Nov. 1921]	T.382	p. 486		Schiff, S.	British Libr.	1	227	177	0.11	Wove			
446	16 Nov. 1921			U.89	Monro, H.	Gallup	1	227	176	0.11	Wove			
447	PM 17 Nov. 1921			U.90	Hutchinson, M.	Texas	1	227	177	0.11	Wove			
448	17 Nov. 1921	T.383	p. 487		Aldington, R.	Texas	3	227	177	0.11	Wove			
449	30 Nov. 1921	T.385	p. 490		Morrell, O.	Texas	1	227	177	0.11	Wove			
450	PM 3 Dec. 1921			U.91	Lewis, W.	Cornell	1	141	90	0.29	Wove			
451	PM 4 Dec. 1921	T.386	p. 490		Hutchinson, M.	Texas	1	136	86	0.32	Wove			
452	5 Dec. 1921			U.92	Rivière, J.	Texas	1	223	177	0.12	Wove			
453	13 Dec. 1921	T.387	p. 493		Eliot, H.	Houghton	2	210	131	0.08	Laid	Horizontal	28	8
454	19 Dec. 1921	T.389	p. 495		Waterlow, S.	Waterlow	1	271	209	0.06	Wove			
455	PM 23 Dec. 1921			U.93	Hutchinson, M.	Texas	1	133	84	0.24	Wove			
456	25 Dec. 1921	T.390	p. 500		Knopf, A.	Texas	1	210	131	0.07	Laid	Horizontal	28	8
457	20 Jan. 1922	T.391	p. 501		Thayer, S.	Beinecke	1	263	203	0.07	Laid	Horizontal	25.5	8
458	24 Jan. 1922	T.393	p. 503		C.-Sanderson, R.	Gallup	1	210	131	0.08	Laid	Horizontal	28	7
459	[26 Jan. 1922]	T.394	p. 504		Pound, E.	Houghton	1	264	203	0.07	Laid	Horizontal	25.5	8
460	29 Jan. 1922	T.395	p. 506		C.-Sanderson, R.	Gallup	1	210	131	0.08	Laid	Horizontal	28	8
461	30 Jan. 1922			U.94	C.-Sanderson, R.	Gallup	1	210	131	0.07	Laid	Horizontal	28	8
462	[1 Feb. 1922]			U.95	C.-Sanderson, R.	Gallup	1	210	131	0.08	Laid	Horizontal	28	8
463	[5 Feb. 1922]			U.96	Rodker, J.	Virginia	1	253	203	0.07	Wove			
464	[5? Feb. 1922]			U.97	Hutchinson, M.	Texas	1	210	131	0.08	Laid	Horizontal	28	8
465	6 Feb. 1922			U.98	Bax, Clifford	Texas	1	252	203	0.08	Wove			
466	17 Feb. 1922			U.99	Aldington, R.	Texas	1	202	126	0.11	Wove			
467	26 Feb. 1922			U.100	Firuski, M.	Williams	1	253	203	0.07	Wove			
468	4 Mar. 1922			U.101	Knopf, A.	Texas	1	202	126	0.10	Wove			
469	PM 8 Mar. 1922			U.102	Thayer, S.	Beinecke	1							
470	12 Mar. 1922	T.397	p. 506		Pound, E.	Lilly	1	252	203	0.07	Wove			
471	12 Mar. 1922	T.398	p. 508		Larbaud, V.	Vichy	1	252	203	0.07	Wove			
472	13 Mar. 1922	T.399	p. 509		Hesse, H.	Schiller	1	265	203	0.06	Wove			
473	13 Mar. 1922	T.400	p. 511		C.-Sanderson, R.	Gallup	1	265	203	0.07	Wove			
474	16 Mar. 1922	T.401	p. 515		Thayer, S.	Beinecke	1	265	203	0.07	Wove			
475	16 Mar. 1922	T.333	p. 441		Lewis, W.	Cornell	1	203	126	0.11	Wove			
476	20 Mar. 1922	T.402	p. 516		Larbaud, V.	Vichy	1	265	203	0.07	Wove			
477	27 Mar. 1922			U.103	Hesse, H.	Schiller	1	144	89	0.27	Wove			
478	27 Mar. 1922			U.104	Thayer, S.	Beinecke	1	202	126	0.11	Wove			
479	[1? Apr. 1922]			U.105	Monro, H.	Gallup	1	265	203	0.06	Wove			
480	[6 Apr. 1922]			U.106	Schiff, S.	British Libr.	1	202	126	0.11	Wove			
481	3 Apr. 1922	T.403	p. 517		Schiff, S.	British Libr.	1	265	203		Wove			
482	3 Apr. 1922	T.404	p. 518		Moore, T. S.	Texas	1	265	203	0.07	Wove			
483	3 Apr. 1922	T.405	p. 519		Knopf, A.	Texas	1	265	203	0.06	Wove			
484	4 Apr. 1922	T.406	p. 519		Beach, S.	Princeton	1	265	202	0.07	Wove			
485	10 Apr. 1922	T.407	p. 520		Moore, T. S.	Texas	1	202	126	0.10	Wove			
486	10 Apr. 1922	T.408	p. 520		Schiff, S.	British Libr.	1	202	127	0.11	Wove			
487	[12 Apr. 1922]			U.107	Hutchinson, M.	Texas	1	265	203	0.07	Wove			
488	[17 Apr.? 1922]	T.409	p. 521		Waterlow, S.	Waterlow	1	202	126	0.11	Wove			
489	[19 Apr. 1922]			U.108	Hutchinson, M.	Texas	1	114	89	0.43	Wove			
490	20 Apr. 1922	T.410	p. 522		Schiff, S.	British Libr.	2	265	203	0.07	Wove			
491	26 Apr. 1922	T.411	p. 522		Morrell, O.	Texas	2	202	126	0.10	Wove			
492	[27 Apr. 1922]	T.412	p. 523		Hutchinson, M.	Texas	2	202	127	0.10	Wove			
493	6 May 1922			U.109	Woolf, L.	Berg	1	265	202	0.06	Wove			
494	7 May 1922	T.413	p. 524		Du Bos, C.	Texas	1	265	202	0.06	Wove			
495	[11 May 1922]			U.110	Aldington, R.	Texas	1	114	89	0.43	Wove			
496	[17 May 1922]	T.414	p. 524		Morrell, O.	Texas	2	203	127	0.10	Wove			
497	17 May 1922	T.415	p. 525		Aldington, R.	Texas	3	203	127	0.10	Wove			
498	19 May 1922			U.111	Jepson, E.	Gallup	1	203	127	0.10	Wove			
499	20 May 1922	T.416	p. 526		Seldes, G.	Beinecke	2	265	203	0.07	Wove			
500	20 May 1922	T.417	p. 527		C.-Sanderson, R.	Texas	1	202	127	0.10	Wove			
501	20 May 1922			U.112	Knopf, A.	Texas	1	265	203	0.07	Wove			
502	20 May 1922			U.113	Woolf, L.	Princeton	1	202	127	0.10	Wove			
503	24 May 1922			U.114	Hesse, H.	Schiller	1	288	191	0.07	Wove			
504	PM 27 May 1922			U.115	Hutchinson, M.	Texas	1	135	88	0.29	Wove			
505	28 May 1922	T.418	p. 527		Morrell, O.	Texas	1	141	90	0.25	Wove			
506	PM 31 May 1922			U.116	Aiken, C.	Huntington	1	140	90	0.26	Wove			

WATERMARK	POSITION	DIMENSIONS	COLOR	PRINTING	LINED PAPER	PC	MS	TS	SCRIPT	TYPEWR.	NOTE	NO.
None			Light yellow brown 76	Post * Card		X	X		Black ink			432
Basildon Bond	Vertical	14 x 129	White				X		Black ink			433
Basildon Bond	Vertical	14 x 129	White					X	Black ribbon 2.10			434
Basildon Bond	Vertical	14 x 129	White					X	Black ribbon 2.10			435
None			Light yellow brown 76	Post * Card		X	X		Black ink			436
Charles Martin	Horizontal	Incomplete	White	Albemarle Hotel			X		Black ink			437
None			White	Albemarle Hotel		X	X		Black ink			438
Basildon Bond	Vertical	14 x 129	White				X		Black ink			439
None			Yellow white 92			X	X		Black ink			440
None			White	Albemarle Hotel		X	X		Black ink			441
Charles Martin	Horizontal	Incomplete	White	Albemarle Hotel			X		Black ink			442
Charles Martin	Horizontal	Incomplete	White	Albemarle Hotel			X		Pencil			443
Charles Martin	Horizontal	Incomplete	White	Albemarle Hotel			X		Black ink			444
Hieratica Bond	Vertical	48 x 45	White				X		Black ink			445
Hieratica Bond	Vertical	48 x 45	White				X		Black ink			446
Hieratica Bond	Vertical	48 x 45	White				X		Black ink			447
Hieratica Bond	Vertical	48 x 45	White					X	Black ribbon 2.10			448
Hieratica Bond	Vertical	48 x 45	White				X		Pencil			449
None			White			X	X		Black ink			450
None			White			X	X		Black ink			451
Hieratica Bond	Vertical	48 x 45	White				X		Black ink			452
H. L. & Co. Ltd	Vertical	Incomplete	Yellow white 92				X		Black ink		4.4	453
None			White		21.234(27).16		X		Black ink			454
None			White			X	X		Black ink			455
H. L. & Co. Ltd	Vertical	Incomplete	Yellow white 92				X		Black ink		4.3	456
Verona Linen	Horizontal	14 x 128	White					X	Black ribbon 2.10			457
H. L. & Co. Ltd	Vertical	49 x 136	Yellow white 92				X		Black ink			458
Verona Linen	Horizontal	14 x 128	White					X	Black ribbon 2.10		6.6	459
H. L. & Co. Ltd	Horizontal	49 x 136	Yellow white 92				X		Black ink			460
H. L. & Co. Ltd	Horizontal	49 x 136	Yellow white 92				X		Black ink		4.4	461
H. L. & Co. Ltd	Horizontal	49 x 136	Yellow white 92				X		Black ink		4.4	462
None			White				X		Black ink			463
H. L. & Co. Ltd	Vertical	49 x 136	Yellow white 92				X		Black ink			464
None			White					X	Black ribbon 2.10			465
Basildon Bond	Vertical	Incomplete	White				X		Black ink			466
None			White					X	Black ribbon 2.10			467
Basildon Bond	Vertical	Incomplete	White				X		Black ink			468
				[Telegram]								469
None			White					X	Black ribbon 2.10			470
None			White					X	Black ribbon 2.10			471
Inglewood Paper	Vertical	129 x 156	White					X	Black ribbon 2.10			472
Inglewood Paper	Vertical	129 x 156	White					X	Black ribbon 2.10			473
Inglewood Paper	Vertical	130 x 156	White					X	Black ribbon 2.10			474
None			White				X		Black ink		4.4	475
Inglewood Paper	Vertical	130 x 156	White					X	Black ribbon 2.10			476
None			Light yellow brown 76			X	X		Black ink			477
None			White				X		Black ink			478
Inglewood Paper	Vertical	130 x 156	White				X		Black ink			479
None			White				X		Black ink			480
Inglewood Paper	Vertical	130 x 156	White					X	Black ribbon 2.10		2.2	481
Inglewood Paper	Vertical	130 x 156	White					X	Black ribbon 2.10			482
Inglewood Paper	Vertical	130 x 156	White					X	Black ribbon 2.10			483
Inglewood Paper	Vertical	130 x 156	White					X	Black ribbon 2.10			484
Basildon Bond	Vertical	14 x 128	White				X		Black ink			485
None			White				X		Black ink			486
Verona Linen	Horizontal	130 x 156	White					X	Black ribbon 2.10			487
None			White				X		Black ink		4.4	488
None			White	Post * Card		X	X		Black ink			489
Inglewood Paper	Vertical	130 x 156	White				X		Black ink			490
Basildon Bond	Vertical	14 x 128	White				X		Black ink			491
Basildon Bond	Vertical	14 x 128	White				X		Black ink			492
Inglewood Paper	Vertical	130 x 156	White				X		Black ink			493
Inglewood Paper	Vertical	130 x 156	White				X		Black ink			494
None			White	Post * Card		X	X		Black ink			495
None			White				X		Black ink			496
None			White				X		Black ink			497
None			White				X		Black ink			498
Inglewood Paper	Vertical	130 x 156	White				X		Black ink			499
None			White				X		Black ink			500
Inglewood Paper	Vertical	130 x 156	White				X		Black ink			501
None			White				X		Black ink			502
None			White	Hotel Bristol Lugano			X		Black ink			503
None			White			X	X		Black ink			504
None			White			X	X		Black ink			505
None			White			X	X		Black ink			506

NO.	DATE	LOTSE	PG. NO.	UNPBD.	RECIPIENT	LOCATION	LVS.	HEIGHT	WIDTH	THICK.	TEXTURE	CHAINLINES	DIST.	NO.
507	PM 31 May 1922			U.117	Hesse, H.	Schiller	1	140	87	0.25	Wove			
508	[5 June 1922]	T.419	p. 527		Schiff, S.	British Libr.	1	203	127	0.10	Wove			
509	10 June 1922			U.118	Rivière, J.	Texas	2	203	127	0.10	Wove			
510	10 June 1922			U.119	Woolf, L.	Princeton	2	203	127	0.10	Wove			
511	11 June 1922	T.420	p. 528		Moore, T. S.	Texas	1	202	127	0.10	Wove			
512	12 June 1922			U.120	C.-Sanderson, R.	Gallup	1	203	127	0.10	Wove			
513	15 June 1922	T.421	p. 528		Morrell, O.	Texas	3	202	127	0.10	Wove			
514	[15 June 1922]			U.121	C.-Sanderson, R.	Gallup	1	113	89	0.26	Wove			
515	18 June [1922]			U.122	Lewis, W.	Cornell	1	203	127	0.10	Wove			
516	PM 21 June 1922			U.123	Quinn, J.	NYPL	1							
517	[23 June 1922]	T.422	p. 529		Hutchinson, M.	Texas	2	202	125	0.11	Wove			
518	PM 25 June 1922			U.124	Quinn, J.	NYPL	1							
519	25 June 1922	T.423	p. 530		Quinn, J.	NYPL	2	265	203	0.07	Wove			
520	25 June 1922	T.424	p. 531		Schiff, S.	British Libr.	1	265	203	0.07	Wove			
521	27 June 1922	T.425	p. 534		C.-Sanderson, R.	Gallup	1	265	203	0.07	Wove			
522	27 June 1922			U.125	Moore, T. S.	Texas	1	265	203	0.07	Wove			
523	30 June 1922	T.426	p. 535		Aldington, R.	Texas	2	265	202	0.07	Wove			
524	1 July 1922			U.126	Woolf, L.	Princeton	1	265	202	0.06	Wove			
525	4 July 1922			U.127	Aldington, R.	Texas	1	266	202	0.06	Wove			
526	4 July 1922	T.427	p. 537		Schiff, S.	British Libr.	1	265	202		Wove			
527	5 July 1922			U.128	Woolf, L.	Princeton	1	265	202	0.06	Wove			
528	9 July 1922			U.129	Curtius, E.	U. of Bonn	2	266	202	0.07	Wove			
529	9 July 1922	T.428	p. 538		Pound, E.	Lilly	4	248	200	0.07	Wove			
530	10 July 1922	T.429	p. 539		Aldington, R.	Texas	1	266	202	0.06	Wove			
531	10 July 1922	T.430	p. 540		Rodker, J.	Virginia	1	266	202	0.07	Wove			
532	11 July 1922			U.130	Schiff, S.	British Libr.	1	202	125	0.12	Wove			
533	13 July 1922	T.431	p. 541		C.-Sanderson, R.	Gallup	1	266	202	0.06	Wove			
534	13 July 1922	T.432	p. 541		Aldington, R.	Texas	2	266	202	0.06	Wove			
535	13 July 1922	T.433	p. 542		Flint, F. S.	Texas	2	266	202	0.06	Wove			
536	13 July 1922	T.434	p. 543		Schiff, S.	British Libr.	1	265	202		Wove			
537	13 July 1922			U.131	Woolf, L.	Princeton	1	266	203	0.06	Wove			
538	17 July 1922	T.435	p. 545		Aldington, R.	Texas	1	266	202	0.06	Wove			
539	[17 July 1922]			U.132	Pound, D.	Lilly	1	201	125	0.11	Wove			
540	18 July 1922			U.133	C.-Sanderson, R.	Gallup	1	266	203	0.06	Wove			
541	18 July 1922	T.436	p. 545		Flint, F. S.	Texas	1	266	202	0.06	Wove			
542	18 July 1922	T.437	p. 546		Morrell, O.	Texas	1	266	203	0.06	Wove			
543	18 July 1922	T.438	p. 547		Read, H.	Victoria	1	266	203	0.06	Wove			
544	18 July 1922			U.134	Woolf, L.	Princeton	1	266	203	0.06	Wove			
545	19 July 1922	T.439	p. 547		Quinn, J.	NYPL	2	266	203	0.06	Wove			
546	19 July 1922	T.440	p. 548		Pound, E.	Lilly	3	266	202	0.07	Wove			
547	21 July 1922	T.441	p. 550		Curtius, E.	U. of Bonn	2	266	203	0.07	Wove			
548	PM 25 July 1922			U.135	Moore, T. S.	Texas	1	114	89	0.26	Wove			
549	PM 28 July 1922			U.136	Moore, T. S.	Texas	1	115	89	0.26	Wove			
550	28 July 1922	T.442	p. 551		Thayer, S.	Beinecke	2	266	202	0.07	Wove			
551	28 July 1922	T.443	p. 552		Pound, E.	Lilly	2	266	202	0.06	Wove			
552	29 July 1922	T.444	p. 553		Moore, T. S.	Texas	1	202	125	0.11	Wove			
553	[end July? 1922]	T.445	p. 554		Morrell, O.	Texas	2	266	203	0.06	Wove			
554	[4 Aug. 1922]			U.137	Pound, D.	Lilly	1	201	125	0.11	Wove			
555	9 Aug. 1922	T.447	p. 556		Randall, A.	McFarlin	1	266	203	0.06	Wove			
556	9 Aug. 1922	T.448	p. 556		C.-Sanderson, R.	Gallup	1	266	202	0.07	Wove			
557	[9 Aug. 1922]			U.138	Pound, D.	Lilly	1	201	125	0.12	Wove			
558	PM 12 Aug. 1922			U.139	Pound, D.	Lilly	1	113	89	0.26	Wove			
559	14 Aug. 1922	T.450	p. 557		Curtius, E.	U. of Bonn	1	266	202	0.07	Wove			
560	14 Aug. 1922	T.451	p. 558		Seldes, G.	Beinecke	1	266	202	0.06	Wove			
561	14 Aug. 1922			U.140	Wilson, Edmund	Beinecke	1	266	202	0.06	Wove			
562	15 Aug. 1922	T.452	p. 559		Flint, F. S.	Texas	1	266	202	0.06	Wove			
563	15 Aug. 1922	T.453	p. 559		Watson, J. S.	Berg	2	266	203	0.06	Wove			
564	PM 17 Aug. 1922			U.141	Watson, J. S.	Berg	1							
565	17 Aug. 1922	T.455	p. 562		Flint, F. S.	Texas	1	266	203	0.06	Wove			
566	20 Aug. 1922	T.457	p. 563		Schiff, S.	British Libr.	1	265	202		Wove			
567	21 Aug. 1922	T.458	p. 563		Quinn, J.	NYPL	2	266	203	0.07	Wove			
568	21 Aug. 1922	T.459	p. 564		Watson, J. S.	Berg	2	266	202	0.06	Wove			
569	21 Aug. 1922			U.142	Wilson, Edmund	Beinecke	1	266	202	0.06	Wove			
570	PM 23 Aug. 1922			U.143	Aldington, R.	Texas	1	138	88	0.40	Wove			
571	PM 23 Aug. 1922			U.144	C.-Sanderson, R.	Texas	1	141	91	0.30	Wove			
572	PM 23 Aug. 1922			U.145	Pound, D.	Lilly	1	140	89	0.26	Wove			
573	23 Aug. 1922			U.146	Read, H.	Victoria	1	263	202	0.09	Wove			
574A	28 Aug. 1922	T.460	p. 565		Curtius, E.	U. of Bonn	1	263	202	0.10	Wove			
574B	28 Aug. 1922	T.460	p. 565		Curtius, E.	U. of Bonn	1	266	203	0.06	Wove			
575	PM 29 Aug. 1922	T.461	p. 566		Read, H.	Victoria	1	113	89	0.29	Wove			
576A	30 Aug. 1922	T.462	p. 567		Pound, E.	Lilly	1	263	202	0.10	Wove			
576B	30 Aug. 1922	T.462	p. 567		Pound, E.	Lilly	1	267	203	0.06	Wove			
577	31 Aug. 1922	T.463	p. 568		C.-Sanderson, R.	Gallup	1	263	202	0.10	Wove			
578	7 Sept. 1922			U.147	C.-Sanderson, R.	Texas	1	263	202	0.09	Wove			
579	10 Sept. 1922	T.464	p. 569		C.-Sanderson, R.	Gallup	1	263	202	0.10	Wove			

WATERMARK	POSITION	DIMENSIONS	COLOR	PRINTING	LINED PAPER	PC	MS	TS	SCRIPT	TYPEWR.	NOTE	NO.
None			White			X	X		Black ink			507
Basildon Bond	Vertical	14 x 131	White				X		Black ink			508
Basildon Bond	Vertical	14 x 131	White				X		Black ink			509
Basildon Bond	Vertical	14 x 132	White				X		Black ink			510
Basildon Bond	Vertical	14 x 131	White				X		Black ink			511
Basildon Bond	Vertical	14 x 131	White				X		Black ink			512
Basildon Bond	Vertical	14 x 131	White				X		Black ink			513
None			White	Post * Card		X	X		Black ink			514
Basildon Bond	Vertical	14 x 130	White				X		Black ink			515
				[Telegram]								516
* Bond	Vertical	27 x 72	White				X		Black ink			517
				[Telegram]								518
Inglewood Paper	Vertical	132 x 156	White					X	Black ribbon	2.10		519
Inglewood Paper	Vertical	132 x 156	White					X	Black ribbon	2.10		520
Inglewood Paper	Vertical	132 x 156	White					X	Black ribbon	2.10		521
Inglewood Paper	Vertical	132 x 156	White					X	Black ribbon	2.10		522
Inglewood Paper	Vertical	131 x 156	White					X	Black ribbon	2.10		523
None			White					X	Black ribbon	2.10		524
None			White					X	Black ribbon	2.10		525
None			White					X	Black ribbon	2.10	2.2	526
None			White					X	Black ribbon	2.10		527
None			White					X	Black ribbon	2.10		528
None			White		29.216(25).3		X		Pencil			529
None			White					X	Black ribbon	2.10		530
None			White					X	Black ribbon	2.10		531
* Bond	Vertical	26 x 72	White				X		Black ink			532
None			White					X	Black ribbon	2.10		533
None			White					X	Black ribbon	2.10		534
None			White					X	Black ribbon	2.10		535
None			White					X	Black ribbon	2.10	2.2	536
None			White					X	Black ribbon	2.10		537
None			White					X	Black ribbon	2.10		538
* Bond	Vertical	27 x 72	White				X		Black ink			539
None			White					X	Black ribbon	2.10		540
None			White					X	Black ribbon	2.10		541
None			White					X	Black ribbon	2.10		542
None			White					X	Black ribbon	2.10		543
None			White					X	Black ribbon	2.10		544
None			White					X	Black ribbon	2.10		545
None			White					X	Black ribbon	2.10		546
None			White					X	Black ribbon	2.10		547
None			Light yellow brown 76	Post * Card		X	X		Black ink			548
None			Light yellow brown 76	Post * Card		X	X		Black ink			549
None			White					X	Black ribbon	2.10		550
None			White					X	Black ribbon	2.10		551
* Bond	Vertical	26 x 72	White				X		Black ink			552
None			White					X	Black ribbon	2.10		553
* Bond	Vertical	26 x 72	White				X		Black ink			554
None			White					X	Black ribbon	2.10		555
None			White					X	Black ribbon	2.10		556
* Bond	Vertical	26 x 72	White				X		Black ink			557
None			Light yellow brown 76				X		Black ribbon	2.10		558
None			White					X	Black ribbon	2.10		559
None			White					X	Black ribbon	2.10		560
None			White					X	Black ribbon	2.10		561
None			White					X	Black ribbon	2.10		562
None			White					X	Black ribbon	2.10		563
				[Telegram]								564
None			White					X	Black ribbon	2.10		565
None			White					X	Black ribbon	2.10	2.2	566
None			White					X	Black ribbon	2.10		567
None			White					X	Black ribbon	2.10		568
None			White					X	Black ribbon	2.10		569
None			White	Post Card		X	X		Black ink			570
None			White	Post Card		X	X		Black ink			571
None			Light gray 264			X	X		Black ink			572
Charta Regia	Horizontal	99 x 94	White	The Criterion				X	Black ribbon	2.10		573
Charta Regia	Horizontal	99 x 94	White	The Criterion				X	Black ribbon	2.10		574A
None			White					X	Black ribbon	2.10		574B
None			White	Post * Card			X		Black ribbon	2.10		575
Charta Regia	Horizontal	99 x 94	White	The Criterion				X	Black ribbon	2.10		576A
None			White					X	Black ribbon	2.10		576B
Charta Regia	Horizontal	99 x 94	White	The Criterion				X	Black ribbon	2.10		577
Charta Regia	Horizontal	99 x 94	White	The Criterion			X		Black ink			578
Charta Regia	Horizontal	99 x 94	White	The Criterion			X		Black ink			579

NO.	DATE	LOTSE	PG. NO.	UNPBD.	RECIPIENT	LOCATION	LVS.	HEIGHT	WIDTH	THICK.	TEXTURE	CHAINLINES	DIST.	NO.
580	13 Sept. 1922			U.148	Hutchinson, M.	Texas	1	273	178	0.11	Wove			
581	15 Sept. 1922	T.465	p. 569		Pound, E.	Lilly	1	267	203	0.06	Wove			
582	21 Sept. 1922	T.466	p. 571		Quinn, J.	NYPL	3	267	203	0.07	Wove			
583	22 Sept. 1922			U.149	Flint, F. S.	Texas	1	263	202	0.10	Wove			
584	26 Sept. 1922			U.150	C.-Sanderson, R.	Gallup	1	264	202	0.10	Wove			
585	27 Sept. 1922	T.467	p. 574		C.-Sanderson, R.	Gallup	1	263	202	0.10	Wove			
586	28 Sept. 1922	T.468	p. 575		C.-Sanderson, R.	Gallup	1	263	202	0.10	Wove			
587	1 Oct. 1922	T.469	p. 575		C.-Sanderson, R.	Gallup	1	263	202	0.10	Wove			
588	1 Oct. 1922			U.151	Wilson, Edmund	Beinecke	1	266	203	0.06	Wove			
589	3 Oct. 1922	T.470	p. 576		C.-Sanderson, R.	Gallup	1	263	202	0.10	Wove			
590	3 Oct. 1922	T.471	p. 576		Murry, J. M.	Northwest.	1	263	202	0.10	Wove			
591	5 Oct. 1922	T.472	p. 577		Larbaud, V.	Vichy	1	263	202	0.10	Wove			
592	6 Oct. 1922	T.473	p. 578		C.-Sanderson, R.	Texas	1	263	202	0.09	Wove			
593	[6 Oct. 1922]			U.152	Hutchinson, M.	Texas	1	202	125	0.11	Wove			
594	11 Oct. 1922	T.474	p. 578		Eliot, H.	Houghton	4	257	203	0.07	Wove			
595	13 Oct. 1922	T.475	p. 581		C.-Sanderson, R.	Gallup	1	263	202	0.10	Wove			
596	13 Oct. 1922	T.476	p. 581		Murry, J. M.	Northwest.	1	263	202	0.10	Wove			
597	15 Oct. 1922			U.153	C.-Sanderson, R.	Gallup	1	263	202	0.10	Wove			
598	16 Oct. 1922	T.477	p. 582		C.-Sanderson, R.	Gallup	1	263	202	0.10	Wove			
599	[16 Oct. 1922]	T.478	p. 582		Schiff, S.	British Libr.	1	262	202	0.10	Wove			
600	16 Oct. 1922	T.479	p. 584		C.-Sanderson, R.	Gallup	1	263	202	0.10	Wove			
601	18 Oct. 1922			U.154	Flint, F. S.	Texas	1	263	202	0.10	Wove			
602	22 Oct. 1922	T.480	p. 585		Pound, E.	Lilly	2	267	203	0.06	Wove			
603	1 Nov. 1922			U.155	Jean-Aubry, G.	Texas	2	267	203	0.06	Wove			
604	[3 Nov. 1922]	T.481	p. 585		Pound, E.	Lilly	2	267	203	0.06	Wove			
605	5 Nov. 1922			U.156	Murry, J. M.	Northwest.	1	267	203	0.06	Wove			
606	6 Nov. 1922	T.482	p. 591		Flint, F. S.	Texas	1	263	201	0.10	Wove			
607	8 Nov. 1922	T.484	p. 593		C.-Sanderson, R.	Gallup	1	263	201	0.10	Wove			
608	8 Nov. 1922	T.485	p. 594		Aldington, R.	Texas	1	267	203	0.07	Wove			
609	8 Nov. 1922	T.486	p. 595		Larbaud, V.	Vichy	1	267	203	0.06	Wove			
610	8 Nov. 1922			U.157	Wilson, Edmund	Beinecke	1	267	203	0.06	Wove			
611	12 Nov. 1922			U.158	C.-Sanderson, R.	Gallup	1	263	201	0.10	Wove			
612	13 Nov. 1922			U.159	C.-Sanderson, R.	Texas	1	113	89	0.30	Wove			
613	14 Nov. 1922	T.487	p. 596		Pound, E.	Lilly	1	138	86	0.27	Wove			
614	15 Nov. 1922	T.488	p. 596		Aldington, R.	Texas	1	267	203	0.06	Wove			
615	[15 Nov. 1922]	T.489	p. 597		Pound, E.	Lilly	4	267	203	0.07	Wove			
616	PM 16 Nov. 1922			U.160	Hutchinson, M.	Texas	1	113	89	0.25	Wove			
617	18 Nov. 1922	T.490	p. 599		Aldington, R.	Texas	2	267	203	0.07	Wove			
618	18 Nov. 1922	T.491	p. 600		Pound, E.	Lilly	2	267	203	0.06	Wove			
619	[20 Nov. 1922]	T.492	p. 600		Aldington, R.	Texas	1	267	203	0.06	Wove			
620	27 Nov. 1922	T.493	p. 601		C.-Sanderson, R.	Texas	1	263	201	0.09	Wove			
621	27 Nov. 1922	T.494	p. 601		Thayer, S.	Beinecke	1	263	202	0.10	Wove			
622	1 Dec. 1922	T.495	p. 603		C.-Sanderson, R.	Texas	1	263	202	0.09	Wove			
623	[1 Dec. 1922]			U.161	Hutchinson, M.	Texas	1	267	203	0.07	Wove			
624	4 Dec. 1922			U.162	Schiff, S.	British Libr.	1	266	202		Wove			
625A	4 Dec. 1922	T.498	p. 606		Woolf, V.	Berg	1	262	201	0.06	Wove			
625B	4 Dec. 1922	T.498	p. 606		Woolf, V.	Berg	1	267	202	0.06	Wove			
626	4 Dec. 1922	T.499	p. 607		Eliot, T. L.	Reed	1	268	203		Wove			
627	7 Dec. 1922			U.163	Aldington, R.	Texas	2	252	204	0.07	Wove			
628	8 Dec. 1922			U.164	Lewis, W.	Cornell	1	254	203	0.08	Wove			
629	12 Dec. 1922	T.501	p. 610		Pound, E.	Lilly	1	251	204	0.07	Wove			
630	12 Dec. 1922	T.502	p. 611		Morrell, O.	Texas	1	253	205	0.04	Wove			
631A	15 Dec. 1922	T.503	p. 612		Pound, E.	Lilly	1	252	204	0.07	Wove			
631B	15 Dec. 1922	T.503	p. 612		Pound, E.	Lilly	1	263	201	0.10	Wove			
632	15 Dec. 1922	T.504	p. 613		Aldington, R.	Texas	1	263	202	0.09	Wove			
633	18 Dec. 1922	T.505	p. 613		Thayer, S.	Beinecke	1	263	201	0.10	Wove			
634	26 Dec. 1922	T.506	p. 614		C.-Sanderson, R.	Gallup	1	263	202	0.10	Wove			
635	27 Dec. 1922	T.507	p. 615		Quinn, J.	NYPL	1	252	204	0.07	Wove			
636	27 Dec. 1922			U.165	Read, H.	Victoria	1	263	203	0.09	Wove			
637	29 Dec. 1922			U.166	Morrell, O.	Texas	1	253	204	0.06	Wove			
638	31 Dec. 1922	T.508	p. 616		C.-Sanderson, R.	Gallup	1	263	202	0.10	Wove			

WATERMARK	POSITION	DIMENSIONS	COLOR	PRINTING	LINED PAPER	PC	MS	TS	SCRIPT	TYPEWR.	NOTE	NO.
None			White	9, Clarence Gate		X			Black ink			580
None			White					X	Black ribbon	2.10		581
None			White					X	Black ribbon	2.10		582
Charta Regia	Horizontal	99 x 93	White	The Criterion		X			Black ink			583
*CRB	Horizontal	133 x 114	White	The Criterion		X			Black ink			584
Charta Regia	Horizontal	99 x 94	White	The Criterion				X	Black ribbon	2.10		585
Charta Regia	Horizontal	99 x 94	White	The Criterion		X			Black ink			586
Charta Regia	Horizontal	99 x 94	White	The Criterion				X	Black ribbon	2.10		587
None			White					X	Black ribbon	2.10		588
Charta Regia	Horizontal	99 x 94	White	The Criterion				X	Black ribbon	2.10		589
Charta Regia	Horizontal	99 x 94	White	The Criterion				X	Black ribbon	2.10		590
Charta Regia	Horizontal	99 x 94	White	The Criterion				X	Black ribbon	2.10		591
Charta Regia	Horizontal	99 x 94	White	The Criterion		X			Black ink			592
* Bond	Vertical	27 x 72	White			X			Black ink			593
None			White					X	Black ribbon	2.10		594
Charta Regia	Horizontal	99 x 94	White	The Criterion				X	Black ribbon	2.10		595
Charta Regia	Horizontal	99 x 94	White	The Criterion				X	Black ribbon	2.10		596
Charta Regia	Horizontal	99 x 94	White	The Criterion				X	Black ribbon	2.10		597
Charta Regia	Horizontal	99 x 94	White	The Criterion		X			Black ink			598
Charta Regia	Horizontal	99 x 94	White	The Criterion		X			Black ink			599
Charta Regia	Horizontal	99 x 94	White	The Criterion				X	Black ribbon	2.10		600
Charta Regia	Horizontal	99 x 94	White	The Criterion				X	Black ribbon	2.10		601
None			White					X	Black ribbon	2.10		602
None			White			X			Black ink			603
None			White			X			Black ink			604
None			White			X			Black ink			605
*CRB	Horizontal	134 x 114	White	The Criterion				X	Black ribbon	2.10		606
*CRB	Horizontal	134 x 114	White	The Criterion				X	Black ribbon	2.10		607
None			White					X	Black ribbon	2.10		608
None			White					X	Black ribbon	2.10		609
None			White					X	Black ribbon	2.10		610
*CRB	Horizontal	134 x 114	White					X	Black ribbon	2.10		611
None			Light yellow brown 76	Post * Card		X	X		Black ink			612
None			Light gray 264			X	X		Black ink			613
None			White					X	Black ribbon	2.10		614
None			White			X			Black ink			615
None			Light yellow brown 76	Post * Card		X	X		Black ink			616
None			White					X	Black ribbon	2.10	5.3	617
None			White			X			Black ink		5.3	618
None			White			X			Black ink			619
*CRB	Horizontal	134 x 114	White	The Criterion				X	Black ribbon	2.10		620
Charta Regia	Horizontal	99 x 94	White	The Criterion				X	Black ribbon	2.10		621
Charta Regia	Horizontal	99 x 94	White	The Criterion				X	Black ribbon	2.10		622
None			White			X			Black ink			623
None			White			X			Black ink		2.2	624
Charta Regia	Horizontal	99 x 94	White	The Criterion				X	Black ribbon	2.10		625A
None			White					X	Black ribbon	2.10		625B
None			White					X	Black ribbon	2.10	2.3	626
None			White					X	Black ribbon	2.10		627
None			White					X	Black ribbon	2.10		628
None			White					X	Black ribbon	2.10		629
None			White					X	Black ribbon	2.10		630
None			White			X			Black ink			631A
*CRB	Horizontal	134 x 114	White	The Criterion		X			Black ink			631B
Charta Regia	Horizontal	99 x 94	White	The Criterion		X			Black ink			632
Charta Regia	Horizontal	99 x 94	White	The Criterion				X	Black ribbon	2.10		633
Charta Regia	Horizontal	99 x 94	White	The Criterion		X			Black ink			634
None			White					X	Black ribbon	2.10		635
Charta Regia	Horizontal	99 x 94	White	The Criterion				X	Black ribbon	2.10		636
None			White			X			Black ink			637
Charta Regia	Horizontal	99 x 94	White	The Criterion				X	Black ribbon	2.10		638

NOTES

1. Variants in Height or Width

1.1 Height and width are conjectured reconstructions; the leaf itself, evenly torn at the top and right margins, measures 208 × 125 mm.

1.2 Paper has deckled edges.

1.3 Height reconstructed; actual size is 178 × 114 mm.

1.4 Height reconstructed; actual size is 176 × 113 mm.

1.5 One side of the leaf has been cut to fit into an envelope; the actual width ranges from 166 to 172 mm.

1.6 The height given here is a conjectural reconstruction; the leaf, which has been cut at the top, actually measures 254 mm. in height.

2. Variants in Thickness

2.1 Letter encased in Mylar; thickness cannot be measured.

2.2 Letter mounted on backing; thickness cannot be measured.

2.3 The original of this letter has not been consulted and therefore there is no information about its thickness. Height and width provided by curators; typewriter measurements from photocopy.

3. Variants in Chainlines

3.1 Leaf B has 5 chainlines.

3.2 Leaf B has 7 chainlines.

3.3 Leaf B has 8 chainlines.

3.4 Leaf C has 7 chainlines.

3.5 Leaves B and C have 7 chainlines.

4. Variants in Watermarks

4.1 Watermark too faint to read, though discernible.

4.2 Watermark legible, but too faint to measure.

4.3 Only part of the watermark is visible, reading "Superior Satin." But other measurements show this is the same kind of paper elsewhere designated with the watermark of "HL Co. Ltd."

4.4 Though no watermark appears on this leaf, other measurements indicate that it is the same kind of paper elsewhere designated with the watermark "HL Co. Ltd."

4.5 Though no watermark appears on this leaf, other measurements indicate that it is the same kind of paper elsewhere designated with the watermark "Basildon Bond."

5. Variants in Typewriting

5.1 Some characters are in red, apparently the result of dual ribbon with black and red halves.

5.2 Traces of black ribbon are discernible, apparently the result of a dual ribbon with black and red halves.

5.3 Leaf B is a carbon copy of Eliot's transcription from an article that appeared in the *Liverpool Daily Post,* 16 November 1922, the text of which is reprinted in *LOTSE,* 555 n. 1.

6. Variants in Dating and Location

6.1 The letter is contained on the verso of a letter from Vivien Eliot to Henry Eliot, 17 October 1918, reported in *LOTSE,* 245.

6.2 *LOTSE,* 260, incorrectly assigns this letter to the Houghton Library at Harvard University.

6.3 T. S. Eliot incorrectly dates this letter 2 December 1921.

6.4 *LOTSE,* 463, mistakenly reports that this letter dates from 8 August, rather than 8 March, 1921.

6.5 *LOTSE,* 449, mistakenly reports that this letter dates from 2 May 1921.

6.6 *LOTSE,* 504, mistakenly assigns this letter to [24? January 1922]. The error results from assigning a date of [24 December 1921] (*LOTSE,* 497) to a letter from Ezra Pound to T. S. Eliot, one that Pound dated "24 Saturnus An I," following an esoteric calendar which he published. In the calendar, "Saturnus" replaces January, and Pound's letter should be dated 24 January 1922. In turn, Eliot's reply, the letter under discussion (T.394), should be dated [26 January 1922].

APPENDIX 1: T. S. ELIOT'S UNPUBLISHED LETTERS, 1914–1922

This appendix lists the 166 unpublished letters by T. S. Eliot, dating from 1914 through 1922, that were used in drawing up Table 1, synthesizing information already contained there and adding each letter's incipit (or opening words), a device that identifies exactly which letter is being designated. Of the 166 letters listed here, forty-four lack a date or a postmark, and I am responsible for assigning them the dates which appear here in square brackets. The rationale used to assign dates to these letters is given in Appendix 2, which immediately follows. When a letter has been dated solely by its postmark, instead, the date is preceded by the abbreviation PM.

NO.	DATE	RECIPIENT	INCIPIT	LOCATION
U.1	2 October 1914	Briggs, L. B. R.	In accordance with the requirements	Harvard
U.2	23 October 1914	Wiener, Norbert	I hear from an American here that	M.I.T.
U.3	[20? December 1914]	Wiener, Norbert	Did you ever get a note from me?	M.I.T.
U.4	PM 7 January 1915	Thayer, Scofield	I forgot to say that Wiener's address	Beinecke
U.5	[16 August 1915]	Woods, J. H.	I forgot to answer your questions	Williams
U.6	17 October 1915	Monroe, Harriet	I have received the cheque for £.3	Chicago
U.7	[2 January 1916]	Russell, Bertrand	Have just found that they have two	McMaster
U.8	27 January 1916	Waterlow, Sidney	It is very kind of you to forward the	Waterlow
U.9	28 September 1916	Monroe, Harriet	Thank you very much for the cheque	Chicago
U.10	27 October 1916	Zimmern, Alfred	I find that I owe you a great debt	Bodleian
U.11	1 January 1917	Hutchinson, Mary	I am glad to be able to accept	Texas

NO.	DATE	RECIPIENT	INCIPIT	LOCATION
U.12	16 January 1917	Huxley, Julian	I am writing this to you, as I fear	Fondren
U.13	28 March 1917	Hutchinson, Mary	I must apologise very deeply for	Texas
U.14	23 September 1917	Huxley, Julian	I got away from the City at 1^{15}	Fondren
U.15	[15? December 1917]	Mother	I don't know whether you saw this	Virginia
U.16	1 May 1918	Hutchinson, Mary	I only got your note late last night	Texas
U.17	1 July 1918	Hutchinson, Mary	I meant to let you know that I had	Texas
U.18	6 July 1918	Monroe, Harriet	Thank you for your appreciation of	Chicago
U.19	4 August 1918	Hutchinson, Mary	Thanks awfully for your letter and	Texas
U.20	15 August 1918	Hutchinson, Mary	Thank you very much for your two	Texas
U.21	[19 August 1918]	Lewis, Wyndham	I want to get at Lady Cunard at once	Cornell
U.22	25 August 1918	Hutchinson, St. John	Thanks awfully for your letter, which	Texas
U.23	25 August 1918	Hutchinson, Mary	Thank you so much for your letter. I	Texas
U.24	27 October 1918	Eliot, Henry	Thank you very much for your kind	Houghton
U.25	7 November 1918	Monroe, Harriet	I have handed your correspondence	Chicago
U.26	9 November 1918	Hutchinson, Mary	J. has I hope explained to you	Texas
U.27	10 November 1918	Hutchinson, St. John	I rang up your office twice last week	Texas
U.28	12 November 1918	Woolf, Virginia	Please pardon me for not having	Berg
U.29	2 December 1918	Rodker, John	I sent you the book several days ago	Virginia
U.30	14 December 1918	Wallas, Graham	I am writing, after a long epidemic	LSE
U.31	22 January 1919	Hutchinson, Mary	Do forgive me if I ask you if you	Texas
U.32	29 January 1919	Woolf, Virginia	I return you the proof, which seems	Berg
U.33	1 April 1919	Hutchinson, St. John	Your hospitality is very unfair	Texas
U.34	[1 May 1919]	Hutchinson, Mary	Are we going to see you before you go	Texas
U.35	16 May 1919	Hutchinson, Mary	Of course I should be delighted	Texas
U.36	[21 May 1919]	Rodker, John	Thanks for your letter. I am sorry	Virginia
U.37	[21 May 1919]	Strachey, Lytton	Don't be absurd—of course I should	BL
U.38	[26 May 1919]	Hutchinson, Mary	I am so sorry about Thursday. It would	Texas
U.39	[10 June 1919]	Hutchinson, Mary	About half a mile further the car	Texas
U.40	[1 July 1919]	Hutchinson, Mary	Thank you for wiring to the ferryman	Texas
U.41	11 July 1919	Jepson, Edgar	We should have loved to come on	Gallup
U.42	PM 7 August 1919	Hutchinson, Mary	Vivian says book were [sic] gift	Texas
U.43	[4 September 1919]	Hutchinson, Mary	I am so sorry and hope it is not a	Texas
U.44	10 September 1919	Squire, John Collins	I have been walking in France, & your	UCLA
U.45	[3 November 1919]	Jepson, Edgar	I wrote and suggested next Sunday	Gallup
U.46	10 November 1919	Hutchinson, Mary	Thank you for the card—I was sorry	Texas
U.47	24 November 1919	Morrell, Ottoline	May we choose the 6th to come to	Texas
U.48	13 December 1919	Jepson, Edgar	I have been meaning to write to you	Gallup
U.49	[17 December 1919]	Jepson, Edgar	I enclose the Playwrights, which I	Gallup
U.50	7 January 1920	Knopf, Alfred	This is merely to thank you for your	Texas
U.51	7 January 1920	Hutchinson, Mary	I am ashamed of the meal you had	Texas
U.52	[14? January 1920]	Morrell, Ottoline	I understood that you were to be at	Texas
U.53	[18? January 1920]	Hutchinson, Mary	Just found your note. We *thought*	Texas
U.54	20 January 1920	Rodker, John	I am sorry that I have not had time	Gallup
U.55	[15 February 1920]	Morrell, Ottoline	I found your card on getting back	Texas
U.56	21 February 1920	Monro, Harold	Here it is, such as it is. If I had	Gallup
U.57	[25 March 1920]	Hutchinson, Mary	I should like very much to meet Tonks	Texas
U.58	PM 4 April 1920	Hutchinson, Mary	Nous y sommes. Quel dommage que	Texas
U.59	[12 April 1920]	Hutchinson, Mary	Mary, how charming of you to ask us	Texas
U.60	[15 April 1920]	Hutchinson, Mary	Mary, thank you for suggesting another	Texas
U.61	[13 May 1920]	Monro, Harold	Can you come to tea tomorrow Friday	Gallup
U.62	PM 6 June 1920	Hutchinson, Mary	Dear Mary, do you think we could have	Texas
U.63	9 June 1920	Aiken, Conrad	I am very sorry I had unexpectedly to	Huntington

NO.	DATE	RECIPIENT	INCIPIT	LOCATION
U.64	[10 June 1920]	Aiken, Conrad	Can you come in to tea *tomorrow*	Huntington
U.65	PM 20 July 1920	Aiken, Conrad	You must get your visa via	Huntington
U.66	[14 August 1920]	Jepson, Edgar	Thank you for your note. I should	Gallup
U.67	[27 August 1920]	Lewis, Wyndham	I sent Fritz a card to say that I would	Cornell
U.68	[5 September 1920]	Schiff, Sydney	After all, if you can have me I should	BL
U.69	23 September 1920	Torrence, Ridgley	I thank you for your letter of the 24th	Princeton
U.70	15 October 1920	Jepson, Edgar	Please forgive my unpardonable delay	Gallup
U.71	18 October 1920	Lewis, Wyndham	You may already have left for Hastings	Cornell
U.72	PM 30 October 1920	Hutchinson, Mary	I am so sorry about these	Texas
U.73	2 November 1920	Methuen, Sir A.	Thank you for your letter about	Lilly
U.74	[5 November 1920]	Monro, Harold	I am writing to de la Mare to	Gallup
U.75	16 November 1920	Green, Russell	Again I should like to help you, but	Texas
U.76	8 December 1920	Jepson, Edgar	I am returning your tickets with	Gallup
U.77	[2 January 1921]	Woolf, Leonard	I shall be very glad to dine and	Berg
U.78	18 January 1921	Woolf, Leonard	Thank you for your letter of the 11th	Berg
U.79	7 April 1921	Aldington, Richard	Thank you very much for your letter.	Texas
U.80	[22 April 1921]	Jepson, Edgar	In the fatigue of last night I failed	Gallup
U.81	18 May 1921	Jepson, Edgar	Thank you very much for sending	Gallup
U.82	[15 June 1921]	Hutchinson, Mary	I have spotted a telephone at 41	Texas
U.83	PM 18 August 1921	Pound, Dorothy	Will dine on Monday or Tuesday	Lilly
U.84	21 August 1921	Pound, Dorothy	Tuesday is excellent, but Clarence	Lilly
U.85	23 September 1921	Jepson, Edgar	We have perpetual bad luck—we	Gallup
U.86	2 October 1921	Cobden-Sanderson, R.	I should have written you much	Gallup
U.87	PM 5 October 1921	Hutchinson, Mary	Thank you *very much* for your letter.	Texas
U.88	PM 1 November 1921	Eliot, Henry	Have been here a 4'night, & may	Houghton
U.89	16 November 1921	Monro, Harold	Thanks very much for your amble	Gallup
U.90	PM 17 November 1921	Hutchinson, Mary	This is a farewell note to tell	Texas
U.91	PM 3 December 1921	Lewis, Wyndham	I wish you wd. send me the criticism	Cornell
U.92	5 December 1921	Rivière, Jacques	Je viens de recevoir votre aimable	Texas
U.93	PM 23 December 1921	Hutchinson, Mary	Pour vous souhaiter la bonne année	Texas
U.94	30 January 1922	Cobden-Sanderson, R.	Since writing to you I have heard	Gallup
U.95	[1 February 1922]	Cobden-Sanderson, R.	Lady Rothermere dines at 8. I shall	Gallup
U.96	[5 February 1922]	Rodker, John	I should have communicated with	Virginia
U.97	[5? February 1922]	Hutchinson, Mary	I am very much distressed by	Texas
U.98	6 February 1922	Bax, Clifford	I must apologise for not replying	Texas
U.99	17 February 1922	Aldington, Richard	You will excuse me, I hope, for	Texas
U.100	26 February 1922	Firuski, Maurice	Your name has been given me by	Williams
U.101	4 March 1922	Knopf, Alfred	Thank you for your letter of the 20th	Texas
U.102	PM 8 March 1922	Thayer, Scofield	cannot accept under !8!56 pounds	Beinecke
U.103	27 March 1922	Hesse, Hermann	I have your manuscript today	Schiller
U.104	27 March 1922	Thayer, Scofield	I discovered when in Switzerland	Beinecke
U.105	[1? April 1922]	Monro, Harold	It was a great pleasure to me	Gallup
U.106	[6 April 1922]	Schiff, Sydney	The only person I have to whom	BL
U.107	[12 April 1922]	Hutchinson, Mary	I rang you up tonight but you were	Texas
U.108	[19 April 1922]	Hutchinson, Mary	Thank you for your suggestion	Texas
U.109	6 May 1922	Woolf, Leonard	I am so sorry and anxious to hear	Berg
U.110	[11 May 1922]	Aldington, Richard	Thanks very much for your 2 letters	Texas
U.111	19 May 1922	Jepson, Edgar	I am very glad to have your book	Gallup
U.112	20 May 1922	Knopf, Alfred	Thank you for your kind letter	Texas
U.113	20 May 1922	Woolf, Leonard	Your letter and MS. arrived just	Princeton
U.114	24 May 1922	Hesse, Hermann	Sie werden sich erinnern, dass	Schiller
U.115	PM 27 May 1922	Hutchinson, Mary	Specialità Asti Spumante fresca	Texas

NO.	DATE	RECIPIENT	INCIPIT	LOCATION
U.116	PM 31 May 1922	Aiken, Conrad	I recommend this place as	Huntington
U.117	PM 31 May 1922	Hesse, Hermann	Ich empfange Ihre Dichtung mit	Schiller
U.118	10 June 1922	Rivière, Jacques	Je viens de rentre à Londres	Texas
U.119	10 June 1922	Woolf, Leonard	I should very much like to publish	Princeton
U.120	12 June 1922	Cobden-Sanderson, R.	I trust that you are back in town	Gallup
U.121	[15 June 1922]	Cobden-Sanderson, R.	Thank you for your card. I	Gallup
U.122	18 June [1922]	Lewis, Wyndham	I am very sorry to find that	Cornell
U.123	PM 21 June 1922	Quinn, John	DISSATISFIED LIVERIGHTS	NYPL
U.124	PM 25 June 1922	Quinn, John	VERY GRATEFUL PLEASE WAIT	NYPL
U.125	27 June 1922	Moore, Thomas S.	Thank you for your letter of the 22nd	Texas
U.126	1 July 1922	Woolf, Leonard	I am waiting hopefully to know	Princeton
U.127	4 July 1922	Aldington, Richard	I was very glad indeed to get your	Texas
U.128	5 July 1922	Woolf, Leonard	Thank you for your letter of the 3d.	Princeton
U.129	9 July 1922	Curtius, Ernst	Ich gestatte mich, Ihnen zu schreiben	Bonn
U.130	11 July 1922	Schiff, Sydney	I have been waiting every day to	BL
U.131	13 July 1922	Woolf, Leonard	Thank you for your letter of the 8th	Princeton
U.132	[17 July 1922]	Pound, Dorothy	I have just come back from Bosham	Lilly
U.133	18 July 1922	Cobden-Sanderson, R.	Thank you very much for your letter	Gallup
U.134	18 July 1922	Woolf, Leonard	Thank you very much for your efforts	Princeton
U.135	PM 25 July 1922	Moore, T. Sturge	I am delighted. This is my address	Texas
U.136	PM 28 July 1922	Moore, T. Sturge	I have your MSS. and am looking	Texas
U.137	[4 August 1922]	Pound, Dorothy	It is very sweet of you to send the	Lilly
U.138	[9 August 1922]	Pound, Dorothy	I arrived back from my weekend at	Lilly
U.139	PM 12 August 1922	Pound, Dorothy	I am indeed very disappointed, but	Lilly
U.140	14 August 1922	Wilson, Edmund	Thank you for your letter of the 1st	Beinecke
U.141	PM 17 August 1922	Watson, James Sibley	PLEASE TAKE NO STEPS AWAIT	Berg
U.142	21 August 1922	Wilson, Edmund	Referring to my letter of the 14th	Beinecke
U.143	PM 23 August 1922	Aldington, Richard	I will be in Monday evening by 9	Texas
U.144	PM 23 August 1922	Cobden-Sanderson, R.	I will answer yr. letter in a day	Texas
U.145	PM 23 August 1922	Pound, Dorothy	I am delighted to hear you are back	Lilly
U.146	23 August 1922	Read, Herbert	Thank you for your postcard with	Victoria
U.147	7 September 1922	Cobden-Sanderson, R.	I am very sorry indeed to hear your	Texas
U.148	13 September 1922	Hutchinson, Mary	I was really dreadfully sorry to	Texas
U.149	22 September 1922	Flint, F. S.	Can you manage to return this to	Texas
U.150	26 September 1922	Cobden-Sanderson, R.	I enclose proof. Saintsbury, Miss	Gallup
U.151	1 October 1922	Wilson, Edmund	Thank you very much for your letter	Beinecke
U.152	[6 October 1922]	Hutchinson, Mary	Vivien has been very ill this week	Texas
U.153	15 October 1922	Cobden-Sanderson, R.	I rang you up on Saturday, simply	Gallup
U.154	18 October 1922	Flint, F. S.	I have had to devote al my	Texas
U.155	1 November 1922	Jean-Aubry, G.	Je viens de rentrer, je trouve	Texas
U.156	5 November 1922	Murry, John Middleton	I should like very much to spend	Northwestern
U.157	8 November 1922	Wilson, Edmund	I have received your letter of the	Beinecke
U.158	12 November 1922	Cobden-Sanderson, R.	As I told you on the	Gallup
U.159	13 November 1922	Cobden-Sanderson, R.	Thank you for your letter and	Texas
U.160	PM 16 November 1922	Hutchinson, Mary	Yes my dear thank you, I shall	Texas
U.161	[1 December 1922]	Hutchinson, Mary	I was *very* sorry not to see you	Texas
U.162	4 December 1922	Schiff, Sydney	Vivien has reported to me a	BL
U.163	7 December 1922	Aldington, Richard	You will not I know think that	Texas
U.164	8 December 1922	Lewis, Wyndham	I should like to see you on a matter	Cornell
U.165	27 December 1922	Read, Herbert	I have at last had time over the	Victoria
U.166	29 December 1922	Morrell, Ottoline	Thank you so much for your present	Texas

APPENDIX 2: RATIONALE FOR DATES ASSIGNED TO ELIOT'S UNDATED
LETTERS, 1914–1922

Letter No.: U.3
Date: [20? December 1914]
Recipient: Norbert Wiener
Incipit: Did you ever get a note from me?
Location: M.I.T.

Eliot notes that he is writing from "Swanage, Dorsetshire." In a letter dated
[9? November 1914] he had informed Wiener that he "was planning to retire
somewhere in the country with books" (*LOTSE*, 66) during the six-week vacation
between terms, and to Eleanor Hinkley on 27 November 1914 he mentioned his
plan to spend "a fortnight or so somewhere in the country with books" (*LOTSE*,
72). Since Eliot was already in London by 31 December, where he planned to stay
until 15 January 1915 and whence he informed Conrad Aiken that he had just
"spent nearly three [weeks] at the seashore in Dorsetshire" (*LOTSE*, 74), the letter
must date from sometime between 10 and 31 December. 20 December is a rough
guess.

Letter No.: U.5
Date: [16 August 1915]
Recipient: James H. Woods
Incipit: I forgot to answer your questions
Location: Williams

Eliot notes that he is writing on "Monday" from "Eastern Point," near Glouces-
ter, Massachusetts. The letter discusses matters omitted in his previous letter to
Woods, written early the same day and dated 16 August 1915 (*LOTSE*, 112–113).

Letter No.: U.7
Date: [2 January 1916]
Recipient: Bertrand Russell
Incipit: Have just found that they have two
Location: McMaster

Eliot notes that he is writing on "Sunday." The letter's contents make clear
that it precedes Russell's arrival in Chichester, which took place on 6 January
according to Valerie Eliot (*LOTSE*, 127 n. 1), and therefore "Sunday" must refer
to 2 January 1916.

Letter No.: U.15
Date: [15? December 1917]
Recipient: Mother
Incipit: I don't know whether you saw this
Location: Virginia

This letter accompanied Eliot's Christmas gift of a book called *Union
Portraits* (Boston: Houghton Mifflin, 1916), by Gamaliel Bradford, a work that

Eliot reviewed in April 1917 for the *New Statesman;* see Donald Gallup, *T. S. Eliot: A Bibliography,* rev. ed. (New York: Harcourt Brace, 1963), C39b, and Lyndal Gordon, *Eliot's Early Years* (New York: Farrar, Straus, 1977), 2.

Letter No.: U.21
Date: [19 August 1918]
Recipient: Wyndham Lewis
Incipit: I want to get at Lady Cunard at once
Location: Cornell

Eliot states that he is writing on "Monday." The letter asks Lewis to help Eliot meet Lady Cunard, and further references appear in U.22, dated 25 August 1918, to St. John Hutchinson, leaving little doubt that "Monday" was 19 August 1918. The letter also mentions an appointment that Lewis had failed to keep the previous Monday, 12 August; the appointment is arranged in a letter from Eliot to Lewis, 11 August 1918 (*LOTSE,* 240).

Letter No.: U.34
Date: [1 May 1919]
Recipient: Mary Hutchinson
Incipit: Are we going to see you before you go
Location: Texas

Eliot states that he is writing to Hutchinson on "Thursday," and notes that he and Vivien must move out of their flat and into separate hotels for a brief period beginning Saturday, 3 May, and ending on Friday, 16 May 1919. "Thursday," therefore, must refer to 1 May. A letter by Vivien Eliot to Mary Hutchinson that is also dated "Thursday" and ascribed to [1 May? 1919] by Valerie Eliot (*LOTSE,* 288) was more likely written on 8 May, since Vivien gives as her return address the hotel to which she had moved, at 39 Inverness Terrace.

Letter No.: U.36
Date: [21 May 1919]
Recipient: Lytton Strachey
Incipit: Don't be absurd—of course I should
Location: British Library

Eliot states that he is writing on "Wednesday." His brief note apparently replies to one by Strachey, who had answered an earlier letter by Eliot dated Monday, 19 May 1919 (*LOTSE,* 295); thus it is likely that "Wednesday" refers to 21 May 1919.

Letter No.: U.37
Date: [21 May 1919]
Recipient: John Rodker
Incipit: Thanks for your letter. I am sorry
Location: Virginia

Eliot notes that his letter dates from "Wednesday." He had first approved Rodker's proposal for a deluxe edition of his recent poetry on Saturday, 17 May 1919 (*LOTSE*, 294), shortly after the publication of his *Poems* with the Hogarth Press on 12 May. This letter, like the earlier one, discusses how many new poems the Rodker volume should contain, allowing one to infer that "Wednesday" must be 21 May 1919.

Letter No.: U.38
Date: [26 May 1919]
Recipient: Mary Hutchinson
Incipit: I am so sorry about Thursday. It would
Location: Texas
Eliot notes that he is writing on "Monday." He mentions that he would enjoy seeing Roger Fry on his forthcoming visit to take place on Whitsun (8 June) at Mary Hutchinson's country house, a prospect first broached in his letter to her of 16 May 1919 (*LOTSE*, 291–292). He also makes reference to his travels at this time on behalf of Lloyds Bank, which allows us to infer that "Monday" refers to 26 May 1921.

Letter No.: U.39
Date: [10 June 1919]
Recipient: Mary Hutchinson
Incipit: About half a mile further the car
Location: Texas
Though dated only "Tuesday" by Eliot, the letter thanks Mary Hutchinson for having him as a guest over Pentecost, which fell on Sunday, 8 June 1919, allowing us to infer that "Tuesday" means 10 June 1919.

Letter No.: U.40
Date: [1 July 1919]
Recipient: Mary Hutchinson
Incipit: Thank you for wiring to the ferryman
Location: Texas
Though dated only "Tuesday" by Eliot, the letter is conserved with an envelope postmarked 2 July 1919, a Wednesday. The letter also refers to "all this trouble about the boat," an incident which took place on the preceding Sunday, 29 June 1919, when Eliot, together with Vivien, Mary Hutchinson, and Sacheverell Sitwell, rented a boat and "got stuck on a sandbank." He recounts the incident in a letter to his mother dated 29 June 1919 (*LOTSE*, 309).

Letter No.: U.43
Date: [4 September 1919]
Recipient: Mary Hutchinson
Incipit: I am so sorry and hope it is not a

Location: Texas

The letter is dated only "Wednesday." However, the letter refers to Eliot's reading during his "lunch time" a book by Flaubert, one given to him by Mary Hutchinson. He had accepted her offer of this book in an earlier letter to her, one assigned to [11? July 1919] by Valerie Eliot (*LOTSE*, 326), and had acknowledged receiving it in yet another postmarked 7 August 1919 (U.42). Eliot was away from work, traveling in France, from 9 to 31 August and had no "lunch time" during this period. "Wednesday" must therefore refer to the week immediately after his return, or 4 September 1919.

Letter No.: U.45
Date: [3 November 1919]
Recipient: Edgar Jepson
Incipit: I wrote and suggested next Sunday
Location: Gallup

The letter is dated only "Monday" by Eliot. In the letter he retracts an offer to meet with Jepson which he had advanced in a previous letter of Friday, 31 October 1919 (*LOTSE*, 343), and therefore "Monday" must be 3 November.

Letter No.: U.49
Date: [17 December 1919]
Recipient: Edgar Jepson
Incipit: I enclose the Playwrights, which I
Location: Gallup

Eliot dates the letter only "Wednesday." However, he refers to the proximity of Christmas and Vivien's impending trip "out of town" on the coming weekend. Vivien's diary shows that she left London for their country cottage in Bosham on Saturday, 20 December 1919, and therefore the letter should be assigned to Wednesday, 17 December 1919.

Letter No.: U.52
Date: [14? January 1920]
Recipient: Ottoline Morrell
Incipit: I understood that you were to be at
Location: Texas

The letter is dated only "Wednesday." However, Eliot addresses Ottoline Morrell as "Lady Ottoline," a formality he abandoned in letters to her after February 1920; and he refers to Wyndham Lewis sending her "his book," most likely the *Fifty Drawings* published in January 1920 by John Rodker and his Ovid Press. The letter is written on paper with a watermark that depicts a crown above the single word "Bond," a watermark also found in his letters of 7 and 11 January 1920 (U.51, T.251 in *LOTSE*, 354). "Wednesday," therefore, is probably Wednesday, 14 January 1920.

Letter No.: U.53
Date: [18? January 1920]
Recipient: Mary Hutchinson
Incipit: Just found your note. We *thought*
Location: Texas

The letter is dated only "Sunday." However, it clearly replies to a note from Mary, one that in turn responded to an earlier letter by Eliot which is assigned to [14 January 1920] by Valerie Eliot (*LOTSE*, 357). "Sunday," therefore, is Sunday, 18 January 1920.

Letter No.: U.55
Date: [15 February 1920]
Recipient: Ottoline Morrell
Incipit: I found your card on getting back
Location: Texas

The letter is dated only "Sunday." However, Eliot refers to a letter soliciting funds for the Phoenix Society, a topic he also mentions in a letter to Mary Hutchinson of 21 February 1920 (*LOTSE*, 367). He also expresses his hopes for an upcoming encounter with Ottoline on "Wednesday evening," an encounter that he later describes to his mother on 22 February 1920 (*LOTSE*, 368). "Sunday," therefore, must refer to 15 February 1920.

Letter No.: U.57
Date: [25 March 1920]
Recipient: Mary Hutchinson
Incipit: I should very much like to meet Tonks
Location: Texas

The letter is dated only "Thursday," but its envelope is postmarked 26 March 1920, a Friday.

Letter No.: U.59
Date: [12 April 1920]
Recipient: Mary Hutchinson
Incipit: Mary, how charming of you to ask us
Location: Texas

The letter is dated only "Monday." But Eliot refers to "the most depressing adventure which Paris turned out to be," a trip to Paris cut short by an attack of influenza. The journey is recounted in an unpublished postcard to Mary Hutchinson, postmarked 4 April 1920 (U.58), and in a letter to Ottoline Morrell, dated Saturday, 10 April 1920 (*LOTSE*, 379). "Tuesday," therefore, must be Tuesday, 12 April 1920.

Letter No.: U.60
Date: [15 April 1920]

Recipient: Mary Hutchinson
Incipit: Mary, thank you for suggesting another
Location: Texas

The letter is dated only "Thursday." However, it mentions a recent review of Paul-Jean Toulet in the *Times Literary Supplement,* one that appeared on Thursday, 15 April 1920, leaving no doubt about the letter's date.

Letter No.: U.61
Date: [13 May 1920]
Recipient: Harold Monro
Incipit: Can you come to tea tomorrow Friday
Location: Gallup

The letter is dated only "Thursday." But in a letter of Sunday, 16 May 1920, to John Rodker (*LOTSE,* 383), Eliot mentions his recent conversation with Monro, presumably the one they had over tea on "Friday," 14 May, the result of this letter of Thursday, 13 May.

Letter No.: U.64
Date: [10 June 1920]
Recipient: Conrad Aiken
Incipit: Can you come in to tea *tomorrow*
Location: Huntington

Eliot's letter is dated only "Thursday." In an unpublished postcard dated Wednesday, 9 June 1920 (U.63), Eliot had invited Conrad Aiken to meet the next day; Aiken must have replied that he could not make it, for in this letter Eliot proposes "*tomorrow* Friday" instead. "Thursday," therefore, must be 10 June 1920.

Letter No.: U.66
Date: [14 August 1920]
Recipient: Edgar Jepson
Incipit: Thank you for your note. I should
Location: Gallup

The letter is dated only "Saturday." However, Eliot mentions his contract with Methuen for *The Sacred Wood,* which places the letter sometime after May 1920, when the contract was finalized, and he notes that he is "off to France this afternoon," which can refer only to 14 August 1920, a Saturday, when he departed with Wyndham Lewis for Paris. There they both met James Joyce.

Letter No.: U.67
Date: [27 August 1920]
Recipient: Wyndham Lewis
Incipit: I sent Fritz a card to say that I would
Location: Cornell

The letter is dated only "Friday." Eliot informs Lewis of the arrangements that he has made for a discussion to take place among Lewis, "Fritz" Vanderpyl, and himself. "Friday" would therefore have been 27 August 1920, when he and Lewis stopped in Paris on their way back from two weeks' holiday in northern France. Eliot also mentions his plan to visit Vanderpyl in a postcard to Ezra Pound, postmarked the preceding day, 26 August 1920 (*LOTSE*, 404).

Letter No.: U.68
Date: [5 September 1920]
Recipient: Sydney Schiff
Incipit: After all, if you can have me I should
Location: British Library

The letter is dated only "Sunday." Signed "Affectionately, T.S.E.," it adopts a form of closing that places it sometime after March 1920, when Eliot first adopts this form in letters to Schiff; and it announces Eliot's acceptance of Schiff's invitation to visit him in Eastborne "for next weekend (11ᵗʰ)," which must mean the weekend of 11 September. The inference that "Sunday" is 5 September 1920, the Sunday immediately preceding "next weekend (11ᵗʰ)" September, is buttressed by the watermark discernible in the letter's paper, "London Bond"; it appears in only two other letters by Eliot, one from [14 August 1920] to Edgar Jepson (U.66), the other from 31 August 1920 (T.301, *LOTSE*, 404–405).

Letter No.: U.74
Date: [5 November 1920]
Recipient: Harold Monro
Incipit: I am writing to de la Mare to
Location: Gallup

The letter is dated only "Friday." It announces Eliot's intention to write immediately to Walter de la Mare, something he did only twice, once on 5 November 1920 (a Friday), and once again on 8 November (*LOTSE*, 420–421).

Letter No.: U.80
Date: [22 April 1921]
Recipient: Edgar Jepson
Incipit: In the fatigue of last night I failed
Location: Gallup

With this letter Eliot sends Jepson a ticket to a performance of *The Witch of Edmonton*, a play by Thomas Dekker, John Ford, and William Rowley. The performance, which starred Sybil Thorndike, took place on 24 April 1921 and was attended by both Eliot and Jepson (see *LOTSE*, xxv).

Letter No.: U.82
Date: [15 June 1921]
Recipient: Mary Hutchinson
Incipit: I have spotted a telephone at 41

Location: Texas

The letter refers to finding lodgings for Eliot's brother Henry, who came to England on 10 June 1921 (together with Eliot's mother and sister, who were staying in Eliot's flat), and the envelope is postmarked "16 Jun 21 / 12:45 AM."

Letter No.: U.87
Date: [4 October 1921]
Recipient: Mary Hutchinson
Incipit: Thank you *very much* for your letter
Location: Texas

Though undated, the postcard is postmarked "5 OCT 1921 / 12:45 AM" and so was written the evening before, on 4 October 1921.

Letter No.: U.95
Date: [1 February 1922]
Recipient: Richard Cobden-Sanderson
Incipit: Lady Rothermere dines at 8. I shall
Location: Gallup

The letter is dated only "Wednesday." Eliot reports a change in dinner plans that had been made with Cobden-Sanderson and Lady Rothermere, plans discussed in two previous letters to Cobden-Sanderson, one dated 29 January 1922 (T.395 in *LOTSE*, 506) and the other 30 January 1922 (U.94), leaving no doubt that "Wednesday" is 1 February 1922, one day before the dinner took place.

Letter No.: U.96
Date: [5 February 1922]
Recipient: John Rodker
Incipit: I should have communicated with
Location: Virginia

The letter is dated only "Sunday," but since Eliot reports on the dinner he had with Lady Rothermere on Thursday, 2 February 1922, and notes that he expects to meet Rodker at her house next Wednesday, 8 February, when he was to give a lecture there, "Sunday" must be 5 February 1922.

Letter No.: U.97
Date: [5? February 1922]
Recipient: Mary Hutchinson
Incipit: I am very much distressed by
Location: Texas

The letter is undated. But Eliot notes that he will be busy "working on my lecture up to Wednesday the 8th," no doubt the lecture he gave on 8 February 1922 at the home of Lady Rothermere. Since Eliot typically did correspondence on a Sunday, that of 5 February 1922 is the letter's most likely date.

Letter No.: U.105
Date: [1? April 1922]
Recipient: Harold Monro
Incipit: It was a great pleasure to me
Location: Gallup

The letter has no indication of its date. In it Eliot thanks Monro for having given him his most recent collection of poems, *Real Property* (London: Poetry Bookshop), which was published in April 1922. The letter is written on paper watermarked "INGLEWOOD / [DESIGN OF SHIELD] / PAPER," which appears frequently in Eliot's correspondence from 13 March to 27 June 1922 and never appears before or after those dates. 1 April is therefore a date of convenience; the letter might date from anytime that month.

Letter No.: U.106
Date: [6 April 1922]
Recipient: Sydney Schiff
Incipit: The only person I have to whom
Location: British Library

The letter is wholly undated. However, in the upper right corner of it Sydney Schiff noted in gray ink: "Ack.ᵈ 7.4.22." As indicated by similar annotations on other letters from Eliot to Schiff, Schiff typically replied at once, allowing us to infer that Eliot's letter was written the day before, or 6 April 1922.

Letter No.: U.107
Date: [12 April 1922]
Recipient: Mary Hutchinson
Incipit: I rang you up tonight but you were
Location: Texas

The letter is dated only "Wednesday." However, it describes in some detail Vivien's most recent illness, with temperatures averaging steadily about one hundred degrees, an account that coincides with his description of it to Sydney Schiff on Monday, 10 April 1922 (*LOTSE*, 520–521).

Letter No.: U.108
Date: [19 April 1922]
Recipient: Mary Hutchinson
Incipit: Thank you for your suggestion
Location: Texas

This postcard is postmarked "20 AP 22 / 12:15 AM" and was evidently written the evening before.

Letter No.: U.110
Date: [11 May 1922]
Recipient: Richard Aldington

Incipit: Thanks very much for your 2 letters
Location: Texas

This postcard is postmarked "12 MY / 22 / 2:15 AM," indicating that it was written the evening before, 11 May 1922.

Letter No.: U.121
Date: [15 June 1922]
Recipient: Richard Cobden-Sanderson
Incipit: Thank you for your card. I
Location: Gallup

This postcard is postmarked "16 JUN / 22 / 2:15 AM," indicating that it was written the evening before, 11 June 1922.

Letter No.: U.122
Date: 18 June [1922]
Recipient: Wyndham Lewis
Incipit: I am very sorry to find that
Location: Cornell

The letter is dated 18 June 1921 by Eliot, an inadvertent error for 18 June 1922. In the letter, plainly written on a Sunday, Eliot regrets that he cannot meet with Lewis "tomorrow afternoon" because on that day he must "meet a furniture remover" so that he can complete his move from 12 Wigmore Street to 9 Clarence Gate Gardens "on Tuesday." All Eliot's letters during the spring of 1922, from 12 March through 15 June (*LOTSE*, 506–529), as well as this one of 18 June, are addressed from 12 Wigmore Street, and it is only on [23 June 1922] that he addresses his letter to Mary Hutchinson from 9 Clarence Gate Gardens. The change of addresses is at first sight confusing only because in 1921 the Eliots also moved briefly to Wigmore Street, then back to Clarence Gate Gardens, this time from circa 10 June to 7 September when Eliot's visiting family occupied the flat at Clarence Gate Gardens. But in 1921 they did not move out the furniture, which was left there for Eliot's family, and did not employ a remover.

Letter No.: U.132
Date: [17 July 1922]
Recipient: Dorothy Pound
Incipit: I have just come back from Bosham
Location: Lilly

The letter is dated simply "Monday," but the envelope is postmarked "18 JUL / 22 / 2:45 AM," indicating that the letter was written the evening before, 17 July 1922, a Monday.

Letter No.: U.137
Date: [4 August 1922]
Recipient: Dorothy Pound

Incipit: It is very sweet of you to send the
Location: Lilly

The letter is dated only "Friday," but the envelope is postmarked "5 AUG / 22 / 12:45 AM," a Saturday, indicating that the letter was written the evening before, 4 August, a Friday.

Letter No.: U.138
Date: [9 August 1922]
Recipient: Dorothy Pound
Incipit: I arrived back from my weekend at
Location: Lilly

The letter is dated only "Wednesday," but the envelope is postmarked "10 AUG / 22 / 12:45 AM," a Thursday, indicating that the letter was written the evening before, 9 August.

Letter No.: U.152
Date: [6 October 1922]
Recipient: Mary Hutchinson
Incipit: Vivien has been very ill this week
Location: Texas

The letter is dated only "Wednesday," but the envelope is postmarked "7 OCT / 22 / 12:45 AM," a Saturday, indicating that the letter was written the evening before, 6 October.

Letter No.: U.161
Date: [1 December 1922]
Recipient: Mary Hutchinson
Incipit: I was *very* sorry not to see you
Location: Texas

The letter is dated only "Friday," but the envelope is postmarked "2 DEC / 22 / 12:45 AM," a Saturday, indicating that the letter was written the evening before, 1 December.

TABLE TWO STUDENT PAPERS, 1910–1915

ALL OF T. S. ELIOT'S student papers are conserved at the Houghton Library of Harvard University. For the purposes of this table they are arranged in chronological order and each given a separate item number (column 1, headed "Item"). Since some of the student papers were notes that Eliot took over extended periods of weeks or months, the date when each begins is used as the basis for ordering. In a few cases, too, curators at the Houghton have grouped together what were originally separate batches of notes on a common theme, such as Eliot's notes on Eastern philosophy. These I have reseparated and arranged according to their chronology. However, to enable scholars who wish to consult them to locate them I have also listed their manuscript number at Harvard (under column two, headed "Ms. No."). In the third column readers will find either Eliot's own titles or, in square brackets, titles which have been furnished for the materials by curators at the Houghton Library.

In the fourth column I have entered the dates of the student papers. Where Eliot's papers have been dated by him, the dates are simply reported, though in some cases a year has been furnished in square brackets. When a date has been furnished by curators at the Houghton, it is reported in square brackets. However, many of the papers have been left undated by the curators; these papers are indicated by the letters "n.d." ("not dated"), a note which is either left standing alone or followed by dates, again in square brackets, which I have furnished. In all cases I have furnished dates by comparing the writing or typing papers used in the student papers with those in Eliot's letters, as registered in Table 1.

In the fifth column is registered the location where Eliot was when he produced these materials. This makes it much easier for readers and scholars interested in Eliot's intellectual growth to distinguish clearly between the Harvard and the Oxford strata of materials.

In the sixth column, headed "Lvs." (for "Leaves"), is registered the number of leaves contained in each manuscript, while the next three columns go on to record the height, width, and thickness of the paper used. The next seven

ITEM	MS. NO.	TITLE	DATE	WHERE WRITTEN	LVS.	HEIGHT	WIDTH	THICK.	TEXTURE	CHAINLINES	DIST.	NO.
1.1	7	Notes on Fine Arts 20b	n.d. [Feb. 1910]	Harvard	1	265	201	0.13	Wove			
1.2	7	Notes on Fine Arts 20b	19 Feb.–26 May 1910	Harvard	43	259	201	0.13	Wove			
1.2	7	Notes on Fine Arts 20b	n.d. [Spring 1910]	Harvard	2	185	117	0.13	Wove			
1.4	7	Notes on Fine Arts 20b	n.d. [Spring 1910]	Harvard	1	254	175	0.12	Wove			
1.5	7	Notes on Fine Arts 20b	n.d. [Spring 1910]	Harvard	2	135	71	0.09	Wove			
2	132	Draft of a Paper on Bergson	[1910–1911]	Harvard	27	263	199	0.11	Wove			
3	130	Notes on Bergson's Lectures	13 Jan.–17 Feb. [1911]	Paris	24	338	226	0.09	Laid	Horizontal	25.5	13
4	131	Notes on Italy	July–Aug. 1911	Italy	20	211	69	0.09	Wove			
5	8	Physiology of Organs of Skin	[Oct. 1911?]	Harvard	2	267	203	0.13	Wove			
6.1	9	Notes on Philosophy 12 [10?]	4 Oct. 1911–27 May 1912	Harvard	108	255	200	0.12	Wove			
6.2	9	Notes on Philosophy 12 [10?]	[Late Jan. 1912?]	Harvard	9	215	140	0.05	Wove			
6.3	9	Notes on Philosophy 12 [10?]	n.d.	Harvard	2	252	203	0.08	Wove			
7	10	[Notes on a Text]	[1912–1913]	Harvard	10	159	133	0.05	Wove			
8	31	Relation Between Politics...	[1913–1914]	Harvard	24	260	198	0.12	Wove			
9	12.6	Perry. Philosophy 25	2 Oct. [1913]	Harvard	1	268	205	0.12	Wove			
10.1	12.1	[Notes on Eastern Philosophy]	3–10 Oct. [1913]	Harvard	2	268	205	0.12	Wove			
10.2	12.2	[Notes on Eastern Philosophy]	10 Oct.–14 Nov. [1913]	Harvard	6	267	204	0.13	Wove			
11	11	[Notes on Logic]	24 Nov.–15 Dec. [1913]	Harvard	15	229	143	0.08	Wove			
10.3	12.3	[Notes on Eastern Philosophy]	25 Nov. [1913]–9 Jan. [1914]	Harvard	6	267	204	0.13	Wove			
10.4	12.4	[Notes on Eastern Philosophy]	9 Jan.–20 Feb. [1914]	Harvard	8	267	204	0.13	Wove			
10.5	12.5	[Notes on Eastern Philosophy]	6 Mar.–27 Apr. [1914]	Harvard	5	267	204	0.13	Wove			
10.6	12.6	[Notes on Eastern Philosophy]	10 Feb.–15 May [1914]	Harvard	14	267	204	0.13	Wove			
12	13	[Notes on Logic]	10 Feb.–23 May [1914]	Harvard	42	267	204	0.13	Wove			
13	14	[Notes on Characters & Plots]	n.d.	Harvard	2	265	202	0.12	Wove			
14	18	[Causality]	n.d.	Harvard	4	275	213	0.09	Wove			
15	22	Suggestions toward a theory...	n.d.	Harvard	5	266	203	0.09	Wove			
16	31	Ethics of Green & Sidgwick	n.d.	Harvard	18	266	202	0.09	Wove			
17	15	[Notes on Logic]	12 Oct.–30 Nov. [1914]	Oxford	34	256	204	0.13	Laid	Horizontal	25.5	10
18	16	[Notes on Aristotle]	13 Oct.–3 Dec. [1914]	Oxford	27	256	204	0.13	Laid	Horizontal	25.5	10
19	17	[Notes on Aristotle]	13 Oct.–3 Dec. [1914]	Oxford	50	256	204	0.13	Laid	Horizontal	26	10
20	16	[Notes on Aristotle]	n.d. [Oct. 1914–Feb.1915]	Oxford	44	256	204	0.12	Laid	Horizontal	25.5	10
21	16	[Notes on Aristotle]	n.d. [Oct. 1914–Feb.1915]	Oxford	1	258	202	0.08	Laid	Horizontal	26	10
22	20	[Eidos]	n.d. [Oct. 1914–Feb.1915]	Oxford	4	258	202	0.06	Laid	Horizontal	26	10
23	21	[On Objects]	n.d. [Oct. 1914–Feb.1915]	Oxford	6	258	201	0.06	Laid	Horizontal	26	10
24	23	[On Objects]	n.d. [Oct. 1914–Feb.1915]	Oxford	5	258	201	0.06	Laid	Horizontal	26	10
25	24	[On Objects]	n.d. [Oct. 1914–Feb.1915]	Oxford	5	258	201	0.06	Laid	Horizontal	26	10
26	25	[Object and Point of View]	n.d. [Oct. 1914–Feb.1915]	Oxford	5	257	202	0.07	Laid	Horizontal	26	10
27	26	[On Definition]	n.d. [Oct. 1914–Feb.1915]	Oxford	4	258	201	0.06	Laid	Horizontal	26	10
28	27	The validity of artificial...	n.d. [Oct. 1914–Feb.1915]	Oxford	7	258	201	0.06	Laid	Horizontal	26	10
29	32	[Ethics]	n.d. [Oct. 1914–Feb.1915]	Oxford	21	258	202	0.07	Laid	Horizontal	26	10
30	15	[Notes on Logic]	18 Jan.–10 Mar. [1915]	Oxford	44	256	204	0.12	Laid	Horizontal	26	10
31	17	[Notes on Aristotle]	19 Jan.–6 Mar. [1915]	Oxford	37	256	204	0.12	Laid	Horizontal	25.5	10
32	15	[Notes on Logic]	27 Apr.–8 June [1915]	Oxford	18	254	204	0.12	Laid	Horizontal	25.5	10
33	17	[Notes on Aristotle]	27 Apr.–10 June [1915]	Oxford	30	254	204	0.12	Laid	Horizontal	25.5	10
34	16	[Notes on Aristotle]	29 Apr.–19 May [1915]	Oxford	40	254	204	0.12	Laid	Horizontal	25.5	10
35	30	[Aristotle: Definition of...]	n.d. [Apr. 1915]	Oxford	4	261	203	0.09	Laid	Vertical	26	8
36	29	[Matter and Form]	n.d. [Apr. 1915]	Oxford	5	261	203	0.09	Laid	Vertical	26	8
37.1	28	[On Matter]	n.d. [Apr. 1915]	Oxford	3	261	203	0.09	Laid	Vertical	26	8
37.2	28	[On Matter]	n.d. [Apr. 1915]	Oxford	4	254	204	0.11	Laid	Horizontal	25.5	10
38	19	[On Change]	n.d. [Apr. 1915]	Oxford	10	254	204	0.11	Laid	Horizontal	25.5	10

NOTES

1   The left edge of this leaf is torn, and the figure provided reflects its actual width rather than a reconstruction.

2   Because these leaves are bound together, I have in this instance (and this instance alone) measured only the vertical lines of the ruled paper, not the horizontal.

3   These two leaves were torn from a larger leaf, and their original height

columns follow the format of Table 1 in recording the paper's texture and information about chainlines and watermarks. The column thereafter records the paper's color, again following the format and principles of Table 1. The last seven columns of this table record the same information and in the same format as Table 1.

WATERMARK	POSITION	DIMENSIONS	COLOR	PRINTING	LINED PAPER	MS	TS	SCRIPT	TYPEWR.	NOTES	ITEM
Linen Ledger	Vertical	Incomplete	White		36.206(19).23	X		Pencil			1.1
Shawmut Mills	Horizontal	51 x 123	White		31.223(28).5	X		Black ink, pencil			1.2
Linen Ledger	Vertical	Incomplete	White		21.159(20).5	X		Pencil			1.2
Linen Ledger	Vertical	39 x 125	White		29.220(26).5	X		Black ink, pencil		1	1.4
None			White			X		Pencil		2	1.5
Shawmut Mills	Horizontal	50 x 123	White	Red line 33 mm. from edge	37.223(23).3	X		Black ink			2
Lorraine	Vertical	110 x 94	White		21.183(38).22	X		Black ink, pencil		3	3
None			White		5.205(43).1	X		Black ink			4
Linen Ledger	Vertical	38 x 123	White		4.262(55).1	X		Black ink, pencil			5
Linen Ledger	Vertical	39 x 125	White		29.220(26).6	X		Black ink, pencil			6.1
None			White			X		Black ink		4	6.2
Old Hampshire	Vertical	Incomplete	White			X		Pencil			6.3
None			White			X		Black ink, pencil			7
Shawmut Mills	Horizontal	50 x 124				X		Pencil			8
Linen Ledger	Vertical	Incomplete	White		3.263(55).2	X		Black ink		5	9
Linen Ledger	Vertical	Incomplete	White		3.263(55).2	X		Black ink		5	10.1
Linen Ledger	Vertical	37 x 125	White	Red line 33 mm. from edge		X		Black ink			10.2
Persian Bond	Vertical	48 x 141	White			X		Black ink			11
Linen Ledger	Vertical	37 x 125	White	Red line 33 mm. from edge		X		Black ink			10.3
Linen Ledger	Vertical	37 x 125	White	Red line 33 mm. from edge		X		Black ink, pencil		6	10.4
Linen Ledger	Vertical	Incomplete	White	Red line 33 mm. from edge		X		Black ink			10.5
Linen Ledger	Vertical	38 x 125	White	Red line 33 mm. from edge		X		Black ink, pencil			10.6
Linen Ledger	Vertical	38 x 125	White	Red line 33 mm. from edge		X	X	Black ink & ribbon, pencil	2.12		12
None			White		52.207(22).6	X		Black ink			13
Minnesota Bond	Horizontal	12 x 129	White			X		Black ink			14
Marcus Ward's	Vertical	12 x 123	White				X	Black & red ribbon	2.12		15
Marcus Ward's	Vertical	12 x 123	White				X	Black ribbon	2.12		16
None			White	Red line 47 mm. from edge	25.216(26).15	X		Black ink			17
None			White	Red line 47 mm. from edge	25.216(26).15	X		Black ink			18
None			White	Red line 47 mm. from edge	25.216(26).15	X		Black ink			19
None			White			X		Black ink			20
Croxley Manifest	Vertical	121 x 156	Yellow white 92			X	X	Black ribbon, ink	2.12		21
Croxley Manifest	Vertical	122 x 156	Yellow white 92			X		Black ink			22
Croxley Manifest	Vertical	122 x 156	Yellow white 92			X		Pencil			23
Croxley Manifest	Vertical	122 x 156	Yellow white 92			X	X	Black ribbon, pencil	2.12		24
Croxley Manifest	Vertical	122 x 156	Yellow white 92				X	Black ribbon	2.12		25
Croxley Manifest	Vertical	122 x 156	Yellow white 92			X		Black ink			26
Croxley Manifest	Vertical	122 x 156	Yellow white 92				X	Black ribbon	2.12		27
Croxley Manifest	Vertical	122 x 156	Yellow white 92				X	Black ribbon	2.12		28
Croxley Manifest	Vertical	122 x 156	Yellow white 92				X	Black ribbon	2.12		29
None			White		25.216(26).15	X		Black ink			30
None			White		25.216(26).14	X		Black ink			31
None			White		25.216(26).12	X		Black ink			32
None			White		26.216(26).12	X		Black ink			33
None			White		26.216(26).12	X				7	34
Excelsior Fine	Horizontal	71 x 125	Yellow white 92			X		Black ink			35
Excelsior Fine	Horizontal	71 x 125	Yellow white 92				X	Black ribbon	2.12		36
Excelsior Fine	Horizontal	71 x 125	Yellow white 92				X	Black ribbon	2.12		37.1
None			White			X		Pencil		7	37.2
None			White		25.216(26).13	X		Black ink, pencil			38

cannot be reconstructed, though their width was not changed by the tear.

Parts of a watermark are discernible, but are not legible because of the tear.

4   Three leaves in this group have smaller heights: 99 mm, 118 mm, 189 mm.

5   The watermark is only partially visible: [125] × 38 mm.

6   The watermark is only partially visible: [125] × 38 mm.

7   There is no text for these "[Notes on Aristotle]." The leaves are blank.

THIS TABLE GIVES A synoptic bibliographical description of the extant manuscripts and typescripts used in Eliot's poems and essays during the period 1910 through 1922—with a few exceptions, to be noted in due course. The chief difficulty in compiling such a table resides in dating, especially the dating of early poems. Those written before 1914, in particular, represent an extreme case of a gap between a documentary date and a compositional date, chiefly because Eliot elected to transcribe all his early poems in a notebook that he purchased in the spring of 1910, now known as *Inventions of the March Hare* and first published in 1996 under the editorship of Christopher Ricks (New York: Harcourt Brace; hereafter *IMH*). Into it Eliot transcribed poems written both before and after that date: and in some cases he included dates with the poems, in others not. I have treated all these as one work, registered in Item 1 of the table that follows, and will forgo any attempt at reconstructing their chronology.

However, in addition to those poems that he transcribed into the notebook, Eliot also made typed and manuscript transcriptions of other poems (or even parts of poems) on separate leaves that he then laid into the notebook. There were five of these, but only two are written on paper that matches papers found elsewhere in Eliot's correspondence or his student papers. "Paysage Triste" and "In the Department Store" (*IMF*, 52, 56) are on the same kind of paper found in letters by Eliot that date from October 1914 to February 1915 (see Table 1: T.18, T.28, T.31) and in student papers that can be dated to the same period (Table 2, Items 21–29). The other three ("Easter: Sensations of April II" [*IMH*, 24], "Abendämmerung" [*IMH*, 335], and "Of those ideas in his head" [*IMH*, 57]) are on papers that have no matches elsewhere, and I have omitted all five from the following table. In addition, I have also omitted all the "Bolo" poems, formerly part of Eliot's notebook but excised from it by him, and now preserved among the Ezra Pound papers at the Beinecke Library at Yale, since they all date from a period much earlier than that of *The Waste Land* manuscripts.

Finally, I have included all the "miscellaneous poems mostly unpublished" that originally accompanied the notebook (*IMH*, 60–91), except for two. "Inside the Gloom" and "Hidden under the Heron's Wing" (*IMH*, 72–73, 82) were "not available" when I visited the Berg Collection, and I have therefore omitted them. I have further included all the typescripts of poems included in *Poems* (1920).

To address the gap between the date of composition and the date of the document that preserves it, so problematic in the earliest poems, I have given three dates: date composed (column three), document date (abbreviated "Doc. Date," column four), and publication date (abbreviated "Pubn. Date"). Under "Composed," a date set between quotation marks is one furnished by Eliot himself on the manuscript. All other dates in this column are my own, with exception of the dates for "La Figlia che piange" and "Morning at the Window," where I have followed the dates urged by Christopher Ricks (*IMH*, xl). The dates I have assigned to the poems are based on correlating the types of paper used for them with those used in Eliot's letters. For the dates which I have assigned to Eliot's essays from 1921, see the headnote to each essay in Lawrence Rainey, ed., *The Annotated "Waste Land" with Eliot's Contemporary Prose* (New Haven: Yale University Press, 2005). In all the cases where transcriptions of poems as given in the Berg Collection manuscripts were included in *Inventions of the March Hare*, I provide the page number where the transcription begins, under the column headed "IMH." Thereafter the table follows the format of the previous tables.

ITEM	TITLE	COMPOSED	DOC. DATE	PUBN. DATE	IMH	LOCATION	LVS.	HEIGHT	WIDTH	THICK.	TEXTURE
1	Inventions of the March Hare	1909–1916	1910	1996	1–58	Berg	60	197	165	0.12	Wove
2	First Debate Between the Body and Soul	"Jan. 1910"	Jan. 1910	1996	64	Berg	1	254	165	0.14	Laid
3	Bacchus and Ariadne: 2nd Debate	"Feb. 1911"	Feb. 1911	1996	68	Berg	1	268	205	0.08	Wove
4	The Smoke That Gathers Blue and Sinks	"Feb. 1911"	Feb. 1911	1996	70	Berg	1	268	205	0.08	Wove
5	He Said: This Universe Is Very Clever	"Mar. 1911"	Mar. 1911	1996	71	Berg	1	268	205	0.08	Wove
6	Rhapsody on a Windy Night	"Mar. 1911"	Mar. 1911	1996	338	Berg	3	268	205	0.08	Wove
7	The Burnt Dancer	"June 1914"	June 1914	1996	62	Berg	1	266	203	0.10	Wove
8	Love Song of St. Sebastian	July 1914	July 1914	1996	78	Maryland	2	266	202	0.10	Wove
9	Love Song of St. Sebastian	July 1914	July 1914	1996	78	Berg	1	266	202	0.10	Wove
10	Oh little voices of the throats of men	July 1914	July 1914	1996	75	Berg	1	266	202	0.10	Wove
11	The Love Song of J. Alfred Prufrock	July 1911	July 1914	June 1915		Maryland	4	277	214	0.08	Wove
12	The Love Song of J. Alfred Prufrock	July 1911	July 1914	June 1915		Chicago	6	266	203	0.10	Wove
13	O lord, have patience			1996	83	Berg	1	267	204	0.07	Wove
14	Do I Know How I Feel?	Jan.–Apr. 1915	Jan.–Apr. 1915	1996	80	Berg	1	256	204	0.12	Laid
15	To Helen	Apr. 1915	Apr. 1915			Beinecke	1	261	203	0.09	Laid
16	Mr. Apollinax [Draft]	Apr. 1915	Apr. 1915	Sept. 1916		Berg	1	261	203	0.09	Laid
17	Mr. Apollinax [Fair Copy]	Apr. 1915	Apr. 1915	Sept. 1916		Berg	1	250	199	0.10	Laid
18	The Engine, II Machinery: Dancers [Draft]	Apr. 1915	Apr. 1915	1996	90	Berg	1	254	205	0.08	Wove
19	The Engine, I–II [Fair Copy]	Apr. 1915	Apr. 1915	1996	90	Berg	1	250	199	0.10	Laid
20	Introspection	July 1915–Aug. 1915		1996	60	Berg	1	286	190	0.12	Laid
21	Conversation Gallante	Nov. 1909	May 1916	Sept. 1916		Chicago	1	257	200		Laid
22	La Figlia che piange	Nov. 1911	May 1916	Sept. 1916		Chicago	1	259	202	0.08	Laid
23	Morning at the Window	Sept. 1914	May 1916	Sept. 1916		Chicago	1	257	200		Laid
24	The Death of St. Narcissus	Apr. 1915	May 1916	1971		Chicago	1	257	200		Laid
25	Mr. Apollinax	Apr. 1915	May 1916	Sept. 1916		Chicago	1	259	202	0.08	Laid
26	Reflections on Vers Libre	Feb. 1917	Feb. 1917	3 Mar. 1917		Beinecke	7	259	203		Laid
27	Tristan Corbière	Mar.–Oct. 1917	Mar.–Oct. 1917	1996	88	Berg	1	251	202	0.07	Laid
28	Tristan Corbière	Mar.–Oct. 1917	Mar.–Oct. 1917	1996	88	Berg	1	251	202	0.07	Laid
29	Airs of Paelstine, No. 2	Mar.–Oct. 1917	Mar.–Oct. 1917	1996	84	Berg	1	252	203	0.07	Laid
30	Airs of Paelstine, No. 2	Mar.–Oct. 1917	Mar.–Oct. 1917	1996	84	Berg	1	252	203	0.07	Laid
31	Petit Epitre	Mar.–Oct. 1917	Mar.–Oct. 1917	1996	86	Berg	1	251	202	0.07	Laid
32	Melange Adultere de Tout	Mar.–June 1917	Mar.–June 1917	July 1917	361	Berg	1	252	202	0.07	Laid
33	Lune de Miel	Mar.–June 1917	Mar.–June 1917	July 1917	362	Berg	1	252	202	0.07	Laid
34	The Hippopotamus	Mar.–June 1917	Mar.–June 1917	July 1917		Beinecke	1	252	203	0.07	Laid
35	Ezra Pound: His Metric and Poetry	May–Sept. 1917	May–Sept. 1917	Jan. 1918		Beinecke	19	252	202	0.07	Laid
36	Dans le Restaurant	Mar.–Oct. 1917	Mar.–Oct. 1917	Sept. 1918	363	Berg	1	252	202	0.07	Laid
37	A Cooking Egg	Mar.–Oct. 1917	Mar.–Oct. 1917	May 1919	358	Berg	1	252	202	0.07	Laid
38	A Cooking Egg	Mar.–Oct. 1917	Mar.–Oct. 1917	May 1919	358	Berg	1	252	202	0.07	Laid
39	Whispers of Immortality [A]	Mar.–Oct. 1917	Mar.–Oct. 1917	Sept. 1918	365	Berg	1	251	202	0.07	Laid
40	Whispers of Immortality [B]	Mar.–Oct. 1917	Mar.–Oct. 1917	Sept. 1918	365	Berg	1	251	202	0.07	Laid
41	Whispers of Immortality [C]	Mar.–Oct. 1917	Mar.–Oct. 1917	Sept. 1918	368	Berg	1	251	202	0.07	Laid
42	Try This on Your Piano: Whispers...[D]	Mar.–Oct. 1917	Mar.–Oct. 1917	Sept. 1918	370	Berg	1	252	202	0.07	Laid
43	Try This on Your Piano: Whispers...[E]	Mar.–Oct. 1917	Mar.–Oct. 1917	Sept. 1918	370	Berg	1	252	202	0.07	Laid
44	Whispers of Immortality [F]	Mar.–Oct. 1917	Mar.–Oct. 1917	Sept. 1918	372	Berg	1	252	202	0.07	Laid
45	Whispers of Immortality [G]	Mar.–Aug. 1918	Mar.–Aug. 1918	Sept. 1918	373	Berg	1	254	204	0.09	Laid
46	Whispers of Immortality [H]	Mar.–Aug. 1918	Mar.–Aug. 1918	Sept. 1918	373	Berg	1	254	204	0.09	Laid
47	Ode on Independence Day, July 4th 1918	July 1918	July 1918	Feb. 1920	383	Berg	1	254	204	0.09	Laid
48	Ode on Independence Day, July 4th 1918	July 1918	July 1918	Feb. 1920	383	Berg	1	254	204	0.09	Laid
49	Mr. Eliot's Sunday Morning Service	Mar.–Aug. 1918	Mar.–Aug. 1918	Sept. 1918	377	Berg	1	254	204	0.09	Laid
50	Sweeney Among the Nightingales	Mar.–Aug. 1918	Mar.–Aug. 1918	Sept. 1918	380	Berg	1	254	204	0.09	Laid
51	Sweeney Among the Nightingales	Mar.–Aug. 1918	Mar.–Aug. 1918	Sept. 1918	380	Berg	1	254	204	0.09	Laid
52	Tarr	Aug. 1918	Aug. 1918	Sept. 1918		Beinecke	4	254	204	0.09	Laid
53	Sweeney Erect	Aug. 1918–Feb. 1919	Aug. 1918–Feb. 1919	June 1919	355	Berg	1	254	204	0.09	Laid
54	Sweeney Erect	Aug. 1918–Feb. 1919	Aug. 1918–Feb. 1919	June 1919	355	Berg	1	264	203	0.06	Wove
55	Bleistein with a Cigar	Aug. 1918–Feb. 1919	Aug. 1918–Feb. 1919	June 1919	353	Berg	1	264	204	0.09	Laid
56	Burbank with a Baedeker; Bleistein...	Aug. 1918–Feb. 1919	Aug. 1918–Feb. 1919	June 1919	353	Berg	1	264	203	0.07	Wove
57	Burbank with a Baedeker; Bleistein...	Aug. 1918–Feb. 1919	Aug. 1918–Feb. 1919	June 1919	353	Virginia	1	263	203	0.07	Wove
58	Ode	Aug. 1918–Feb. 1919	Aug. 1918–Feb. 1919	Feb. 1920	383	Berg	1	263	203	0.07	Wove
59	Gerontion	Feb. 1919	Feb. 1919	Feb. 1920	349	Berg	2	254	204	0.09	Laid
60	Gerontion	Feb. 1919	Feb. 1919	Feb. 1920	349	Berg	2	263	203	0.07	Wove
61	Gerontion	Feb. 1919	Feb. 1919	Feb. 1920	349	Berg	2	259	203	0.07	Laid
62	Autour d'une traduction d'Euripede	Feb. 1919	Feb. 1919			Berg	1	259	203	0.07	Laid
63	A Brief Treatise on the Criticism of Poetry	Dec. 1919–Feb. 1920	Dec. 1919–Feb. 1920	Mar. 1920		Gallup	4	228	177	0.12	Wove
64	London Letter: May, 1921	Apr. 1921	Apr. 1921	June 1920		Beinecke	6	264	203	0.08	Wove
65	London Letter: September, 1921	10–25 Aug. 1921	10–25 Aug. 1921	Oct. 1921		Beinecke	5	264	203	0.07	Laid
66	London Letter: September, 1921	10–25 Aug. 1921	10–25 Aug. 1921	Oct. 1921		Beinecke	5	264	203	0.07	Laid
67	London Letter: April, 1922	1–15 Mar. 1922	1–15 Mar. 1922	May 1922		Beinecke	5	253	203	0.06	Wove
68	London Letter: June, 1922	15–30 May 1922	15–30 May 1922	July 1917		Beinecke	14	248	200	0.06	Wove
69	London Letter: August, 1922	15–30 July 1922	15–30 July 1922	Sept. 1922		Beinecke	4	266	203	0.06	Wove
70	London Letter: November, 1922	15–30 Oct. 1922	15–30 Oct. 1922	Dec. 1922		Beinecke	6	267	203	0.06	Wove

NOTES

1   Paper has a printed letterhead reading "U.S.M.S. St. Louis."

2   Paper mounted on backing; thickness cannot be measured.

CHAINLINES	DIST.	NO.	WATERMARK	POSITION	DIMENSIONS	COLOR	LINED PAPER	MS	TS	SCRIPT	TYPEWR.	CORRECTIONS	NTS.	ITEM
			Manomet Ledger	Horizontal	81 x 123	White	22.166(21).9	X		Black ink, pencil				1
Horizontal	24	10	Harvard Coop	Vertical	65 x 103	Yellow white 92		X		Pencil				2
			None			Yellow white 92		X		Pencil		Black ink		3
			None			Yellow white 92		X		Pencil				4
			None			Yellow white 92		X		Pencil		Black ink		5
			None			Yellow white 92		X		Pencil				6
			Marcus Ward's	Vertical	12 x 123	White			X	Black, red ribbon	2.12	Pencil		7
			Marcus Ward's	Vertical	13 x 123	White			X	Black ribbon	2.12			8
			Marcus Ward's	Vertical	12 x 123	White			X	Black ribbon	2.12	Black ink, pencil		9
			Marcus Ward's	Vertical	13 x 123	White			X	Black ribbon	2.12	Black ink, pencil		10
			Falcon Bond	Vertical	25 x 119	Yellow white 92			X	Black ribbon	2.12			11
			Marcus Ward's	Vertical	13 x 122	White			X	Black ribbon	2.12			12
			Merchants Pure	Horizontal	13 x 179	White		X		Pencil				13
Horizontal	25.5	10	None			White	26.216(26).13	X		Pencil				14
Vertical	26	8	Excelsior Fine	Horizontal	Incomplete	Yellow white 92		X		Black ink				15
Vertical	26	8	Excelsior Fine	Horizontal	71 x 125	Yellow white 92		X		Pencil				16
Vertical	27	7	None			White	30.207(24).13	X		Black ink				17
			Croxley Manifest	Vertical	113 x 146	White		X		Pencil			1	18
Vertical	27	8	None			White	30.207(23).13	X		Black ink				19
Horizontal	25.5	11	Waldorf Club [A]	Vertical	34 x 208	Blue White 189		X		Black ink				20
Vertical	25	8	None						X	Black ribbon	2.12		2	21
Vertical	25.5	8	None						X	Black ribbon	2.12			22
Vertical	25	8	None						X	Black ribbon	2.12		2	23
Vertical	25	8	None						X	Purple carbon	2.12		2	24
Vertical	25.5	8	None						X	Black ribbon	2.12			25
Horizontal	27	9	None						X	Black carbon	2.12			26
Vertical	27	8	Silver Linen [A]	Horizontal	18 x 155	Yellow white 92			X	Black ribbon	2.12			27
Vertical	27	8	Silver Linen [A]	Horizontal	18 x 156	Yellow white 92			X	Black ribbon	2.12			28
Vertical	27	8	Silver Linen [A]	Horizontal	18 x 156	Yellow white 92			X	Black ribbon	2.12			29
Vertical	27	8	Silver Linen [A]	Horizontal	Incomplete	Yellow white 92			X	Black carbon	2.12			30
Vertical	27	8	Silver Linen [A]	Horizontal	Incomplete	Yellow white 92			X	Black ribbon	2.12			31
Vertical	27	8	Silver Linen [A]	Horizontal	Incomplete	Yellow white 92			X	Black carbon	2.12			32
Vertical	27	7	Silver Linen [A]	Horizontal	Incomplete	Yellow white 92			X	Black carbon	2.12			33
Vertical	27	8	Silver Linen [A]	Horizontal	18 x 156	Yellow white 92			X	Black ribbon	2.12			34
Vertical	27	8	Silver Linen [A]	Horizontal	18 x 156	Yellow white 92			X	Black ribbon	2.12			35
Vertical	27	8	Silver Linen [A]	Horizontal	Incomplete	Yellow white 92			X	Black carbon	2.12			36
Vertical	27	7	Silver Linen [A]	Horizontal	Incomplete	Yellow white 92			X	Black ribbon	2.12			37
Vertical	27	8	Silver Linen [A]	Horizontal	Incomplete	Yellow white 92			X	Black carbon	2.12			38
Vertical	27	8	Silver Linen [A]	Horizontal	Incomplete	Yellow white 92			X	Black ribbon	2.12	Pencil		39
Vertical	27	8	Silver Linen [A]	Horizontal	Incomplete	Yellow white 92			X	Black carbon	2.12	Pencil		40
Vertical	27	8	Silver Linen [A]	Horizontal	Incomplete	Yellow white 92			X	Black carbon	2.12	Pencil		41
Vertical	27	8	Silver Linen [A]	Horizontal	Incomplete	Yellow white 92			X	Black ribbon	2.12	Pencil		42
Vertical	27	8	Silver Linen [A]	Horizontal	Incomplete	Yellow white 92			X	Black carbon	2.12	Pencil		43
Vertical	27	7	Silver Linen [A]	Horizontal	Incomplete	Yellow white 92			X	Black ribbon	2.12	Pencil		44
Vertical	27	8	Silver Linen [B]	Horizontal	18 x 155	Yellow white 92			X	Black ribbon	2.12	Pencil		45
Vertical	27	8	Silver Linen [B]	Horizontal	18 x 155	Yellow white 92			X	Black carbon	2.12	Pencil		46
Vertical	27	8	Silver Linen [B]	Horizontal	18 x 155	Yellow white 92			X	Black ribbon	2.12			47
Vertical	27	8	Silver Linen [B]	Horizontal	18 x 155	Yellow white 92			X	Black carbon	2.12			48
Vertical	27	7	Silver Linen [B]	Horizontal	18 x 155	Yellow white 92			X	Black carbon	2.12	Pencil		49
Vertical	27	8	Silver Linen [B]	Horizontal	18 x 155	Yellow white 92			X	Black carbon	2.12	Pencil		50
Vertical	27	8	Silver Linen [B]	Horizontal	18 x 155	Yellow white 92			X	Black carbon	2.12			51
Vertical	27	8	Silver Linen [B]	Horizontal	18 x 154	Yellow white 92			X	Black ribbon	2.12			52
Vertical	27	8	Silver Linen [B]	Horizontal	18 x 155	Yellow white 92			X	Black ribbon	2.12			53
			None			White			X	Purple carbon	2.12			54
Vertical	27	8	Silver Linen [B]	Horizontal	18 x 155	Yellow white 92			X	Black ribbon	2.12			55
			None			White			X	Purple carbon	2.12			56
			None			White			X	Purple carbon	2.12			57
			None			White			X	Purple carbon	2.12			58
Vertical	27	8	Silver Linen [B]	Horizontal	18 x 155	Yellow white 92			X	Black ribbon	2.12	Pencil		59
			None			White			X	Purple carbon	2.12	Pencil		60
Horizontal	27	9	None			Yellow white 92			X	Black carbon	2.12			61
Horizontal	27	9	None			Yellow white 92			X	Black carbon	2.12	Black ink, pencil		62
			* Bond	Vertical	72 x 27	White		X		Black ink, pencil			3	63
			British Bond	Horizontal	65 x 125	White			X	Black ribbon	2.12	Black ink, pencil		64
Vertical	25.5	8	Verona Linen	Horizontal	14 x 128	White			X	Black ribbon	2.10	Black ink, pencil		65
Vertical	25.5	8	Verona Linen	Horizontal	14 x 128	White			X	Black carbon	2.10			66
			None			White			X		2.10	Black ink, pencil		67
			None			White	29.216(25).3	X		Black ink				68
			None			White			X	Black ribbon	2.10	Black, red ink, pencil		69
			None			White			X	Black carbon	2.10	Black ink, red crayon, pencil		70

3 Paper has a printed letterhead reading "18, CRAWFORD MANSIONS, / CRAWFORD STREET, W." and is therefore the same paper as found in Table 1, T.244, T.251, and T.265, all from December 1919 though early March 1920.

TITLE	LVS.	HEIGHT	WIDTH	THICK.	TEXTURE	CHAINLINES	DIST.	NO.	WATERMARK
After the turning	1	267	205	0.12	Wove				Linen Ledger
So through the evening	1	267	205	0.12	Wove				Linen Ledger
I am the Resurrection	1	267	205	0.12	Wove				Linen Ledger
The Death of St. Narcissus [Draft]	1	262	203	0.09	Laid	Vertical	26	8	Excelsior Fine
The Death of St. Narcissus [Fair Copy]	1	250	198	0.10	Laid	Vertical	27	8	None
The Death of the Duchess	2	258	202	0.07	Laid	Horizontal	27	9	None
Song [for the Opherion]	1	263	200	0.07	Laid	Vertical	26	8	British Bond [B]
Those are pearls	1	263	203	0.07	Wove				British Bond [C]
The Burial of the Dead	3	264	203	0.08	Wove				British Bond [C]
A Game of Chess [Top Copy]	3	264	203	0.08	Wove				British Bond [C]
A Game of Chess [Carbon Copy]	3	264	203	0.08	Wove				British Bond [C]
Elegy/Dirge [Draft]	1	227	177	0.11	Wove				Hieratica Bond [D]
O City, City/London, the swarming	1	228	176	0.11	Wove				Hieratica Bond [D]
The river sweats	1	228	177	0.11	Wove				Hieratica Bond [D]
Highbury bore me	1	228	177	0.11	Wove				Hieratica Bond [D]
On Margate Sands	1	228	177	0.11	Wove				Hieratica Bond [D]
The Fire Sermon [Top Copy]	5	265	203	0.06	Laid	Vertical	25.5	8	Verona Linen
The Fire Sermon [Carbon Copy]	5	265	203	0.06	Laid	Vertical	25.5	8	Verona Linen
Exequy	1	265	202	0.06	Laid	Vertical	25.5	8	Verona Linen
Death by Water [Autograph Fair Copy]	4	271	208	0.06	Wove				None
What the Thunder Said [Autograph Fair Copy]	6	271	208	0.06	Wove				None
Dirge [Autograph Fair Copy]	1	270	208	0.06	Wove				None
From which a Venus Anadyomene	1	271	208	0.06	Wove				None
Death by Water [Typescript Fair Copy]	4	267	208	0.05	Wove				None
What the Thunder Said [Typescript Fair Copy]	2	389	303	0.07	Wove				None
The Waste Land [Title Page]	1	263	203	0.06	Laid	Vertical	25.5	8	Verona Linen

POSITION	DIMENSIONS	LINED PAPER	COLOR	MS	TS	TYPEWR.	SCRIPT	CORRECTIONS	DATE
Vertical	38 x 124	4.262(55).2	White	X			Black ink	Black ink	2–10 Oct. 1913
Vertical	38 x 124	4.262(55).2	White	X			Black ink	Black ink, pencil	2–10 Oct. 1913
Vertical	38 x 124	4.262(55).2	White	X			Black ink	Black ink	2–10 Oct. 1913
Horizontal	72 x 124		White	X			Pencil	Blue crayon, pencil	April 1915
		29.207(24).14	White	X			Black ink	Black ink	May 1915
			White		X	2.12	Black ribbon	Black ink, pencil	September 1916
Horizontal	66 x 125		White		X	2.12	Black ribbon	Black ink, pencil	23–30 Jan. 1921
Horizontal	66 x 122		White	X			Pencil	Pencil	Feb.–May 1921
Horizontal	66 x 123		White		X	2.12	Black ribbon	Black ink, pencil	Feb.–May 1921
Horizontal	66 x 123		White		X	2.12	Black ribbon	Black ink, pencil	Feb.–May 1921
Horizontal	66 x 123		White		X	2.12	Black carbon	Pencil	Feb.–May 1921
Vertical	45 x 48		White	X			Pencil	Blue pencil, pencil	1–12 Nov. 1921
Vertical	45 x 48		White	X			Pencil	Pencil	1–12 Nov. 1921
Vertical	45 x 48		White	X			Pencil	Pencil	1–12 Nov. 1921
Vertical	45 x 48		White	X			Pencil	Black ink, green crayon, pencil	1–12 Nov. 1921
Vertical	45 x 48		White	X			Pencil	Pencil	1–12 Nov. 1921
Horizontal	14 x 128		White		X	2.10	Black ribbon	Black ink, pencil	12–18 Nov. 1921
Horizontal	14 x 128		White		X	2.10	Black ribbon	Black ink, pencil	12–18 Nov. 1921
Horizontal	14 x 128		White		X	2.10	Black ribbon	Black ink, pencil	12–18 Nov. 1921
		21.234(27).16	White	X			Black ink	Black ink, pencil	19 Nov.–31 Dec. 1921
		21.234(27).16	White	X			Pencil	Black ink, green crayon, pencil	19 Nov.–31 Dec. 1921
		21.234(27).16	White	X			Black ink	Black ink	19 Nov.–31 Dec. 1921
		21.234(27).16	White	X			Pencil	Pencil	19 Nov.–31 Dec. 1921
			White		X	2.54	Purple ribbon	Pencil	2–10 Jan. 1922
			White		X	2.54	Purple ribbon	Black ink, pencil	2–10 Jan. 1922
Horizontal	14 x 128		White		X	2.10	Black ribbon	Black ink	17–22 Jan. 1922

INDEX